Deleuze and Design

D1615527

Deleuze Connections

'It is not the elements or the sets which define the multiplicity. What defines it is the AND, as something which has its place between the elements or between the sets. AND, AND, AND – stammering.'

Gilles Deleuze and Claire Parnet, *Dialogues*

General Editor
Ian Buchanan

Editorial Advisory Board

Keith Ansell-Pearson
Rosi Braidotti
Claire Colebrook
Tom Conley

Gregg Lambert
Adrian Parr
Paul Patton
Patricia Pisters

Titles Available in the Series

Ian Buchanan and Claire Colebrook (eds), *Deleuze and Feminist Theory*
Ian Buchanan and John Marks (eds), *Deleuze and Literature*
Mark Bonta and John Protevi (eds), *Deleuze and Geophilosophy*
Ian Buchanan and Marcel Swiboda (eds), *Deleuze and Music*
Ian Buchanan and Gregg Lambert (eds), *Deleuze and Space*
Martin Fuglsang and Bent Meier Sørensen (eds), *Deleuze and the Social*
Ian Buchanan and Adrian Parr (eds), *Deleuze and the Contemporary World*
Constantin V. Boundas (ed.), *Deleuze and Philosophy*
Ian Buchanan and Nicholas Thoburn (eds), *Deleuze and Politics*
Chrysanthi Nigianni and Merl Storr (eds), *Deleuze and Queer Theory*
Jeffrey A. Bell and Claire Colebrook (eds), *Deleuze and History*
Laura Cull (ed.), *Deleuze and Performance*
Mark Poster and David Savat (eds), *Deleuze and New Technology*
Simone Bignall and Paul Patton (eds), *Deleuze and the Postcolonial*
Stephen Zepke and Simon O'Sullivan (eds), *Deleuze and Contemporary Art*
Laura Guillaume and Joe Hughes (eds), *Deleuze and the Body*
Daniel W. Smith and Nathan Jun (eds), *Deleuze and Ethics*
Frida Beckman (ed.), *Deleuze and Sex*
David Martin-Jones and William Brown (eds), *Deleuze and Film*
Laurent de Sutter and Kyle McGee (eds), *Deleuze and Law*
Arun Saldanha and Jason Michael Adams (eds), *Deleuze and Race*
Rebecca Coleman and Jessica Ringrose (eds), *Deleuze and Research Methodologies*
Inna Semetsky and Diana Masny (eds), *Deleuze and Education*
Hélène Frichot and Stephen Loo (eds), *Deleuze and Architecture*
Betti Marenko and Jamie Brassett (eds), *Deleuze and Design*

Visit the Deleuze Connections website at
www.euppublishing.com/series/delco

Deleuze and Design

Edited by Betti Marenko and
Jamie Brassett

EDINBURGH
University Press

Edinburgh University Press Ltd
The Tun – Holyrood Road, 12(2f) Jackson's Entry, Edinburgh EH8 8PJ

www.euppublishing.com

Typeset in 10.5/13 Adobe Sabon by
Servis Filmsetting Ltd, Stockport, Cheshire,
and printed and bound in Great Britain by
CPI Group (UK) Ltd, Croydon CR0 4YY

A CIP record for this book is available from the British Library

ISBN 978 0 7486 9153 1 (hardback)
ISBN 978 0 7486 9155 5 (webready PDF)
ISBN 978 0 7486 9154 8 (paperback)
ISBN 978 0 7486 9156 2 (epub)

Contents

Schizo Tea Set © Khairul Islam 2006

Introduction

Jamie Brassett and Betti Marenko

Everything depends on Design.
Vilém Flusser, *The Shape of Things: A Philosophy of Design*

What matters to experimenters are the objections and the tests to which their propositions will be subjected, and the future it makes it possible to envisage.
Isabelle Stengers, *Thinking with Whitehead*

Assembling Deleuze and Design

The subtitle to this 'Introduction' might well be *How to catalyse an encounter between philosophy and design*, as one of the main drivers of this project has been how to bring to the fore possible connections between the two practices that this book interrogates: Gilles Deleuze's philosophy, as the practice of creating concepts, and design, as the practice of materialising possibilities. Deleuze's work offers a way of thinking about the encounter between philosophy and design, as they are both concerned with expressing the creation of the *not yet* in impactful ways. Furthermore, for Deleuze and Guattari in *What is Philosophy?*, a creative philosophy is pitched as dealing in *use, profit, interest, value* and *success*, and certainly not truth. 'We will not say of so many books of philosophy that they are false', they write, 'for that is to say nothing, but rather that they lack importance or interest, precisely because they do not create any concept' (1994: 82–3). This language brings us close to that used in design, especially when its creative influence is articulated in terms of innovation (Flynn and Chatman 2004; Cox 2005). An interesting, important, successful philosophy deals not in truth or falsity, but in engaging with different creative activities in many different registers having multiple layers of affect.

This should declare our editorial intentions by providing the overall intellectual framework to which this book intends to abide: that *if* there is a way of designing that both affects and is affected by Deleuze's philosophy, it will be found at the intersection of said practices. Design and philosophy, and other creative practices, are massively entangled and it is time, therefore, to investigate some of the ways in which this occurs. This need is driven not only by Deleuze's intellectual proximity to issues that are relevant to design practice (including its own theoretical and historical contextualisation), but also by the changing nature of design, which as a process enacts a way of thinking and doing philosophy (Giaccardi 2005; Binder et al. 2011; Kimbell 2011, 2012; Tonkinwise 2014). Both design and philosophy are creative practices. The relationship between them is akin to the relation between theory and practice. Each is a way of doing the other, using particular materials, skills and experiences, as well as engaging with particular discourses. We are interested not only in doing philosophy – as a practical process with which the possibilities of new futures can be thought and materialised – but also in articulating concepts through creative, tangible, embodied, material, *designed* means.

Philosopher of science Isabelle Stengers has encountered similar concerns when thinking of how to write about Alfred North Whitehead. 'What is at stake' in writing about Whitehead, she says, 'is not to share a vision, nor to provide a definitive interpretation of Whiteheadian thought, but to experiment/experience in the present what it means to ask the question "What has happened to us?" in the way he suggests' (2011: 22). In this way Stengers expresses her adventure with Whitehead, engaging not with his thought in its place, but creating new milieus for his concepts. Her subtitle, 'a free and wild creation of concepts', quoting from Deleuze and Guattari's *What is Philosophy?*, shows how her thinking with Whitehead will progress: as a no-holds-barred experiment and experience. Even without Stengers's explicit reference to Deleuze and Guattari on the cover of her book (and the proximity of her philosophy to theirs), we are close not only to Deleuze's own work on philosophy's creativity but also to the approach we are taking in this book. In thinking design with Deleuze we might substitute Stengers's use of a Whiteheadian question 'What has happened to us?' for 'What might our possibilities be?' That Deleuze's philosophy and design express ontogenetic processes of becoming will be posited not only later in this introduction, but also at moments throughout this book.

Somehow, the potential of examining design in relation to Deleuze's work has not been explored in a sustained manner until now, notwithstanding the fact that other fields have benefited from encountering

Deleuze: most notably architecture (of which more below), and art (see especially Anne Sauvagnargues's recent work (2006)). For us the creative power of Deleuze's thought should be channelled by design: not as a theoretical fad soon to be outmoded, and neither as an instrument with which to guide applied thinking. Rather: to inform – to seep through all matter on its way to allowing forms to emerge; to strategise – simultaneously to map the topology of complex space and constitute that space with the material of its future actualisation; to make and to develop – that is, to *create* and let these creatures run wild and free. In so doing, we are certain that an encounter with design will be as creatively fruitful for Deleuze's work as vice versa. The challenge we have set for ourselves with this project, then, is to push Deleuze's work beyond the well-known and well-rehearsed notion of 'a toolbox' – where philosophical concepts are simply applied in other practices – towards a new assemblage whose parts are so intertwined that it is difficult to see what is affecting what. Where concepts, emotions, screams, whispers, profits and losses, insights, foresights and oversights, all broil in an endless morass where simple cause and effect are not only impossible to judge, but meaningless when imposed. We would like this machine to re*design* Deleuze in the same way in which through Deleuze we re*think* design. For if we take seriously Deleuze's assertion of a pragmatic philosophy creating concepts immanently intertwined with other creative practices, then we must find that 'his' concepts will be knocked into new directions by the encounter. It will be as insightful for us to see how connections with designing in all its forms effect swerves in Deleuze's thought as it is to watch his concepts steam into design's placid landscape disrupting its deeply held beliefs. We will see how to undo design's reliance upon form (Antonioli, Crawford, Marenko) and function (Beaubois) and the ways in which they can be used to dominate one another, as well as considering the machinic, socio-political and creative constructs determined in the design machine's relation to the art machine (Sauvagnargues) and craft-making machines (Crawford), to social activist machines (Hroch) or capitalist machines (Brassett). We will see encounters with Deleuze swerve speculative hardware design (Hales) and the milieu of illustration (O'Reilly). And in all these cases, whether Deleuze's, or Deleuze and Guattari's, creative thought is overt in driving these disruptions of design or is one set of concepts among many (including those launched from Georges Canguilhem, Stuart Kauffman, Gilbert Simondon, Isabelle Stengers, Lars Spuybroek, to name but a few), we will find that we must think differently about Deleuze. The Deleuze-design machine's affects have no privileged direction of impact.

Let us be clear from the start: *no matter in which form it happens to be materialised, design is here not considered a thing, but a process.* A process of change, invention and speculation always possessing tangible implications that cannot but affect behaviours and lives. Designing describes a field concerned not only with the creation and materialisation of possible worlds, but also a way of thinking and critically responding to current issues and concerns. Whether we are dealing with products or scenarios, packaging or experiences, things or digital platforms, services or territories, organisations or strategies, designing traverses, creates, manipulates and affects all of these expressions of human inventiveness. As a process, designing mobilises the many materials, methodologies, semiotic regimes and imaginary worlds along ways that intersect with the already fluid but sometimes concrete or totally evaporated process of capital. Indeed, it is its proximity to the flows of capital constituted as such by the global Capitalist Machine that leads to its (design's) critics bemoaning its friendliness with capitalism, if not its collusion. In 1971, the designer and social activist Victor Papanek led such a critique of design in his *Design for the Real World*, famously stating in its Preface that:

> There are professions more harmful than industrial design, but only a very few of them. And possibly only one profession is phonier. Advertising design, in persuading people to buy things they don't need, with money they don't have, in order to impress others who don't care, is probably the phoniest field in existence today. Industrial design, by concocting the tawdry idiocies hawked by advertisers, comes a close second. (Papanek 1985: xi)

Firmly in the pocket of advertising in materialising 'harmful' 'idiocies', the 'phony' industrial design Papanek rails against fuels the motor of surplus-value generation and capitalist growth through its delivery of a 'Kleenex Culture'. For many, the design professions are so deeply involved in the Capitalist Machine that it is difficult to see the difference between them. For others, there are ways in which designers whose social consciences have been pricked can articulate their practice either steeped in criticality (Dunne and Raby 2013), or direct activism (Julier 2013b, 2013c; Manzini 2014).

Design's critics may have Deleuze and Guattari on their side. In *What is Philosophy?* they write:

> Finally the most shameful moment came when computer science, marketing, design, and advertising, all the disciplines of communication, seized hold of the word *concept* itself and said: 'This is our concern, we are the

creative ones, we are the *ideas men!* We are the friends of the concept, we put it in our computers' (1994: 10; original emphases)

To engage in the creation of concepts, and store them in computers for the purposes of communication, design (along with other capitalist cogs, marketing, advertising and computer science) engages in a similarly phony, indeed *shameful* activity. Some of our contributors will examine the relation of design to the Capitalist Machine in a little more detail (Brassett, Hroch), but it is worth mentioning now how we respond to Deleuze and Guattari's comment quoted above. As philosophers working in design contexts we might simply say 'sorry'. But we are not in a discussion with Deleuze and Guattari *about* design. Philosophy is not about debate after all (Deleuze and Guattari 1994: 28). We are *not* even *interested* in what they *say* about design: not simply because their attitude to the design profession is antipathetic, or even because what design might have been at the end of the 1980s and the beginning of the 1990s is quite different to what design is today, but because *they* are not the point. Their concepts and the creative opportunities they allow are. There seem to be two ways in which anyone with an interest in both Deleuze and design might approach the topic, steeled against their criticism: either by examining their antipathy, locating it in its critical context and evaluating the impact of their position on the practice – this does not appear to have happened yet, and may prove fruitful for further investigation. Or one could unpack and examine the moments where design seems to get a better press in their work: see O'Reilly in this volume, who does this in relation to Illustration, and Matthew Kearnes, who emphasises design's 'ontological incompleteness' (2006: 74) in relation to the question of nanotechnology and the works of Deleuze and Simondon. We shall return to the dynamic opportunities of design's 'ontological incompleteness' below, but it is also worth noting at this point that Deleuze and Guattari express designing in this way. In their book on Kafka they write: 'Two problems enthral Kafka: *when can one say that a statement is new? . . . and when can one say that a new assemblage is coming into view?*' (1986: 83; original emphasis). This second clause is as follows in the French: '*quand peut-on dire qu'un nouvel agencement se dessine?*' (Deleuze and Guattari 1986: 149). '*Se dessine*', translated in the English publication as 'coming into view', is an interesting phrase for us. '*Dessiner*' is the French word that captures 'to draw' as well as 'to design', 'to make' and 'to form'; '*se dessiner*' gives us 'to stand out', 'to *emerge*'. The autopoietic emergence of form that happens when an assemblage self assembles is an important aspect of designing and one that we emphasise in this book, across all of the chapters in many different ways. It is also a key feature of the assemblage that forms itself as we bring Deleuze and designing together.

There is yet another way of dealing with this bringing together of Deleuze and designing, clearly expressed by Deleuze and Guattari when they write: 'What is the best way to follow the great philosophers? Is it to repeat what they said or *to do what they did*, that is, create concepts for problems that necessarily change?' (1994: 28). This collection of essays attempts to follow Deleuze and Guattari by 'doing what they do' and to create concepts in a philosophical plane that cuts through the plane of designing. As these planes 'interfere' (1994: 216–8), we strive to allow for a new becoming for Deleuze-designing, which emerges autopoietically as its own assemblage. This book is therefore the outcome of the exploratory effort to create such a construct, and offers a glimpse of the possible networks elicited by the emerging assemblages of Deleuze and designing. It is neither the first nor last word on the topic, but inserts itself in the middle, in an experimental fashion that allows both designing and Deleuze to become on multifarious trajectories.

We might, therefore, also be following the thought: 'Never interpret; experience, experiment' (Deleuze 1995: 87). For us, and the authors participating in this book, this is not a difficult or strained task, since designing – defined (provisionally here) as the momentary coalescence of future possibilities materialised today, whether this might take the form of things, images, experiences, services or strategies – operates as a profoundly disruptive force in contexts increasingly marked by complexity and contingency. Already, designing operates in a milieu of experience and experiment, connected to futures, presents and histories, in the middle of the psycho, social and ecological materialities that it constructs and that it is constructed by. In the multiform entanglement of commercial practices, theoretical discourses, industrial agendas, consumer lifestyles and behaviours, at the intersection of material cultures, object theories, marketing requirements, craftsmanship models, creativity and innovation paradigms, entailing a set of skills enabling designers to recognise, address and negotiate complex and often conflicting demands. Designing is optimally positioned to delineate, reflect and question the ways in which the relationships between human and non-human agencies elicit affects, tell stories and ultimately make us think by doing. Designing experiments and experiences in ways that Deleuze and Guattari create for philosophy. Sometimes both come close to the Capitalist Machine[1] and at others they clash in opposition. Neither serves as a point at which other creative practices should be rigidified and condemned. Indeed, the complex milieu in which any creative practice exists (as mentioned above) currently appears to demand a similarly complex approach to its interrogation, experimentation and experience. This volume offers one such approach.

This complex nest of intertwining concepts delineated by the coming together of Deleuze and designing does not produce easily defined affective relationships. While it has been important to highlight the impacts upon ways of thinking about Deleuze that his work's encounter with designing offers (along with the more simple mapping of the use value of Deleuze's concepts to designing), the relationship Deleuze–designing does not allow of simple biunivocity. As soon as we allow for the double disruption that this new assemblage produces, we will notice that the ripples of creative affect radiate across a wider landscape than that delimited by Deleuze and designing alone. To understand this it might be necessary to unpack this notion of 'disruption' a little more.

In innovation studies (which spans business, technology and economics, organisational psychology and sociology, as well as creativity and design studies), the concept of disruption has a very specific use. Coined by Clayton Christensen (1997), the term describes the way that smaller technology companies innovate radically through the creative use of old technology. While disruption is not often the *aim* of any innovative act, it can be the *affect*. A business can feel the affects of disruption without being its target, and can realise the disruptive power of its activities without them being the aim. Deleuze and Guattari have shown throughout their work together that the Capitalist Machine's tendency to schizophrenise at the edges and imperialise at the centre, and for pockets of schizophrenising resistance to develop throughout, with drives to control at the edges, does not allow for easy dichotomisations where one is good and another bad. The same holds for disruption/radical/revolutionary innovation and its 'opposite' incremental/sustaining/evolutionary. These concepts operate in a much more complex (and interesting) space.[2] Organisation theorists Michael Tushman and Charles O'Reilly, in an article called 'The Ambidextrous Organisation: Managing Evolutionary and Revolutionary Change' (2004), recognise this complexity in mapping a way for organisations to be 'ambidextrous' and to be open to engaging with both types of innovation activities. Félix Guattari in *Les Trois écologies* (1989) writes similarly, albeit not quite so biunivocally. For him it is necessary sometimes for activists in their struggle against Integrated World Capitalism to adopt identity positions, rigidifying themselves at moments of active opposition, coalescing under familiar, and historically problematic, subject positions. For both the Capitalist Machine and those positioned oppositionally to it, taking conceptual sides is not so simple (as Brassett discusses in this volume). For us, then, in approaching Deleuze and design, taking sides is also not an option. Deleuze's work – 'Deleuze' – must be as open to disruption out of its well-wrought identity position as the 'design' he and Guattari malign so much, even at those moments when their very identities are being reified.

We are not, therefore, prescribing a new breed of 'Deleuzian design'. Indeed, *is there a Deleuzian way of designing?* is a question that is worth investigating. While some of the chapters found here (Crawford's in particular) address this question head-on, we invite readers to draw their own conclusions. As stated earlier, this book is about thinking design *with* Deleuze, by exploring the possible alignments, discordances and crosspollinations between the two creative practices: to assemble a Deleuze-designing machine. To think design with Deleuze does not mean extracting ideas from an established philosophical corpus and then applying them to design. The point is not a philosophy 'applied' to design; or worse, a philosophy wanting to stand in normative authority over design to monitor its activities. Rather, this is about a processual, becoming way of proceeding (albeit not a method), a way of re*designing* the relationship between thinking and making through a nonlinear, emergent, open perspective; as comes through strongly regarding Deleuze, and Guattari's, discussions of pragmatics and practical philosophy (Deleuze and Guattari 1987; Deleuze 1988). Deleuze's empiricism is the opposite of an applied philosophy: 'Empiricism starts with an entirely different assessment: analyzing states of things so as to bring out previously nonexistent concepts from them' (Deleuze 2006: 304). In a radical disruption of canonical philosophy what now comes to the fore is an existent state of things out of which new concepts – and new practices – are to be extracted. This is the nature of Deleuze's empiricism. States of things are multiplicities, and in multiplicities what goes on between points is more important than the points in themselves (Deleuze 1995: 147). For Deleuze it is not the beginning or the end that counts but the middle, the multiple middles, and the milieus they describe: intersections, crossings, inflections, where a multilinear complex folds back on itself and where philosophy can interconnect with what is outside itself. 'I tend to think of things as sets of lines to be unravelled but also to be made to intersect. I don't like points; I think it's stupid summing things up' (Deleuze 1995: 160). Thus, one of our motivations for promoting the encounter between philosophy and design comes from considering the ways that philosophy might insert itself in the middle of what is already happening in designing. In many ways, we have noted, design as a cluster of practices and disciplines is having a stronger role in shaping the world. Design's current concern for co-creation, openness, nonlinearity and experimentation suggests that there exist already points of connection to Deleuze's thought. Indeed, we believe that a philosophy as an open empirical system is particularly suited to articulate some of the phenomena and concerns currently informing and transforming the theory and practice of design.[3] Designers, practitioners, critics and theorists are increasingly coming together to reflect on, and to respond to, the changes traversing established modes of practice within design, either by rethinking the economic models upon which design is predicated (inbuilt obsolescence, anyone?), pushing the technological boundaries within which it operates, or questioning the traditional top-down attitude of designers and manufacturers towards end-users. The practice of design is shifting to collaborative, multi-authorial platforms. New networks for sharing knowledge are creating communities that work in collaboration, and this open source movement is questioning the boundaries between user and producer (for example, *FabLabs*, a global network of small-scale workshops offering cutting-edge digital fabrication technologies to communities in dozens of cities and countries). The DIY culture of the make and repair movement, enabled by 3D printing and low-cost, miniaturised electronics, is redefining the relationship between making and thinking, theory and practice; new business models emerge with crowdfunding platforms like *kickstarter*; a surge of upstream and interdisciplinary design means that the traditional distinctions between different disciplines seem increasingly obsolete; finally, design is becoming more and more concerned with social innovation (Manzini 2014), social change and activism (Lees-Maffei 2012; Julier 2013b, 2013c; Steenhuisen 2013), and used as an investigative tool in the field of speculative design and design fictions (Hales 2013) and critical design (Dunne and Raby 2013; Malpass 2013) and as a way of catalysing strategies of innovation. All of these cases show design (traditionally thought) shifting its loci of impact on the world, and at the same time undergoing (or exacerbating already contained tendencies to) ontological disruption.

What is remarkable is that we are witnessing a profound shift, no longer based on what design *is*, but on what design is becoming because of what it can do: a shift from design as problem solving to design as problem finding. The former – where design is thought as the act of finding solutions to problems – is the rational and linear interpretation that evaluates design's activities in terms of efficiency and performance, and has dominated the world of design since the advent of modernity.

In this sense, design is a task-oriented, performance-measured, linear exercise that ultimately reduces uncertainty by promoting functional competence. This is the conventional view of design as enforcing and reproducing market ideologies and working as a technology of affective capture.

On the other hand, design as *problem finding* has to do with increasing complexity, problematising the existent, developing a critical and conceptual perspective, first of all on design itself. For example, design for debate and critical design use their materials, whether objects or concepts, to raise discussion on specific issues and to frame new problems. We will return to the matter of 'problems' in relation to design in more detail below, but would like next to turn to the issue of defining design, or rather to consider what design has been and what its becoming might offer.

A Thousand Tiny Definitions of Design

We have stated that for us designing is a process by which future possibilities tend to coalesce in/as the present, no matter the singular form this coalescence might take. While everyday usage might position design as a thing – 'this is a terrible design!' – there is a history of discussion of it both as an evolving practice, a multiplicity of (evolving) practices, and as a process. For design theorist Richard Buchanan, 'No single definition of design, or branches of professionalised practice such as industrial or graphic design, adequately covers the diversity of ideas and methods gathered together under the label' (1992: 5). IDEO's head of Human Factors, Jane Fulton-Suri (2003) and practitioners/theorists Alain Findelli and Rabah Bousbaci (2005) have highlighted the changing nature of designing. Furthermore, design and any research associated to design has no single definition but must be taken instead as an 'interdisciplinary form of inquiry' (Almquist and Lupton 2010: 3). This makes for a complex space of what Matthew Kearnes calls design's 'ontological incompleteness' (2006: 74).

Before beginning to embark into this complex space and seeing what forms a Deleuze-designing assemblage might take, it is worth charting some of design's definitions. We start with what design is conventionally taken to be, namely, the intentional planning, the ideal blueprint, even the cunning deceit. For philosopher Vilém Flusser the very word 'design' contains in itself the roots of cunning action, deception and trickery, and a designer is 'a cunning plotter laying his traps' (1999: 17). It is worth quoting Flusser at length here, not simply for his insight on the etymology of the word (an etymology picked up by Anne Sauvagnargues in this volume, but with different affect), but for the questions he raises about the proliferation of the word 'design' in contemporary culture:[4]

> In English, the word *design* is both a noun and a verb (which tells one a lot about the nature of the English language). As a noun, it means – among other things 'intention', 'plan', 'intent', 'aim', 'scheme', 'plot', 'motif', 'basic structure', all these (and other meanings) being connected with 'cunning' and 'deception'. As a verb ('to design'), meanings include 'to concoct something', 'to simulate', 'to draft', 'to sketch', 'to fashion', 'to have designs on something'. The word is derived from the Latin *signum*, meaning 'sign', and shares the same ancient root. Thus, etymologically, *design* means 'de-sign'. This raises the question: How has the word *design* come to achieve its present-day significance throughout the world? This question is not a historical one, in the sense of sending one off to examine texts for evidence of when and where the word came to be established in its present-day meaning. It is a semantic question, in the sense of causing one to consider precisely why this word has such significance attached to it in contemporary discourse about culture. (Flusser 1999: 17)

Design theory offers a wealth of definitions, from Herbert Simon's *The Sciences of the Artificial* (1969), to Richard Buchanan's notion of 'wicked problems', to design consultancy IDEO's 'design thinking'. In *The Sciences of the Artificial* Simon identifies design as ultimately a problem-solving activity 'concerned with how things ought to be, with devising artefacts to attain goals' (1969: 59). His notion – to this day one of the most quoted definitions of design – states: 'Everyone designs who devises courses of action aimed at changing existing situations into preferred ones' (1969: 55). Compare this with another equally influential notion of design as form-giving activity (Alexander 1971), where design is seen eminently as the activity of making things. These two positions embody well the tension historically traversing design, as design theorist Lucy Kimbell points out:

> On the one hand, following Alexander's thesis, designers give form to things; they are privileged makers whose work is centrally concerned with materiality. This is the tradition of craft and professional design fields that create specific kinds of objects, from furniture, to buildings, to clothing. Simon, on the other hand, suggests that designers' work is abstract; their job is to create a desired state of affairs. This way of thinking about design is the core of all professions, not just the work of engineers and designers of artifacts. (Kimbell 2011: 291)

For Simon design is an activity that seeks to change existing situations into preferred ones. However, while Simon is concerned with design's prescriptive outcome, design theorist Richard Buchanan's influential paper 'Wicked Problems in Design Thinking' (1992) borrowed the notion of wicked problems (Rittel and Webber 1973) in order to shift design discourses from the tangible (artefacts) to the intangible (systems, organisations, experiences), in so doing opening the way for further developments of the practice, notably towards 'design thinking'.[5] Buchanan argues that 'designers are concerned with conceiving and planning a particular that does not yet exist' (1992: 17), thus insisting on the open-ended future implications of design. For both Simon and Buchanan the implications are clear: design is always future oriented, as it is constantly engaged with turning what is into what *could*, *might* or *ought* be.[6]

Along with the future-orientation of design, or maybe because of it, these definitions also have in common their postulation of a connection between design and change. If this seems rather obvious, it also throws into the open, and openly questions, the models, paradigms and tacit knowledge that often underpin ideas of 'change': the methods deployed to achieve it, the practices that can enable it, and those that might prevent it. In short, the multiple entanglements associated with materialising the 'not yet' now.

This book wishes to suggest other ways of thinking about design. If design has the potential to reveal the richness of the world, this richness gets diluted when design is taken to be a thing, linearly designed, representing an equally linear path. If, as we state repeatedly, design is not a thing but a process, the question will therefore be not what design *is*, but rather *how* its process can be thought, articulated, embodied and practised. We contend that such a thinking about design will offer myriad more ways of expressing the opportunities in which future, present (and past) are created through designing than do simple, deterministic or static notions. While it may be that such thinking will demand a departure from current definitions, it may be that we engage with or cut through them; our having quoted them already has shown this. As we work designing through Deleuze, we might at times favour an oblique and less representational approach, a *minoritarian* line that eschews the normativity of given definitions, that is able to account for the mutations that the field of design is – and has always been – dramatically undergoing. By advocating an open-ended enquiry that reflects the participation with the practices of 'making worlds' and 'creating futures' found in designing, we will highlight those aspects of the Designing Machine that are both ontologically dynamic and create dynamic ontologies. For us, the more design is expanding its remit and scope, the more it becomes significant to offer *not* a normalising or normative definition of design, but rather a working, flexible, negotiable, situated framework within which any practice might be considered to be that of design*ing*. The gerund form here is chosen to indicate the inherent processual nature of design and the continuity it connotes projected into the future. Nevertheless, as mentioned, and like Guattari's 'little soldiers' (1989), it may sometimes suit us to retrench upon well-understood forms of design, if only to see where they might be unravelled and opened up to new creative possibilities, or as activist forms intent on disrupting other areas.

We will engage more fully in the following section with Deleuze's idea that philosophy is a creative and revolutionary practice precisely *because* it is always creating new concepts. We see this resonate with our positioning of designing as the material expression now of future opportunities: where designing as a creative act has the possibility to disrupt the present. Briefly now, we would like to highlight that this type of designing is already partaking of an approach to pragmatics outlined by Deleuze, where *immanence* and *becoming* are important moments in its practice. This liberates us from the normative imposition of *a* fixed definition and allows us to consider designing as a way of investigating the possible via material means. In this sense it becomes an articulation of myriad creative responses to any (proposed) opportunity space: in other words, the tangible embodying of speculative operations upon possible futures. Thought in this way, designing as creative process comes close to philosophy as creative process. Which is not to say that they become equivalents, but that the different planes upon which they operate have a momentary connection. In 'On Philosophy' Deleuze says: 'That's what it's like on the plane of immanence: multiplicities fill it, singularities connect with one another, processes or becomings unfold, intensities rise and fall' (1995: 146–7). Design's unfolding into so many different arenas of activity, its multiplicitous guises and disguises leading to its ontological incompleteness, show the points at which it interacts with the plane of immanence as constructed and expressed by philosophy. Later in the same conversation Deleuze, after citing poets, painters, novelists, composers, and philosophers of course, says: 'The whole thing is a crossroads, a multiple connectedness' (1995: 155). We will add designing, designers and other related thinkers and do-ers to this, as you will see in the book that follows. Furthermore, within this broiling mass of 'multiple connectedness' designing becomes a form of theoretical-practical research process to investigate and interrogate core issues and questions of contemporary culture, be they digital technologies and new media, politics and social conflict, the intersection between science and art, social responsibility and citizen participation. As we highlight the creative, immanent and, above all, practical philosophical assemblage that Deleuze and designing becomes, we will see designing assert itself as a questioning and investigative tool. Designing offers not only the interface between the material and the immaterial, the motor for innovation, the expression of the tangible form of possible futures, but also the critical embodying of all these concerns in their practical resonance.

Mapping the Themes of the Book

If we were to map where the lines of creative opportunity might emerge from navigating the entanglements of Deleuze and Guattari with designing, we would do well to acknowledge where such connections have already been highlighted. First, with only a few shining examples,[7] there is the philosophical engagement with designing. Second, the ways in which the field of design articulates itself as a critical and theoretical – often highly conceptual[8] – practice, which indicates both the tensions and questions already pervading the world of design, and the further conceptual articulation sought. Finally, we cannot ignore the malleability that Deleuze's thought has shown to possess in relation to what is perhaps the closest field to design to have been exposed to a dialogue with Deleuze's thought: architecture (Eisenman 1992a, 1992b, 1992c; Cache 1995; Rajchman 1998; Williams 2000; Ballantyne and Smith 2001; Grosz 2001; Lynn 2004; Ballantyne 2007; Brott 2011; Carpo 2011; Frichot and Loo 2013). While some of the authors collected in this volume do engage with some thinkers about architecture (Crawford, Hales, Marenko) we have been eager to keep our focus on designing.

This broad landscape of intellectual and practical discourses (philosophy of design, critical design, Deleuze and architecture) offers a milieu within which *Deleuze and Design* can emerge. In other words, we would imagine this project in a space in the philosophy of design where Deleuze can be foregrounded, as well as in a practice of critical design driven by Deleuze's thought and practice of creative philosophy, and a highlighting of the spaces relating to design that have been forgotten when architecture has constructed its own assemblage with Deleuze. *Deleuze and Design*, then, aims to interrogate the rapidly evolving world of design as an aggregate of material practices that demands new and flexible bodies of theorisations capable of articulating its mutating nature and propensity to capture the future. Emerging discourses within design that are of particular relevance here concern practices of co-design, open design,

design thinking, speculative and critical design. We will do this by encountering philosophy, critical design practice and speculative spaces but in ways not offered in other related milieus. We propose these as interventions within these discourses, not necessarily oppositional, but sometimes singular and partial.

One of the ways into this construction is from the thought that design needs to be alert to what is circulating outside its familiar domain. Not a surprisingly original thought, but one that it is often necessary to rethink as some notions have quickly become canonised: form and function, the role of the user, the ethics of designing, designing as problem solving, and so on. To open up onto thought and practice from outside might either bring in completely new issues with which to contend, or rework these tired old authoritative positions. For example, the existing design-mediated, but also somatic and cognitive, relationship between users and increasingly sentient digital devices demands a theoretical shift that can reflect what is already taking place within design-mediated practices and entanglements between the human and non-human, something that the notion of 'user' as a clearly separate and distinct entity from the object used is no longer able to capture (see Marenko in this volume). The centrality of the user in design has been questioned as too reductive of the richness of the interaction between humans and things, and as a tool of instrumentalisation by design (Almquist and Lupton 2010). It has also been critiqued as the product of an over-deterministic object-centric perspective that leaves little space for *people* (rather than users) to act and improvise in their fluid interaction with designed artefacts (Redström 2006). Another example would be the way in which not only Deleuze and Guattari's work but also other creative philosophies affirm the distribution of the agency of material things and the symmetry between human and non-human actors, pointing to the kind of reflection that should concern directly – and in doing so redefine – the theory and practice of design.[9] And so, as the chapters of this book collectively chart, we urge design to look eagerly to those concepts and practices that can assist its theorising, given that the entanglements of matter and meaning we are part of are no longer resolved by well-trodden formulas such as 'form follows function', or by straightforward paradigms based on usability and the modernist assumption of the centrality of the user.

Deleuze and Design stems, in one part, from the fundamental consideration that design would do well to mongrelise its diktats. The more design changes, expands and broadens its scope and field of action, the more it needs to be conversant with what philosophers, critical thinkers, theorists, and designers of concepts are developing. Furthermore, as design theorist Victor Margolin writes, designers 'need early warning systems to alert them to social trends that might have a bearing on what they design, and they require the intellectual tools to reflect on the meaning of these trends and their ethical implications' (2007: 14). Design is exquisitely located to embody in a creative, experimental and innovative way the questions and tensions circulating in these ideas and the way they are reformatting the paradigms of the world we inhabit. It has done so for many years (Flusser 1999), incorporating many other forms of practice and thinking into its remit (Kimbell 2011, 2012) as well as offering for other disciplines ways of thinking and doing that open up creative opportunities (Tonkinwise 2014). Our urge for the need for designing to look beyond its boundaries and engage with Deleuze's thinking comes not because being open is anathema to it (though it can, at times, coalesce strongly around certain dogmas), but because a Deleuze-designing assemblage might itself provide singular materialities worth noticing. By engaging, for example, with the creative and transformative practice of giving shape to concepts, the critical thinking emerging from this process is in turn taken further to explore processes of designing, challenging the meaning and values of existing creative practices, all the while expressing the seductive power of philosophy to affect existence, provoke responses and destabilise the known. Even when that creative practice is Deleuze's own work. As mentioned above, we are as eager for his work to be as open to creative impact from design as the other way around.

In pursuit of this, the book's contributions as a whole address a number of Deleuze's concepts, especially those that might prompt design to rethink some of the notions it tends to assume as immutable. For example, the ways in which the creation of the new and ideas on the future are thought and materialised are central to any design discourse. Deleuze's actualisation of the virtual provides a counterpoint to the conventional design dictum 'form follows function' to explain and conceptualise how objects come into being. The concept of becoming resonates strongly with designing seen as a process of ontogenetic dynamism, and reinforces design's own inbuilt relationality; that is, it emphasises the way in which design keeps on proliferating through the agential power of each and every designed object, either tangible or intangible, to be not only a meaning-making machine but a receptacle of further actions, behaviours and events. Indeed, design keeps on designing. Connected to the above is another key point that design needs to take on board, which concerns ways in which Deleuze provides a springboard to overcome the narrow impositions of the hylomorphic model. If in general Deleuze's brand of vitalist nonorganic materialism ought to affect the way design (as a complex nexus of theories, practices, cultures, discourses and industries, each with its own material entanglements) theorises its own presence in the world, and formalises its own agenda of speculative and tangible interventions, it is imperative that the limitations of hylomorphism are grasped and reflected upon with the means that Deleuze offers (among others, especially Simondon, as Crawford, Hales and Sauvagnargues show in this volume). The expression of matter as generating its own form, and how this capacity for self-organisation allows different models that describe the creation of the new and the emergence of objects from matter, provides the opportunity for a critical reformulation of design's theoretical and practical positioning.

Some thoughts about actualisation are relevant here. Deleuze affirms that only the transition from the virtual to the actual is based on genuine innovation (Deleuze 1991). While a process of realisation allows only a limited number of possibilities to be reproduced and there is no space for novelty to manifest itself (an apt description of the hylomorphic model), actualisation on the other hand engenders the emergence of new forms, of the 'not yet' through the unfolding of matter and the interaction of forces at play (see Beaubois, Hales, Marenko and Sauvagnargues in this volume). In what can be read as a warning to overplanning by design, Deleuze writes:

> We give ourselves a real that is ready-made, preformed, pre-existent to itself, and that will pass into existence according to an order of successive limitations. Everything is already completely given: all of the real in the image, in the pseudo-actuality of the possible. Then the sleight of hand becomes obvious: if the real is said to resemble the possible, is this not in fact because the real was expected to come about by its own means, to 'project backward' a fictitious image of it, and to claim that it was possible at any time, before it happened? In fact, it is not the real that resembles the possible, it is the possible that resembles the real, because it has been abstracted from the real once made, arbitrarily extracted from the real like a sterile double. Hence, we no longer understand anything either of the mechanism of differentiation or of the mechanism of creation. (Deleuze 1991: 98)

The only true 'difference, divergence or differentiation' (Deleuze 1994: 212) happens in what Deleuze calls the 'inventive drama' of actualisation – the movement from the virtual to the actual, where a contraction of virtuality takes place, whilst containing the germs of yet more virtual events to come. Only actualisation is genuine creation because it breaks with the principle of identity, whilst opening up new problem frames that question the existent. Actualisation can be thought of as a *prob-lematic* and problematising event, and it is creative precisely because of this. If actualisation is the (problematic and problematising) relationship between what is and what could be it has certainly plenty to offer to design.

These are just a few examples of the many themes that occur through-out this book, but already we can see how these encounters between Deleuze and designing manifest an impact on the boundaries of design as a discipline. What we are finding, then, is a milieu that theory and practice are constructing as a critical, contested space where multiple ways of theorising design and practising philosophy might be imagined.

Theory and Practice

Because of our position as philosophers (with an interest in Deleuze) immersed in the theory and practice of design, we are both intimately motivated to reflect on what might possibly emerge from an encounter between Deleuze and design, on what mutating shapes the Deleuze-designing assemblage might take. Another creative impulse for this book was given by the awareness that a field like design, steeped in tricky, always complicated, and never linear modes of expressing the relation-ship between theory and practice, could benefit greatly from a remap-ping of such a relationship informed by Deleuze's analyses. 'No theory can develop without eventually encountering a wall', says Deleuze in conversation with his friend Michel Foucault, 'and practice is necessary for piercing this wall' (Foucault 1977: 205). And furthermore he adds:

> Possibly we're in the process of experiencing a new relationship between theory and practice. At one time, practice was considered an application of theory, a consequence; at other times, it has an opposite sense and it was thought to inspire theory, to be indispensable for the creation of future theoretical forms. In any event, their relationship was understood in terms of a process of totalization. For us, however, the question is seen in a dif-ferent light. The relationships between theory and practice are far more partial and fragmentary. On one side, a theory is always local and related to a limited field, and it is applied in another sphere, more or less distant from it. The relationship which holds in the application of a theory is never one of resemblance. Moreover, from the moment a theory moves into its proper domain, it begins to encounter obstacles, walls, and blockages which require its relay by another type of discourse (it is through this other discourse that it eventually passes to a different domain). Practice is a set of relays from one theoretical point to another, and theory is a relay from

one practice to another ... Representation no longer exists; there's only action – theoretical action and practical action which serve as relays and form networks. (Foucault 1977: 205)

As each one is necessary to the development of the other, theory and practice must be seen as an integrated assemblage. What matters are the connections between them and the creative opportunities that their capacities for affecting and being affected by each other promote, rather than their synthesis, the hierarchy of their positions or their relationship of direct causality. This immanence of theory and practice allows us to get closer to a practical and materialistic philosophy capable of examining matter without ever presupposing its structure, and capable of investigating both the uncharted territories of design processes as much as the elsewhere of thought (Deleuze 1988). A great deal of Deleuze's work focuses on the problem of practice, specifically how the force of creativity can be triggered, and how a philosophy can be truly a practice. His insistence on philosophy as a practical and experimental enterprise, as the creative act of inventing concepts, and always outside of itself, traverses all his work. Deleuze's idea that philosophy is creative and revolutionary precisely because it is always creating new concepts deeply resonates with the demands of designing, always engaged as it is with thinking about the 'not yet'. Even more pertinent to designing is Deleuze's affirmation that new concepts should be both necessary and unfamiliar, as well as being a response to real problems (Deleuze 1995: 136), and express an event (of which more later). Deleuze's discussion of the notion of a problem in his book on Bergson (1991) is of particular relevance here. In relation to what he regards as the misconception that thinking is the search for solutions to problems, Deleuze writes that 'True freedom lies in a power to decide, to constitute problems themselves ... the truth is that in philosophy and even elsewhere it is a question of finding the problem and consequently of positing it, even more than solving it' (Deleuze 1991: 15). Positing a problem has therefore to do with invention, rather than uncovering solutions that already exist; it is about creating the space, the milieu in which problems may become, along with the solutions that go with them. It is about creating the terms by which a problem will be stated. Problems have no given solution; they must generate solutions by a process whereby what did not exist, what might never have happened, is invented.

Deleuze compares the force of inventing concepts to a feedback loop, to an echo chamber, where in order to get moving an idea has to traverses different filters, different fields. Philosophy clearly needs non-philosophy: 'philosophy needs not only a philosophical understanding, through concepts, but a nonphilosophical understanding, rooted in percepts and affects. You need both. Philosophy has an essential and positive relation to nonphilosophy: it speaks directly to nonphilosophers' (Deleuze 1995: 139–40). This has two main implications both relevant to the theory and practice of design, as well as to design's problematising of their relationship: first, that there is no thinking without doing; and then, that there is no hierarchy between thinking and doing. This has an impact upon how we consider philosophy, especially in its relation to designing.

The key question is no longer what *should* philosophy do, but what *can* philosophy do? What sort of impact can it have on other disciplines? On design itself? Indeed, this is a philosophy that is concerned not with justifying established notions, but with exploring the unthought-of, not simply a way of thinking existing problems anew, but a way of formulating entirely new ones. Philosophy for Deleuze is no longer a set of injunctions: *you should think this*, but an exploratory machine, a voyaging in the possible, an adventure in inventing concepts and experimenting with experiences: *what thoughts does it allow me to think*? Which new problems does it allow me to formulate? The problems are not the point of philosophy, but the milieu in which problems are problematised is. Here we find the creative sparks from the connection of the Deleuze machine to the designing machine most illuminating. Designing thought similarly not only untethers itself from the teleological demands of *problem solving*, but pushes beyond even repositioning itself as *problem generating*, to an even wider scope of *possibility creation*.

In 'What is the Creative Act?' (2006), Deleuze maintains that ideas must be taken as potentials already *engaged* with a specific mode of expression, and inseparable from it, so to think an idea means being already engaged with a certain milieu, be it philosophy or the arts or sciences. Or, design: as O'Reilly examines in this volume in relation to illustration practice. And this engagement is necessary. Not only does philosophy have the same status as the arts and sciences and therefore cannot exert any claim of superiority over other disciplines, it must also continuously forge alliances, even rudimentary ones, with them. Without alliances with other disciplines, philosophy cannot be properly practised. Again, philosophy needs nonphilosophy with which to form networks of mobile relations – be they sciences or the arts or design. Design, in turn, needs its own network of connections, junctions and conduits, not least – as Sauvagnargues shows here – with the art machine.

One of the aims of *Deleuze and Design* as a whole, then, is to bring to the fore some of these rudimentary alliances, to tap into these emerging networks and foster new transversal relations to show the multiplicitous ways that the two creative practices of philosophy and design can assemble new machines. This is why we are convinced that philosophy needs design. Likewise, design needs philosophy, if it wants to capture and problematise some of the concerns that are turning it more and more into a magnifying lens with which to observe and critique the existent.

The Creation of the New

In a way, this whole book is about this topic, and some contributors address it specifically (in particular Brassett), but it's worth mentioning here some of the key thoughts about the creation of the new that help orientate this work as a whole. For Deleuze one of the key tasks of philosophy is to figure out not what should be thought, but under which conditions the new is created – in other words to explore the process of creation. Thus, the key question is: how is it possible to think about the production of the new? Bound up with a creative evolution, the production of the new is not something transcendent, a mysterious founding break, or a drastic interruption, but something completely immanent happening in time. It is always about virtualities being actualised. What is important to underline here is the extent to which the virtual is always process and production, rather than a product; a container of manifold tendencies or propensities that can be actualised, rather than a fixed sequence with a teleologically predetermined goal; an urgent, insistent, unpredictable force that can insert itself into (and break apart) the tangibility of concrete reality.

If 'to design' means always to engage with the making of the new, designing involves having a powerful perspective on the future. Where some design theorists argue that there is a future *only* by design (Fry 2009), we might say that design makes possible futures materially present now. It is in a crucial creative position that generates present experiences and the futures that they might become, by engaging with those future becomings. Designing creates the milieus where future, present and, indeed, past enter into being as process. Alfred North Whitehead writes: 'Immediate existence requires the insertion of the future in the crannies of the present' (1961: 191). It seems to us that this existence is one that is designed, in that it is constructed upon the manifold affects and effects of designing; and that this process of designing existence also requires the milieu of the present (and all its crannies) as it inserts the future.

With all its own 'middles' (see O'Reilly here on milieu), designing also produces vectors that intersect a multiplicity of other forces – political, economic, social, cultural, experiential, institutional, and, as we have been arguing here, philosophical – and in so doing complexifies even further the processes engaged in the construction of present, future and past. It is not the future in itself but participates in its creation through becoming; it is not an event in itself but participates in its generation; it is not history itself that is designed, but the becoming past of the present. To be a designer, then, means to occupy the extraordinary space between the world as it is, the world as it could be, and the world that was. It means always to be ready to leap into the unknown. Which is, of course, not without risk.

There is a steadily growing awareness from within the world of design that the faster the pace of change (see Hroch and Marenko in this volume), the more engaged designers need to be, precisely because of the position they occupy in-between so many problem spaces, future-present-past complexes, and other social, cultural, political, economic entanglements. So: if designers are key agents directly and actively involved in this process of making worlds, they will need an array of theories, tested methods, strategic positions, figurations and fabulations with which to think. The aim of this book is to suggest that these can be found by connecting with Deleuze's philosophy, and its own multi-tude of middles. Design theorist Victor Margolin (2007) believes that only few calls for social change have come from designers, and that the design community is yet to produce its own arguments about the kinds of changes it would like to see, though in the years since he said this, design has made more effort in impacting in this area (as Hroch discusses here). Unlike Margolin however, we think that the world of design is already traversed by terrific debates and is continuously in the process of re-assessing itself, its role and its aims. Margolin's call for a deeper engagement of designers who face increasing complexity not only in terms of the array of products they design, but also in terms of the issues emerging from new practices, behaviours, lifestyles and relation-ships with the designed world, is not falling on deaf ears.

Genesis of the Book

We have already mentioned how our fortunate position working in theory and practice has contributed greatly to foment the reflections that culminated in this book. Here we would like to chart some of the events and opportunities that informed the evolution of this project. Some of the material that has found a location here has come from a number of interventions that have kept us occupied and thinking in the past few years.

Betti Marenko was invited to present a paper at the *Deleuzian Futures* conference hosted by The Porter Institute for Poetics and Semiotics, Faculty of Humanities, Tel Aviv University in May 2011. This event constituted the ideal backdrop that enabled the initial idea of working design through Deleuze to develop forward and acquire unexpected articulations. Thanks must go to Ian Buchanan who was the first to suggest that a book on Deleuze and Design was indeed due for the Deleuze Connections series. While working on our book proposal a call for papers was issued and we received a huge number of abstracts and proposals. This gave us a clear indication of the appetite (in both the world of design and that of Deleuze studies) for a project that could combine them in original and innovative ways. The project started to acquire a 'shape by debate' during events and occasions both in London – where a series of talks and seminars with our postgraduate students at Central Saint Martins helped us to refine ideas and keep on sharpening our theoretical tools – and abroad. Like our ideas, we travelled far and wide, taking these interrogations to various parts of the world. In February 2013 we hosted in New York – together with fellow contributor Derek Hales – the *Design Studies Forum* panel on the theme of *Deterritorialising Design: Rethinking the Relationship Between Theory and Practice*. This event, which took place at the 2013 College Art Association conference, allowed us to test some of the initial lines of flight of the book with an audience of design theorists, practitioners and educators. Thanks to Stuart Kendall for graciously inviting us to share ideas in this forum. Further and equally stimulating discussions took place during the First Deleuze Studies in Asia Conference, *Creative Assemblages* at Tamkang University, Taipei, Taiwan in May 2013, when we hosted a panel titled *Deterritorialising Futures: Deleuze and Design*, with Derek Hales and John O'Reilly.

Conclusion

One of the main ideas driving this book is that design is a profoundly disrupting force that can be used to disrupt the Deleuzian paradigm, or what the field of Deleuzian Studies is becoming. Thus, the aim is twofold: to use Deleuze to disrupt design, while simultaneously using design to disrupt Deleuze – taken as the complex of discourses coalescing around the name. It is a tenet both of Deleuze's use of 'becoming' and of theoretical discussions of creativity (in the sciences as well as arts), that the act of becoming/creativity should allow others the space and energy to become/create. It is for this reason that an encounter between Deleuze and design must allow for the creative disruption of each element and that each is not positioned as a totalising discourse with power over the other. We might even say that the title should have been *Re-designing Deleuze*, that is, how to deterritorialise Deleuze through and with the disruptive force of design.

Acknowledgements

JB: Thanks, first, to Betti for reconnecting me with Deleuze; having dropped out of the Deleuze Machine since the Warwick conferences in the mid-1990s, my intellectual focus has been elsewhere (even though it has always had a strong whiff of Deleuze). I first encountered Deleuze while a postgraduate student at University of Warwick in 1988. My doctorate was supervised by Nick Land, whose genius was unfathomable and whose influence still affects me like radiation burn. I owe him much more than I can imagine. My colleagues and students on both BA Product Design and MA Innovation Management at Central Saint Martins have taught me much; I would like especially to thank two colleagues, Nick Rhodes and Monika Hestad, without whom my thoughts on design and innovation would be poorer. Another colleague, Dominic Stone, has been very supportive of my work on this project, as well as providing a space for discussion about design, management and complexity. In all my years at Central Saint Martins Lorraine Gamman has supported and cajoled me in so many ways. Working with Ruth Clarke on translating Anne Sauvagnargues's chapter was an absolute joy.

Some of my thoughts collected here have been test-driven elsewhere. My chapter-specific thanks are found with that piece. Finally thanks to my family, Joanna, Ewelina, Tomasz and Jacek, for creating a productive milieu for this work with patience and much support.

BM: Thanks to the colleagues and scholars met at the numerous Deleuze Studies conferences I took part in during the past five years. The countless inspiring conversations I had in different parts of the world and the dazzling atmosphere of heady brainwork and free-spirited concept-making stayed with me long after the conferences were over, and inform obliquely this entire project. In particular I want to thank Nir Kedem, Patricia Pisters and Anne Sauvagnargues. All my colleagues on the team of BA Product Design, Central Saint Martins and in the Programme of Ceramic, Industrial and Product Design have been instrumental, each one in their own often idiosyncratic way, in shaping my understanding and love of design, and making me question it, always. They are too numerous to mention. Thanks to Lorraine Gamman for her unfailing support. Thanks to the research team at CSM, in particular the Associate Dean of Research, Janet McDonnell, for believing in this project and supporting us with a research grant that allowed us to carve some precious time to think and write. Thanks to Carol MacDonald at EUP for her immense patience and for sticking with us even when the project seemed to be moving exceedingly slowly. I am grateful to, and humbled by, my students at Central Saint Martins. They are my most challenging audience yet. Finally, a very special and felt thanks to Piero Ricci, my former Professor of Sociology of Culture at the University of Urbino, who in 1990 one day told me: 'It is time you read Deleuze.'

JB and BM: This book is dedicated to our colleague and friend Nic Hughes who died when this book was beginning to take shape. Nic was a formidable designer and educator, and he had unfailing enthusiasm and dedication towards this book project. We wish to remember him by including here the abstract of the chapter he never had time to write:

Nic Hughes, 'Chattering Objects'. This chapter takes Deleuze and Guattari's connected notions of 'schizo flux' (1984) and assemblage and identifies their presence within various critical design collaborations. It shows how these concepts can be mutated through practise, culminating in alternative design approaches and new methodologies. In a 1972 issue of *L'Arc*, Deleuze describes how Guattari treated writing as a highly productive 'schizo flux' – a generative tool that produces numerous lines of flight. Transpose this idea into design and one immediately destabilises its key teleological mandates; design as 'schizo flux' is no longer primarily concerned with either achieving goals or solving problems. In fact, it neatly inverts the classic design formulae of providing answers, favouring instead a continuous flow of questions. Design as 'schizo flux' can be developed further by introducing the related concept of assemblage. This is useful if you take the view that design is an act of terraforming. It brings forth new worlds and artefacts. Seen through a Deleuzian lens these whole worlds are constructed from disparate heterogeneous parts – assemblages. In this 'flat ontology' the designer is only one of many entities contributing to the wider design matrix. Under this model designers essentially curate patterns, clusters and networks in order to establish worlds and spaces that pose questions. They re-order the existing furniture in order to produce question-factories. The two concepts from Deleuze and Guattari will be supported by three case studies from critical design: Dunne and Raby, DWFE and DSG. In their commitment to innovation and 'creating concepts' (Deleuze and Guattari 1994), Deleuze and Guattari augmented and re-patterned the work of many philosophers, practitioners and outsiders, using their ideas as DNA and giving birth to some wonderfully monstrous offspring. This chapter seeks to promote a similar approach within design, outlining existing progressive design trajectories and accelerating them further through a Deleuzo-Guattarian framework.

Notes

1. We have encountered design's collusion with capitalism a little above, for philosophy's see Deleuze and Guattari's *What is Philosophy?* 'Modern philosophy's link with capitalism, therefore, is of the same kind as that of ancient philosophy with Greece: *the connection of an absolute plane of immanence with a relative social milieu that also functions through immanence*' (1994: 98; original emphasis).
2. Management theorists Haridamos Tsoukas and Robert Chia take concepts from chaos and complexity theories deep into management and organisation theories (Tsoukas 1998; Tsoukas and Chia 2002). See also Brassett (2013).
3. See *Open Design Now* (Van Abel et al. 2011), a collaborative effort of Creative Commons Netherlands, Premsela, the Netherlands Institute for Design and Fashion and Waag Society, and events such as The Future in The Making: Open Design Archipelago (Milan Triennale 2012).
4. See Binder et al. 2011 for an excellent analysis of the meanings of design and its current transformations.
5. This is a practice promoted by IDEO (Brown 2008, 2009) and others (Berger 2009; Martin 2009; Neumeier 2009) as a way of incorporating design into business practices (as well as public and third sector organisations) in ways that were not traditional. It has been argued by these people that design offers ways of doing business (strategically, organisationally and culturally) that is necessary because traditional approaches (as taught on MBA courses (Neumeier 2009)) are inadequate. Some designers have found this liberating as it offers them new avenues for developing their own creative offers. Others have criticised it as cheapening their skills by saying that quick-fix workshops for CEOs on 'design thinking' involving post-it notes and brainstorming can be equated with designing (McCullagh 2010). Excellent overviews/critiques of this idea can be found in Kimbell 2011, 2012; Johansson-Sköldberg et al. 2013; Tonkinwise 2014.
6. We should note here that the difference embodied by each of these modals maps entirely different design scenarios, agendas and values, partially reflected in the distinction between Simon's and Buchanan's positions above.
7. See, for example, Centre for Philosophy and Design (CEPHAD), The Royal Danish Academy of Fine Arts, and *Design Philosophy Papers* (DPP), founded by Tony Fry, Professor, Design Futures Program at Griffith University, Queensland College of Art Australia, to name some of the most influential and established. Some notable design journals are open to more philosophical expressions: *Design and Culture* and *Design Issues* for example.
8. See, for example, Anthony Dunne and Fiona Raby's work (2013). Dunne was Professor and Head of the Design Interactions programme at the Royal College of Art in London, and Raby is Professor of Industrial Design at the University of Applied Arts in Vienna.
9. Signs of these affinities and alignments are evident, for example, in the way a dialogue has recently emerged between design and Bruno Latour's agential theory (2008) and Jane Bennett's radical materialism (2010). See also Kimbell 2013. Though this position is not without its critics too. See Hables Gray who writes: 'Like all subcultures, STS [Science and Technology Studies] has a number of shibboleths, conventional wisdoms that are charming, even though they are ridiculous if interrogated closely. The "agency of things" is one of the most annoying' (2014: 375).

References

Alexander, Christopher (1971), *Notes on the Synthesis of Form*, Cambridge, MA: Harvard University Press.

Almquist, J. and J. Lupton (2010), 'Affording Meaning: Design-Oriented Research from the Humanities and Social Sciences', *Design Issues*, 26:1, pp. 3–14.

Ballantyne, A. (2007), *Deleuze and Guattari for Architects*, London and New York: Routledge.

Ballantyne, A. and C. Smith (eds) (2001), *Architecture in the Space of Flows*, London and New York: Routledge.

Bennett, Jane (2010), *Vibrant Matter: A Political Ecology of Things*, Durham, NC and London: Duke University Press.

Berger, Warren (2009), *Glimmer: How Design Can Transform Your Business, Your Life, and Maybe Even the World*, London: Random House Business Books.

Binder, Thomas, G. De Michelis, P. Ehn, G. Jacucci, P. Linde and I. Wagner (2011), *Design Things*, Cambridge, MA and London: The MIT Press.

Brassett, J. (2013), 'Networks: Open, Closed or Complex. Connecting Philosophy, Design and Innovation', in J. Cai, T. Lockwood, C. Wang, G. Tong and J. Liu (eds), *Design-Driven Business Innovation. 2013 IEEE-Tsinghua International Design Management Symposium Proceedings*, Beijing: IEEE, pp. 1–11.

Brott, Simone (2011), *Architecture for a Free Subjectivity: Deleuze and Guattari at the Horizon of the Real*, Farnham and Burlington, VT: Ashgate.

Brown, Tim (2009), *Change by Design: How Design Thinking Transforms Organizations and Inspires Innovation*, New York: Harper Collins Publishers.

Brown, T. (2008), 'Design Thinking', *Harvard Business Review*, June, pp. 84–92.

Buchanan, R. (1992), 'Wicked Problems in Design Thinking', *Design Issues*, 8:2, pp. 5–21.

Cache, Bernard (1995), *Earth Moves: The Furnishing of Territories*, Cambridge, MA and London: The MIT Press.

Carpo, Mario (2011), *The Alphabet and the Algorithm*, Cambridge, MA and London: The MIT Press.

Christensen, Clayton (1997), *The Innovator's Dilemma: The Revolutionary Book That Will Change the Way You do Business*, Boston: Harvard Business School Press.

Cox, Sir George (2005), *Cox Review of Creativity in Business: Building on the UK's Strengths*, Norwich: Her Majesty's Stationery Office.

Coyne, R. (2005), 'Wicked Problems Revisited', *Design Studies*, 26, pp. 5–17.

Deleuze, G. (2006), 'What is the Creative Act?', in G. Deleuze, *Two Regimes of Madness: Texts and Interviews 1975–1995*, trans. A. Hodges and M. Taormina, New York: Semiotext(e), pp. 312–24.

Deleuze, Gilles [1990] (1995), *Negotiations 1972–1990*, trans. M. Joughin, New York: Columbia University Press.

Deleuze, Gilles [1968] (1994) *Difference and Repetition*, trans. P. Patton, London: Athlone.

Deleuze, Gilles [1966] (1991), *Bergsonism*, trans. H. Tomlinson and B. Habberjam, New York: Zone Books.

Deleuze, Gilles [1970] (1988), *Spinoza: Practical Philosophy*, trans. R. Hurley, San Francisco: City Lights Books.

Deleuze, Gilles and F. Guattari [1991] (1994), *What is Philosophy?* trans. G. Burchell and H. Tomlinson, London: Verso Books.

Deleuze, Gilles and F. Guattari [1980] (1987), *A Thousand Plateaus. Capitalism and Schizophrenia 2*, trans. B. Massumi, London: Athlone.

Deleuze, Gilles and F. Guattari [1975] (1986), *Kafka: Toward a Minor Literature*, trans. D. Polan, Minneapolis: University of Minnesota Press.

Deleuze, Gilles and F. Guattari [1972] (1984), *Anti-Oedipus. Capitalism and Schizophrenia 1*, trans. R. Hurley, M. Seem and H. Lane, London: Athlone.

Deleuze, Gilles and F. Guattari (1975), *Kafka: Pour une litterature mineure*, Paris: Éditions de Minuit.

Dunne, Anthony and F. Raby (2013), *Speculative Everything: Design, Fiction, and Social Dreaming*, Cambridge, MA and London: The MIT Press.

Eisenman, P. (1992a), 'A _ _ Way From/To Architecture', in C. C. Davidson (ed.), *Anywhere*, New York: Rizzoli, pp. 108–15.

Eisenman, P. (1992b), 'K Nowhere 2 Fold', in C. C. Davidson (ed.), *Anywhere*, New York: Rizzoli, pp. 218–29.

Eisenman, P. (1992c), 'Unfolding Events', J. Crary and S. Kwinter (eds), *Incorporations*, New York: Zone Books, pp. 423–6.

Frichot, Helene and S. Loo (eds) (2013), *Deleuze and Architecture*, Edinburgh: Edinburgh University Press.

Flusser, V. (1999), 'About the Word Design', in V. Flusser, *The Shape of Things: A Philosophy of Design*, London: Reaktion Books, pp. 17–21.

Flynn, F. J. and J. A. Chatman [2001] (2004), 'Strong Cultures and Innovation: Oxymoron or Opportunity?', in M. L. Tushman and P. Anderson (eds), *Managing Strategic Innovation and Change: A Collection of Readings*, 2nd edition, Oxford: Oxford University Press, pp. 234–51.

Foucault, Michel (1977), *Language, Counter-memory, Practice: Selected Essays and Interviews*, Oxford: Blackwell.

Fry, Anthony (2009), *Design Futuring: Sustainability, Ethics and New Practice*, Oxford: Berg.

Fulton Suri, J. (2003), 'The Experience Evolution: Developments in Design Practice', *The Design Journal*, 6:2, pp. 39–48.

Giaccardi, E. (2005), 'Metadesign as an Emergent Design Culture', *Leonardo*, 38:4, pp. 342–9.

Grosz, Elizabeth (2001), *Architecture From the Outside: Essays on Virtual and Real Space*, Cambridge, MA and London: The MIT Press.

Guattari, Félix (1989), *Les Trois écologies*, Paris: Editions Galilée.

Hables Gray, C. (2014), 'Agency, (Re)Invention, and the Internet: The Limits of High Theory', *Science as Culture*, 23:3, pp. 375–81.

Hales, D. (2013), 'Design Fictions: An Introduction and Provisional Taxonomy', *Digital Creativity*, 24:1, pp. 1–10.

Johansson-Sköldberg, U., J. Woodilla and M. Çetinkaya (2013), 'Design Thinking: Past, Present and Possible Futures', *Creativity and Innovation Management*, 22:2, pp. 121–46.

Julier, G. (2013a), 'Design Activism: Introduction. Material Preference and Design Activism', *Design and Culture*, Special Issue: 'Design Activism', 5:2, pp. 145–50.

Julier, G. (2013b), 'From Design Culture to Design Activism', *Design and Culture*, Special Issue: 'Design Activism', 5:2, pp. 215–36.

Julier, Guy (2013c), *The Culture of Design*, 3rd edition, London: Sage.

Kearnes, M. (2006), 'Chaos and Control: Nanotechnology and the Politics of Emergence', *Paragraph*, 29:2, pp. 57–80.

Kimbell, L. (2013), 'The Object Fights Back: An Interview with Graham Harman', *Design and Culture*, 5:1, pp. 103–17.

Kimbell, L. (2012), 'Rethinking Design Thinking: Part 2', *Design and Culture*, 4:2, pp. 129–48.

Kimbell, L. (2011), 'Rethinking Design Thinking: Part 1', *Design and Culture*, 3:3, pp. 285–306.

Kolko, Jon (2012), *Wicked Problems: Problems Worth Solving: A Handbook and A Call to Action*, Austin: Austin Center for Design.

Latour, B. (2008), 'A Cautious Prometheus? A Few Steps Toward a Philosophy of Design (with Special Attention to Peter Sloterdijk)', in F. Hackney, J. Glynne and V. Minton (eds), *Proceedings of the 2008 Annual International Conference of the Design History Society*, Falmouth (3–6 September 2008), e-books, Universal Publishers, pp. 2–10.

Lees-Maffei, G. (2012), 'Reflections on *Design Activism and Social Change*: Design History Society Annual Conference (7–10 September), Barcelona', *Design Issues*, 28:2, pp. 90–2.

Lynn, Greg (ed.) (2004), *Folding in Architecture (Architectural Design)*, revised edition, New York: Wiley.

McCullagh, K. (2010), 'Design Thinking: Everywhere and Nowhere, Reflections on the Big Re-think'; available at http://www.core77.com/blog/featured_items/design_thinkingeverywhere_and_nowhere_reflections_on_the_big_re-think__16277.asp (accessed 12 September 2014).

Malpass, M. (2013), 'Between Wit and Reason: Defining Associative, Speculative and Critical Design in Practice', *Design and Culture*, 5:3, pp. 333–56.

Manzini, E. (2014), 'Making Things Happen: Social Innovation and Design', *Design Issues*, 30:1, pp. 57–66.

Margolin, V. (2007), 'Design, the Future and the Human Spirit', *Design Issues*, 23:3, pp. 4–15.

Margolin, Victor and R. Buchanan (eds) (1996), *The Idea of Design*, Cambridge, MA and London: The MIT Press.

Martin, Roger (2009), *The Design of Business: Why Design Thinking is the Next Competitive Advantage*, Boston: Harvard Business Press.

Neumeier, Martin (2009), *The Designful Company: How to Build a Culture of Nonstop Innovation*, Berkeley: New Riders.

Papanek, Victor (1985), *Design for the Real World: Human Ecology and Social Change*, 2nd edition, London: Thames and Hudson.

Rajchman, John (1998), *Constructions*, Cambridge, MA and London: The MIT Press.

Redström, J. (2008), 'RE:Definitions of use', *Design Studies*, 29, pp. 410–23.

Redström, J. (2006), 'Towards User Design? On the Shift from Object to User as the Subject of Design', *Design Studies*, 27:2, pp. 123–39.

Rittel, H. and M. Webber (1973), 'Dilemmas in a General Theory of Planning', *Policy Sciences*, 4:2, pp. 155–69.

Sauvagnargues, Anne (2006), *Deleuze et l'art*, Paris: Presses Universitaires de France.

Simon, Herbert A. (1969), *The Sciences of the Artificial*, Cambridge, MA and London: The MIT Press.

Spuybroek, Lars (2008), *The Architecture of Continuity: Essays and Conversations*, Rotterdam: V2_Publishing/NAi Publishers.

Steenhuisen, B. (2013), 'How to Design for Social Change: A Template', *Journal of Design Research*, 11:4, pp. 301–16.

Stengers, Isabelle (2011), *Thinking with Whitehead: A Free and Wild Creation of Concepts*, Cambridge, MA and London: Harvard University Press.

Tonkinwise, C. (2014), 'Design Studies – What is it Good For?', *Design and Culture*, 6:1 pp. 5–43.

Tsoukas, H. and R. Chia (2002), 'On Organizational Becoming: Rethinking Organizational Change', *Organization Science*, 13:2, pp. 567–82.

Tsoukas, H. (1998), 'Chaos, Complexity, and Organization Theory', *Organization*, 5:3, pp. 291–313.

Tushman, M. L. and C. O'Reilly III [1996] (2004), 'The Ambidextrous Organization:

Managing Evolutionary and Revolutionary Change', in M. L. Tushman and P. Anderson (eds), *Managing Strategic Innovation and Change. A collection of Readings*, 2nd edition, Oxford: Oxford University Press, pp. 276–91.

Van Abel, Bas, l. Evers, R. Klaassen and P. Troxler (eds) (2011), *Open Design Now: Why Design Cannot Remain Exclusive*, Creative Commons, Netherlands: BIS Publishers.

Verganti, Roberto (2009), *Design-Driven Innovation: Changing the Rules by Radically Innovating What Things Mean*, Cambridge, MA and London: Harvard Business Press.

Williams, J. (2000), 'Deleuze's Ontology and Creativity: Becoming in Architecture', *Pli*, 9, pp. 200–19.

Whitehead, Alfred N. [1933] (1961), *Adventures of Ideas*, New York: The Free Press.

Chapter 1

Poised and Complex:
The Becoming Each Other of Philosophy, Design and Innovation

Jamie Brassett

Action in an open-ended world is potentially creative, in so far as individuals need to improvise . . . to act coherently.

Haridamos Tsoukas, 'On Organizational Becoming'

There is no stable difference between explanation and description, but only distinctions dealing with what matters, and with the environments required by what matters.

Isabelle Stengers, *Thinking with Whitehead*

All of this means that the strategy that we must adopt in our hand-to-hand combat with apparatuses cannot be a simple one.

Giorgio Agamben, 'What is an Apparatus?'

Introduction: Design and Innovation

To define 'design' is always to do it a disservice: there will always be something that either exceeds or is marginalised by any definition. Roberto Verganti, management scholar and champion of 'design-driven innovation', finds problematic the lack of a normative definition of design around which a community can converge (2009: 22). That design is a mass of opportunities, possibilities and activities undergoing constant change, and is therefore difficult to identify, is a problem he wants to solve. He proposes, early on in his book *Design-Driven Innovation* to pin-down design, to stop it being 'fluid and slippery' (2009: 22). Once defined and identified in its ontological certainty, design can more readily be shown to have operational value for areas that otherwise have viewed it with suspicion, at best, or hostility, at worst: areas such as management and business are of particular interest to Verganti. So he aims 'to show how managers can *leverage* design to enable their organizations to innovate' (2009: 25; original emphasis). In doing this he comes up with some interesting propositions outside of the 'traditional' views of design as dealing with form and function and material (at various levels of priority and degree) – namely that designers are mediators of interpretation, communication and meaning-generation. But in his drive to stasis Verganti seems also to tether such a practice too much to systems, organisations: *firms*, in business school parlance, unrepentant in manifesting discourses of order and control. For him, meaning is formed by designers as interpreters, at the behest of visionary leaders (of studios or other firms) and delivered through semiotic objects whose meanings are delivered to people as passive consumers.[1]

There is much to critique in this position, although to do so adequately would require more space than is available here. Nevertheless, I would like to focus a little on the 'problem' (as Verganti sees it) of a slippery design. The fluidity of design's ontology may not only be *unproblematic*, but also the marker of its success. Design, as Matthew Kearnes shows well in 'Chaos and Control: Nanotechnology and the Politics of Emergence' (2006), is always in a process of ontogenesis because it is in a complex relationship to a world that is itself complex and in motion: design contributes to such dynamism at the same time as being affected by this world of becoming. Design – and the innovation that it may drive – is not *firm*. Not only is this what design *is*, it is what it *does*: it makes the coherent ambiguous and the chaotic consistent, all the while offering its outcomes as elements of a flow that will become more, or less, than what they are (through use, understanding, affect). While design has many concrete expressions, these should be seen as fleeting moments of stability in a more general dynamism. Design not only takes us inside and outside boxes, it provides the boxes too. Design is fluid and makes fluid.[2] This reflects, also, some thoughts from designers and design researchers over the past fifteen years or so, regarding the changing nature of design practice, its practitioners, and the context in which together they generate value (for example: Fulton Suri 2003; Findeli and Bousbaci 2005; Julier 2013c). No longer mere stylists or salespeople, designers' ranges of influence and impact stretch into many areas. Design's constant reappraisal of the terms and conditions under which it operates points to a set of practices, and principles for practising, that remain far from equilibrium and massively open and connected to the world in which it works. Design is neither an easily identified, or identifiable, thing, nor are things designs. It is more than the sum of its parts, and some of its parts have the opportunity to take it into other areas. In fact this ability to make sideways, spreading, illogical (or differently logical) connections is itself seen as an important skill transferable from designing into other areas.

In the world of design-driven innovation, particularly that branded as 'design thinking',[3] this ability has been linked to philosopher Charles Sanders Peirce's notion of 'abductive logic', which management professor Roger Martin describes as: 'not declarative reasoning; its goal is not to declare a conclusion to be true or false. It is modal reasoning; its goal is to posit what could possibly be true' (2009: 64–5). So design is a process that engages with possibilities and the dynamic and complex ways that they may actualise. Design is becoming designing. While it is not the purpose of this chapter to provide an in-depth critique of abductive logic in particular, or of 'design thinking' in general,[4] the very fact that such discourses abound currently shows us that we are living at a time when the conditions for the possibility for designing (its meaning, value and very being) are evolving in exciting ways.

Bruno Latour made reference to this in a recent conference keynote address, saying that contemporary design is no longer about matters of *fact*, but matters of *concern*. No longer are *objects* designed but *things*. He explains:

> artefacts are becoming conceivable as complex assemblies of contradictory issues (I remind you that this is the etymological meaning of the word 'thing' in English – as well as in other European languages). When things are taken as having been well or badly designed then they no longer appear as matters of fact. So as their appearance as matters of fact weakens, their place among the many matters of concern that are at issue is strengthened. (Latour 2008: 5)

As designed things become more than (simple) objects, highlighting their complexity through the nest of affects within which they sit, then the forces that converge in creating such artefacts must similarly be complexified. Aspects of these forces I want to focus on here are philosophy, design and innovation, and a more fulsome engagement would encounter politics, economics, ethologies, histories, geographies and a whole host of relevant concerns too.

Designing things (products, processes, systems, garments, images, experiences, and so on) involves the material coagulations of affects, stories, and issues, with insight, foresight and hindsight inserted in their many folds. The intertwining of designer, what is designed, and for whom – involving matter at different levels of expression of its energies, with spaces and times entering, directing and transformed by their participation in all of this – delivers a multiplicity of levels, layers, agencies and energies of which 'complexity' is the simplest description.

Designers must be concerned with complexity because this complexity, I will argue, calls for *poise*.

These conditions are mutually determining for innovation too. As Andy Dong states in his broad review of 'design-led innovation' literature, design and innovation are mutually relevant in so far as they present 'design as set of deliberate activities to create new products (goods and services) that are novel and significantly valuable, a broadly acceptable definition of innovation', and 'because of the value of designers who, by nature of their education, have skills that match the requirements of innovation such as experimentation and invention' (Dong 2014: 2). The changing definitions of design allow greater scope for it to impact innovatively in different sectors. If design is 'ontologically dynamic', definitions of innovation have been remarkably static, until recently.[5] One of its most concise yet open descriptions is Sir George Cox's (2005), which builds upon work done in organisational psychology, notably by Flynn and Chatman (2004). Innovation is, Cox states, 'the successful exploitation of new ideas' (2005: 2). Innovation is creative, then, but not all creativity is innovative. To become innovative a creative act and its expressions need to be pitched somewhere and their impact judged to be successful.[6] Designing's innovation comes through its outputs (*what* it designs), processes (*how* it designs) and the nature of its impacts (what *happens* to/with its designs). The criteria for determining successful impact, manners of exploitation and conditions of creativity are open to interpretation, contestation and development, and it is one of the purposes of this chapter to interrogate some of them.

Success has been examined well in innovation literature over the past thirty years or so (see Porter 1985, 1990; Christensen 1997; Tushman and O'Reilly 2004, to name a few), and here I will focus in more detail upon *creativity* and *exploitation*. *Creativity*, as it is expressed in the work of Deleuze and Guattari, as well as Stuart Kauffman's work (particularly 1993 and 2008), is located at the complex boundary zone between chaos and order. *Exploitation*, with its connotations of power, control, putting to work, imperialism (Lyotard 1993) and overcoding (Deleuze and Guattari 1984, 1987, 1994),[7] points to Deleuze and Guattari's critiques of capitalism, design and, I will add, innovation.

The question of capitalism is not one that can be ignored by anyone involved in design and innovation. The dominant discourses of the latter have determined innovation as an activity that serves only to further the economic growth of its participants through the creation of surplus value (Schumpeter 1934): be they organisations, nation states, collections of individuals, companies, and so on. The word 'exploitation' in the definition above brings innovation close to the signifying regimes of the Capitalist Machine. It may be rather glib at this stage merely to state that it does not have to be so. That Cox's formulation of innovation does not constrain it to economic growth through surplus-value generation is one of the benefits of its use: it allows us to consider, therefore, that creativity can be used to produce impact in wider senses. But the shortcomings of its discourses need also to be challenged: a challenge I hope to begin here.

This chapter, then, will investigate creativity and exploitation in designing and innovating, to begin a way of thinking and practising these activities that emphasise design and innovation's dynamic ontologies. To do this I will first examine creativity as it is expressed in complexity biologist and philosopher Stuart Kauffman's work, particularly *Order out of Chaos* (1993) and *Reinventing the Sacred* (2008), finding creativity *poised* between chaos and order in a complex space. I will then explore the value in Deleuze and Guattari's work of complex mixtures of order and chaos, focusing on their example of bodies without organs.[8] These discussions will allow us to articulate the opportunities for creative processes for innovation and design that go beyond exploitation.

Critically Complex Creativity

Kauffman identifies three types of network, each characterised by different regimes of behaviour (1993; 2008: 112–19): order, chaos and critical complexity. A network that exhibits order is largely frozen. Any perturbation within its components, or the introduction of anything new, never gets the chance to have an affect, as the tendency towards freezing scales quickly through the system (2008: 112) and the network soon becomes stagnant. In the chaotic regime, Kauffman explains, 'small changes in initial conditions unleash avalanches of changes which propagate to many unfrozen elements' (1993: 174). Creativity here is impossible, because any new impact in such a network rapidly, and radically, changes everything: with disastrous results. ('Chaos is not order for free', Kauffman writes – where 'order for free' refers to self-organising emergence – 'I do not want my liver cells doing that, nor do you' (2008: 112). This caveat will return below in Deleuze and Guattari's work.) While chaos may be thought as a type of organisation (Tsoukas 1998; Tsoukas and Chia 2002), it is one where novelty has a tendency to impact catastrophically throughout the entire space.

Kauffman gives this all a *critical* spin, speaking of order and chaos in terms of sub- and supracritical systems respectively.[9] He writes:

If adaptive evolution requires heritable variation, subcritical organisations cannot vary enough to evolve well . . . Supracritical systems are so radically altered by any novel molecular input that they cannot stop varying. If evolution requires heritable variation, profoundly supracritical systems vary too much and too unendingly. (1993: 391)

For systems caught in the chaotic region any tendency towards change spirals out of control too quickly, leaving any semblance of consistency dissolved. On the other hand, a rigidly ordered space allows of no variation, change is stifled and stagnation tends towards death. This leaves the complex zone of emergent creativity 'poised' critically between order and chaos.[10] To consider these three regimes as sitting in a systematic relation, with the complex zone neatly buffering the ordered and the chaotic, does not do justice to the complexity of the system. To poise is not only to balance, serenely, between two opposing forces, but also to generate the opportunities for creative expression that come when seeming opposites collide, merge and repel. In *Reinventing the Sacred: A New View of Science, Reason and Religion*, Kauffman explains that the ordered regime contains within it small pockets of complex, critical, dynamic, creative emergence, operating in isolation from the general tendency towards frozenness of the whole (2008: 112). Similarly, within the chaotic regime, 'a twinkling sea of genes following tremendously long state cycles spreads across the network, leaving behind frozen islands' (2008: 113). As the general tendency towards chaos transforms in places into small, isolated islands of order (Serres 1982), we can note that the moment of change where order comes from an otherwise chaotic mess is complex, critical and creative. Both systems becoming poised is a complex matter. The evolution of life – and so with all creativity – Kauffman explains, occurs at the moment when one system changes into another. The space and time of critical complexity is mapped and instantiated at this moment. And here, too, is highlighted not the *being* of order, chaos or even criticality, but the *becoming* of each into the others; *complexity* happens not only at the boundaries, but also at the simultaneous creation and passing through of boundaries.

This is also the space of design and innovation. The American designer Charles Eames once stated in an interview conducted at the time of an exhibition of his work at the *Musée des Arts Decoratifs* (Paris 1969) that design always has constraints (Eames and Eames 2005). And it is something of a cliché in innovation circles to talk about 'thinking outside the box', which, while advocating the need to be free of constraints, does so in relation to them. Deleuze's position matches Eames's – 'creation takes place in bottlenecks' (1995: 133) – and Kauffman too shows that constraints provide important conditions for creativity. A cell that evolves is one that generates its own constraints in order to determine its consistency (Kauffman 2008: 85, 92), at the same time as it seeks to profit from opening up into new areas to provide opportunities for growth and change. A critical network is one poised in this moment of boundary setting and spanning, order production and chaos negotiation. This space of complex consistency and immanence engages a network of connected concepts, including those created by Deleuze and Guattari. Whilst it is enticing, even useful, to see Deleuze and Guattari's concepts oppositionally (those familiar with their work will recognise rhizomes and trees/roots, smooth and striated space, molecular and molar, minor and major literature, and many others), it may come as no surprise that I say their work is much more complex than this. They also poise creativity where order and chaos blur into and out of one another.

Deleuze and Guattari's final collaboration, *What is Philosophy?*, contains so much concerning the relationship between chaos, order and creative complexity that this could be said to be a point of the book. Throughout they show creation – philosophy's concepts, science's functives and art's affects – relating to both chaos and order. In ways that connect with Kauffman's discussion of biological processes, Deleuze and Guattari's articulations of chaos, order and a zone of indiscernibility between them deal with issues of emergence, complexity and the creative opportunities afforded by both.

Deleuze explains in 'On Philosophy' that 'multiplicities fill [the plane of immanence], singularities connect with one another, processes or becomings unfold, intensities rise and fall' (1995: 146–7). The plane of immanence is the creative milieu that forms as concepts are created, and the medium upon which creativity bases its activities. It is the space of poise. While the concept of milieu itself is too involved to investigate fully here, it is worth noting how this term is useful at this point. A milieu 'is made up', Deleuze writes in 'What Children Say', 'of qualities, substances, powers, and events . . . The trajectory merges not only with the subjectivity of those who travel through a milieu, but also with the subjectivity of the milieu itself, in so far as it is reflected in those who travel through it' (1998: 61).[11] Here the milieu hosts the coming together of children as subjects that become within it – the trajectories they take – in such a way that these dynamic trajectories also constitute the milieu itself. Deleuze focuses on children as subjects becoming with the space of their stories here, but the things of designing and the ways they innovate are as relevant. This coming together in mutual creativity defines immanence, and this is why Deleuze and Guattari talk of the 'plane of immanence' as a space, a milieu and its mapping: the plane of immanence is already in-between, in the middle, and has no beginning or end other than what it creates. Here becoming, *autopoiesis*,[12] self-organisation and emergence come to the fore, as long as they are poised on the edge of chaos.

Chaos provides philosophy with energy, and order provides consistency. The complexity of the resulting acts – the plane of immanence with its concepts roaming, attracting, pulsating, affecting, impacting – establishes the space of creativity. As this is everywhere in *What is Philosophy?* I will provide other lines of flight that may affect my discussion in different ways by drawing attention next to Deleuze and Guattari's body without organs (BwO). A challenging concept on its own, it is entangled with many of Deleuze and Guattari's other concepts so as to make it topologically complex. The BwO is the body stripped of all acts of organisation. It is the fluid mass of matter and energy considered not in any organised state. It is, in terms Spinoza (1955) uses for the body, the speeds and slownesses of a body's particles, and affective capacities, considered on their own. This is of course a little simplistic and the more complex aspects I will draw out next.

Designing, Innovating and the Body without Organs

Infiltrating their work from Artaud, the BwO appears first in the second section of the introduction to *Anti-Oedipus*, where it references Artaud, Marx, Freud, Beckett, Kant, God, and the psychoanalyst Victor Tausk. For Artaud, the BwO unpicked the blockages and organisation demanded by God in his desire to control us, and thereby reduced any capacity bodies had for His Judgement. Deleuze and Guattari explain:

> In order to resist organ-machines, the body without organs presents its smooth, slippery, opaque, taut surface as a barrier. In order to resist linked, connected and interrupted flows, it sets up a counterflow of amorphous, undifferentiated fluid. In order to resist using words composed of articulated phonetic units, it utters only gasps and cries that are sheer unarticulated blocks of sound. (1984: 9)

An agent of resistance, and a champion of chaos, the BwO prowls seductively throughout Deleuze and Guattari's work on capitalism and schizophrenia. Its expressions of liberation, subversion and creative destruction speak both of the times in which Deleuze and Guattari first used the concept (post-1968) and in a timeless way, in the engagement of activism. Deleuze writes further in 'To Have Done With Judgement' that the BwO 'is an affective, anarchist body that consists solely of poles, zones, thresholds, and gradients. It is traversed by a powerful, nonorganic vitality' (1998: 131). A determined opener of systems, and chaos inducer, the BwO still has some faces pointed towards order. It stalks the edge of ordered and chaotic systems, bringing both to each other but settling in neither. Interestingly Deleuze and Guattari describe the BwO as the 'pivot' (1984: 281) between massive, molar aggregates (where all tends to order and authoritative normalisation) and molecular and submicroscopic phenomena (where particular or partial investments cannot be overcoded into unified wholes). It lurks at the limits, 'haunts all forms of the socius' (1984: 281). The BwO marks the boundary between each side, and what lies beyond; it is the box and the dangerous thinking outside.

This is taken further in *A Thousand Plateaus*. The BwO 'swings between two poles, the surfaces of stratification . . . on which it submits to the judgement, and the plane of consistency in which it is open to experimentation' (Deleuze and Guattari 1987: 159). As it stalks the boundaries of order and chaos it becomes aligned with the plane of immanence upon which all flows, it spreads in all directions at speeds approaching the infinite (Deleuze and Guattari 1994). The BwO is creative becoming in all its terrifying glory: mixing, influencing, dissolving order and making chaos consistent. It opposes order with 'disarticulation . . . experimentation . . . and nomadism', as well as housing occurrences of the 'alluvions, sedimentations, coagulations, foldings and recoilings that compose an organism' (Deleuze and Guattari 1987: 159). The BwO might be the enemy of the organism (as was evident in *Anti-Oedipus*) but the processes of organisation into ordered wholes exist as strata upon the BwO. On one side it becomes ordered and organised when the lines of flight upon which it is constituted rebound from any boundaries it meets and fall 'back into the most miserable territorialities of the modern world' (Deleuze and Guattari 1984: 283).[13] On another it is chaotic and dissolved, heading towards untrammelled schizophrenisation and pure deterritorialisation. As a 'pivot' between the terrifying catastrophic opportunities of utter creative freedom, and the consistent but stultifying demands of order, the BwO is poised.

The BwO is complex and folded: this is its consistency. Its sides facing opportunities for opening onto creative chaos as well as those folding back onto the consistencies of order are in a dynamic, ever changing flux that makes achieving poise difficult. Thus the BwO provides complex opportunities for expressing design and innovation beyond any simplistic modelling of processes and actions. The complexity of a creative philosophy, pure abstractions and generalised movement, of strategies[14] forming at the boundaries of tendencies to consistency and dissolution that encompass the BwO, is the space of design, innovation and philosophy. The becoming of the BwO expresses creativity poised between order and chaos. It is worth, here, seeing how this might be of relevance to designing and innovating.

The UK Design Council's famous 'double diamond' of divergence 'Discover', convergence 'Define', divergence 'Develop', convergence 'Deliver' – experimentally and heuristically connecting and spreading, then analytically solving and delivering outcomes (The Design Council 2005: 6) – provides a teleological, linear and normative account of the design process. The brief denotes the opening onto this process, and the designed outcome the end. The 'double diamond' appears a simple, homogenising act coordinating order and chaos into a repeatable process model. As an assemblage, the 'double diamond' appears close to Deleuze and Guattari's description of the Capitalist Machine: territorialising (understanding the task at hand), deterritorialising (questioning assumptions, experimenting with ideas, decoding cultural and design languages), and reterritorialising (folding back onto the demands of the project). It is as if the Design Council uncovered the BwO in designing and tamed it for proper modelling. Innovation is home to even stricter models: the 'innovation funnel' and the 'stage-gate process' are the most dominant. In the funnel, the large open end represents a research department containing many personnel generating the new. The small tube represents the development section of the organisation, from which just one of the projects generated in the research phase will eject to market (with the others being shelved).[15] The 'stage gate' model is similarly linear, with the many generated projects being filtered through successive gates, in well-defined stages, before one well-managed outcome gets to market. While some iteration is allowed in these models, they are resolutely linear, and in the innovation sector, though funnels and stages may stretch or compress giving different values to research and development, their archetypes are still recognisable. Design and innovation processes, it seems, are places for what Deleuze and Guattari call intense axiomatisation and (over)coding, stratification and (re)territorialisation: to which I will return below.

A Designing Machine modelled by the Design Council will have moments when its becoming associates with that of the BwO, though in the end it will drift towards order; while an Innovation Machine seems rarely to approach the BwO. A question emerges for innovation: how do you make yourself a body without organs? While this question could capture what is happening in this chapter, I would like briefly to mention one other attempt if not to answer this question of innovation, then to pose it in a related field.

Drawing on philosophers and scientists of process and creative uncertainty (Deleuze, Whitehead, Bergson, Prigogine), management and organisation theorist Robert Chia works well to push his practices toward the BwO. In 'A "Rhizomic" Model of Organizational Change and Transformation: Perspective from a Metaphysics of Change', he writes:

> The ontological act of organization is an act of arresting, stabilizing and simplifying what would otherwise be the irreducibly dynamic and complex character of lived-experience. Organization is an inherently simplifying mechanism, and the idea of 'complex' organization(s) is in effect an oxymoron. (Chia 1999: 224)

There is much here that allies with the arguments of the current chapter, but Chia appears to be working on organisation and complexity as pure states. The complexity as I have been working with it is much more fluid, as are order and chaos. Thought of not as ideals, but as tendencies towards pure versions, these concepts are constantly swerved off course towards others. Even when they approach purity, in the most frozen or catastrophic states, moments of dissolution or self-organisation can occur. Pure complexity, one that is perfectly poised and unable to move unless pushed, seems also to be impossible. Kauffman shows that for creative evolution to flourish, poised complexity needs to drift towards chaos without ever going too far (1993: 286). Chia writing on his own (1998) and with Tsoukas (2002) ask their disciplines to consider organisation as something that happens to flux, rather than the stable basis upon which change impacts. The same suggestion needs to be considered by innovation – though it is in a more favourable position, because innovation is already a process of change and flux, and more difficult to capture unless through the imposition of rigid models of behaviour. The question posed of innovation above – how do you make yourself a body without organs? – is better put: 'how might your body without organs be set free?' And one of the responses might be, following Kauffman, Chia and Tsoukas: 'to recognise that organisation happens to change, not the other way around'.

An attempt to map the BwO's multiplicity of facets – with strata tending to order, lines fleeing to terrifying chaos – might illustrate it as 'a multiply spread and connected bunch of Xs' rather than 'double diamonds' or 'funnels'. Designing and Innovation Machines have capacities to dissolve and organise, create and signify, among a multitude of other affects: for example, to brand, make invisible, snoop, cajole, help, frustrate and relieve, and so on. An attitude to *points* is one determinant of their ontological status: points directed and determined, and attracted to being, stasis and identity; or smearing through points generating lines to be followed in many directions, and becoming.[16] The becoming-BwO of any assemblage will map the points and lines that constitute it, to see where clusters of assembling will emerge. This must accompany every act of designing or innovating.

Creative complexity is the proof of becoming, and also generates becoming. Complexity is not a zone where the relation between order and chaos can be policed. It is rather the name for the instances of order and chaos becoming each other. And when these instances spread at infinite speeds, the BwO is made. Designing and Innovation Machines reveal their BwOs through their production, when their becomings are mapped via points and lines, processes of experimentation and experience-production: even when these becomings tend towards the 'most miserable territorialities of the modern world' (Deleuze and Guattari 1984: 283), as these are also products of these machines. Indeed, these 'miseries' might be fundamental to designing and innovating. The constraints so important to designing could be seen as the *intensive products* of a designing seen as becoming. The BwOs of designing or innovating are fabricated as soon as the blocks and flows that traverse them are created through experimentation (Deleuze and Guattari 1987: 149). Each of their modes, modalities and models spring up as the blockages of flows to extract a surplus value of intensity (that is, exploitation of creativity for whatever means), and fluid opportunities emerge from opening and spreading into new realms, even 'double diamonds' and stage gates with their gatekeepers. 'In each case' of intense blockage, Deleuze and Guattari write, 'we must define what comes to pass and what does not pass, what causes passage and prevents it . . . something flows through channels whose sections are delimited by doors with gatekeepers, passers-on. Door openers and trap closers' (1987: 152–3). Blockages or disruptions are not necessarily damaging to the functioning of these creative activities, but spur creative experiment. A brief to design a 330ml water bottle may well be seen as the beginning of a process, and a constraint towards which all creative activity should converge. Re-positioning the brief in the middle of a creative process, allowing constraints (sociocultural and economic, as well as technical, material and formal) to *emerge* from the process, shows that designing can be mapped in ways that highlight disordered, creative, possible directions.

Henry Chesbrough (2003) pushes innovation practice outside of simplistic, closed, linear models and places all organisations involved in this practice in the middle of a landscape of creative practice in which they are all linked as nodes. His purportedly new paradigm for conducting business – open innovation – however, brings innovation back to familiar organisational constructs in so far as it locates the fruits of innovation as being controlled by familiar business forms (Brassett 2013a). The nodal points become attractors in the system and, like the 'double diamond', Chesbrough's model opens to become closed once more.

These models of designing and innovating should not serve as proof of their anathema to Deleuze and Guattari's philosophical creations, but as sites for a creative philosophical interjection. Those engaged in any creative task – not least designing or innovating or philosophising – should ask of these machines: who holds the whips? What passes across these machines? What does the blocking? How are they made? What are their modes? Where do they face order and chaos? How do their BwOs pivot? How can they be poised? Creativity, then, is a complex undertaking that has to be poised between utter dissolution of everything at infinite speed and the freezing of all possibilities into immovable lumps. Creativity is the product of a BwO pivoting between the sides looking to the miseries of order and those facing terrifying chaos; and there are BwOs of designing and innovating as of anything, they only need to be found/constructed.

It remains for the rest of this chapter to take some steps towards constructing BwOs of designing and innovating in so far as they open onto each other. As has been discussed, the BwO is a mix of the becomings into each other of all its possible faces, strata and trajectories that cross, form and border it. It is poised, complex and critical, forming from the processes that it promotes: an *autopoietic* autocatalysis that simultaneously fosters the creativity of its neighbours and milieu. In the following section I will map the concept of *exploitation* that is so closely wedded to a definition of innovation, highlighting its overcoding by the Capitalist Machine, as well as ways out of this towards something approaching the BwO.

On Exploitation

It is worth recalling the expression of Deleuze and Guattari's ire regarding design:

> Finally the most shameful moment came when computer science, marketing, design, and advertising, all the disciplines of communication, seized

hold of the word *concept* itself and said: 'This is our concern, we are the creative ones, we are the *ideas men!* We are the friends of the concept, we put it in our computers.' (1994: 10; original emphases)

Design and the other 'disciplines of communication' have captured and exploited philosophy's creative output and made it work for them. 'We do not lack communication', Deleuze and Guattari continue. 'On the contrary, we have too much of it. We lack creation. *We lack resistance to the present*' (1994: 108; original emphasis). As one of the disciplines of communication, for Deleuze and Guattari, design is no more than a conduit through which already created meanings are transmitted to the world for consumption; not far from Verganti's claim (2009). While it is an important principle for Deleuze and Guattari's creative philosophy that it does not deal in meanings or their interpretation (Deleuze entreats, 'Never interpret; experience, experiment' (1995: 87)), the pragmatic mapping of semiotic regimes[17] – wherein meaning generation and its imposition operate as functions of assemblages (see also DeLanda 1997, 2006) – can be an important, oppositional, practice. An oppositional stance for designing or innovating will come from reinvigorating their dynamism, allowing them to hunt down tendencies to interpret or deliver meaning, and replace them with urges to existence, or practices of experimentation. Through the redistribution of their workings towards acts of experiment and experience, designing and innovation work as creative cartographies resisting the present (Julier 2013a, 2013b; Brassett 2014).

This is a complex undertaking, first because of the relationship between capitalism – the Capitalist Machine – and the flows that it codes as Capital. There is no easy, temporally bound system of cause and effect here, but an open dynamic of self-generation/organisation; an ontogenesis of the Capitalist Machine that emerges from its constituents, their contexts and their relationships. This describes the immanence of capitalism axiomatising flows it has decoded in the production of Capital in order to make them work in the production of surplus value. 'Capitalism functions as an immanent axiomatic of decoded flows (of money, labour, products)', Deleuze and Guattari write; 'National States are no longer paradigms of overcoding but constitute the "models of realisation" of this immanent axiomatic' (1994: 106). This contains two aspects that need drawing out in regard to innovating and designing.

On one hand, organisations, businesses and firms for whom innovation is an important concern can be seen operating as the 'national states' of this quotation. Such organisations are neither paradigm-building (for

example, open or closed systems of innovation (Chesbrough 2003)),
nor paradigm-locked: they do not exist in relation to some transcendent
system according to which they are in a relation of subordination (even
if they generate that system). What they are and how they organise are
'models of realisation' of the immanent axiomatics of the Capitalist
Machine: they are micro-cogs of that machine, produced by and productive of it. This is the core definition of innovation as overcoded by this
Capitalist Machine: it (capitalism) is a machine generating surplus value
realised in various forms necessary to power its growth (Schumpeter
1934). It is upon and through this that 'success', 'exploitation' and
'creativity' are all overcoded.

On the other, Deleuze and Guattari mention 'products' here as an
example of decoded flows (along with money and labour): providing a
second moment of designing and innovation as a complex undertaking.
As the outcomes of innovation processes of design, strategy, management, and so on, products have not only been decoded but also overcoded by the Capitalist Machine, and as such are important aspects of
capitalism's self-construction. Further, as work done by Elizabeth Shove
and colleagues has shown (Shove et al. 2007), the practices these products become inserted into are neither mere vehicles for the transmission
of someone else's meaning, nor simply articles through which the many
are controlled by the few. Products (and anything that has emerged from
designing and innovating) can undergo decoding through their use that
instantiates them as loci of opposition, antagonism and activism, even
if they also become overcoded by tendencies to belonging as subcultural
markers of identity (Brassett and Booth 2008). An example of this
might be the safety pins used as jewellery by punks in the late 1970s:
decoded from their regimes of care, comfort and babies' nappies and
inserted into pierced body parts, or as overt decoration of clothing. They
soon became a punk brand identifier. Or: urban furniture designed to
facilitate skateboard tricks; graffiti as vandalism becoming markers of a
city's cultural identity; any viral marketing taking the disruptive, heterogeneous and rhizomatic affective possibilities of the early internet and
folding it into brand-driven commercial activity. These examples show
what Deleuze and Guattari, throughout their work, call capitalism's
reterritorialisation: its ability to take the disruptive, decoded aspects of
flows and fold them back into itself, recode them as Capital and use them
to drive profit. The moments of control, activism, identity production,
power and subversion (among many others) that exist in these examples
simultaneously, testify to a complexity beyond any simple identification
of 'good' and 'bad' practices. The Capitalist Machine is *poised*, taking

advantage of the cascading possibilities that proximity to chaos affords, while prioritising the faces it turns towards order, where it will be able to generate surplus value most easily. Its success comes from its ability to be poised, without being destroyed by the forces of creativity it needs.

Is this discussion further pushing design and innovation deep into the Capitalist Machine, as the only home of their work? The overcoding of all material and energetic flows by capitalism into Capital sounds very much like the 'successfully exploiting creativity' of innovation; and as innovation is often tied to powering economic growth through profit generation (Schumpeter 1934), it is not difficult to see how its treatment of creativity is allied with the workings of the Capitalist Machine in general. So what then for this discussion?

Capitalism does not have an opposite, but moments of disruption in its machinic constructions, even when they are oppositional. Just as we saw in relation to chaos, order and complexity above, capitalism operates a much more complex relationship to that upon which its being is determined. The Capitalist Machine decodes and overcodes, deterritorialises and reterritorialises, frees-up and constrains, dissolves and freezes: it produces Capital from surplus value generated by its complex interplaying of forces of chaos and order. Design and innovation may be important aspects of the way in which the Capitalist Machine does this (as are many others: education, collective action, philanthropy, and so on), but they are not necessarily capitalistic. Innovation is not necessarily tied to growth, though any innovating body may articulate, contingently, the conditions for its success this way. And growth may not necessarily be tied to its capitalist coding. The same goes for design. The Designing Machine may churn out products, images, garments, services and so on, as it is captured and aligned with the Capitalist Machine, such that they fuel profit growth. But designing (products, images, garments, services and so on) is not necessarily a capitalistic act.

Socially responsible design and social innovation, for example, use their creativities to make an impact in milieus that are not tied to profit (Thorpe and Gamman 2011). Clear Village (www.clear-village.org) – a charity based in London but with projects across many geographical locations – marries architecture, urban planning, social innovation, designing in a number of modes (fashion, product, service), collective and individual enterprise production, in different ways to achieve a range of aims that are particular to any given circumstance. Zamek Cieszyn (www.zamekcieszyn.pl) is based in a castle on the border between Poland and the Czech Republic. Simultaneously delivering design education, social and regional development opportunities, and commercial consultancy, its assemblage emerges from the many flows it accesses and modes of expression that it uses. Other design and innovation consultancies have functions that allow them to face in different directions. The South African designer Gustav Praekelt, for example, diverts funds generated by his commercial consultancy to a foundation, a function of which is to muster mobile technologies to engage in socially responsible work across Africa (http://praekeltfoundation.org). These three examples show different modes of operating Innovation and Designing Machines that are not, or not wholly, overcoded in terms of profit making. The conditions for success are not simply commercial growth. This is an important point. The criteria according to which these organisations attribute success (or failure) to their creativity emerge from the processes in each particular context. 'Exploitation' is simply one way of describing how creative activities and their outcomes, the organisational structures, their cultures and material expressions, are matched to the points in the world where they will impact. As such the most important issue is not whether designing or innovating are tied to 'exploitation' as modes of expression of the Capitalist Machine, but the machinic affects, the capacities for being affected, the blockages they experience and the leakages that seep from their multiplicitous, complex arrangements. The term 'exploitation' as used in innovation should be reinserted into the assemblage in which it was produced to see how it works, to identify the other assemblages that it fosters or blocks, and the semiotic regimes that it enforces or denies. This, as we saw above, is how to make yourself a BwO: map modes, create opportunities to be creative, experiment and experience, and poise.

The 'last words' that follow will point towards ways of poising Designing and Innovating Machines at the moments where order and chaos become each other, in relentless, dynamic change, where innovation and designing are poised in a becoming each other, and philosophy too. These last words are not meant to close the issue, but to point in directions for future development.

Last Words: Poised Designing Innovating Assemblages

'Gently tip the assemblage, making it pass over to the side of the plane of consistency', Deleuze and Guattari tell us in *A Thousand Plateaus*, it 'is only there that the BwO reveals itself for what it is: connection of desires, conjunction of flows, continuum of intensities. You have constructed your own little machine, ready when necessary to be plugged into other collective machines' (1987: 161). Assemblages, BwOs, machines for desiring, designing, innovating and philosophising, tip over the edges between order and chaos, always into and out of one or the other. A tipping that is poised as balance, poised as composed, but also poised as the act of chaos and order becoming each other: where the dissolute tends towards consistency, and the frozen dissolves into an oozing mess. Each movement changes the nature of the whole assemblage, and array of possible assemblages, that are so poised. Which repositions us (designers, innovators, philosophers, educators and all) – our 'little machines' – in new locations, ready to find new poise and to be pitched elsewhere. With innovating mapping and generating the spaces of strategic engagement, and designing expressing ways of becoming as things in these spaces (tipping the processes of innovation and spatial generation in new directions), the whole creative assemblage maintains a dynamic fluidity: coalescing here and there, becoming undone on occasions also. As Deleuze and Guattari note:

> Dismantling the organism has never meant killing yourself, but rather opening the body to connections that presuppose an entire assemblage, circuits, conjunctions, levels and thresholds, passages and distributions of intensity, and territories and deterritorializations measured with the craft of a surveyor. (1987: 160)

We need poise and positioning in a field of open possibilities, not ill considered, craft-less dissolution into death. Dismantling the organism far enough to find the openings, the points of cross-fertilisation or co-catalysis, the ways out of organisation without losing consistency of practice. Assemblages are those non-organised organisations, self-organising from chaos. Out of control enough to allow multiplicitous connective, conjunctive and disjunctive opportunities, and this side of chaos enough to construct productive, creative, consistent machines. The quantity and quality of these machines' drive to code, decode and over-code will define an assemblage's tendency: capitalist, militant, and so on. Such tendencies are not necessary either to the nature of the flows they engage, or the constructs they engender. Rather they emerge as contingent operations of the acts of constructing themselves: whether they align to massive, molar or micro-fascist machines, or whether fascism (for example) emerges from the particularities of the matter-energy-context encountered. It serves now to consider what a non-exploitative innovation and design might be, to uncover their BwOs, map their assemblages and find the ways they can be poised between order and chaos.

Simply stated, a poised innovation might occur when it has been complexified, where its tendencies to order and chaos mix. Unravelling but not dissolving, it is a practice that has consistency but is neither gaseous, solid, nor liquid, but all three in different constitutions at different times. It encompasses processes of making little machines with minor strategies that have to articulate their surroundings anew at every instantiation of themselves; micro assemblages that join together in loose collectives as they roll over their landscapes. Innovation thus expressed will drift, not grow imperially (Lyotard 1993). Its creative engine emerging as little innovation machines thread between chaos and order, in the boundary zone where anything can happen.

Insert 'design' for 'innovation' here and it will still work: designing at the creative, complex, poised edge, is the promotion of its own becoming. The concept of design 'digestion' (Brassett and Booth 2008) sought to place design-innovation in this complex zone. To disrupt the familiar stage-gate/funnel/'double diamond' models that direct creative practice to given ends, and insert positive feedback loops from people 'digesting' their products into a distributed process of designing. By reconsidering the boundaries between designers, clients, people, spaces and so on, we delivered a way of designing and innovating that was disruptive, aleatory and reconstituted passive users and consumers as active agents in never-ending innovation. Design digested focused on its creative process, the matter, values, practices and thoughts that it unleashed, without retrenching on any specific order or definition of positions within that process.[18]

To be poised in this way is not only to occupy a position of balance between two seemingly violently opposed dangers, but to become both of those dangers, in all possible gradations of mixture and difference, simultaneously. In their dynamic, ontogenetic states, designing and innovating contain all the opportunities and possibilities of their being at once. To fall back onto the certainties of any definition while offering firmness or infinity, restricts creative opportunity. Layered, interleaved and connecting into and out of each other, machines so poised operate in and construct simultaneous states, zones of admixture, complex regions of critical conditions, the creative spaces where multiplicitous flows of matter-energy cross and are coded, decoded or overcoded. They poise between order and chaos.

Furthermore, Deleuze and Guattari write in *A Thousand Plateaus*, 'Capitalists may be the masters of surplus value and its distribution, but they do not dominate the flows from which surplus value derives. Rather, power centres function at the points where flows are converted into segments: they are exchangers, converters, oscillators' (1987: 226). It is from here that a non-capitalist expression of innovative growth might come.

Capital can be decoded, deterritorialised, unpicked and diverted into new assemblages, for its matter-energy combinations to constitute non-capitalist formations. Unhinged from the need to exploit, the creative forces can be pitched elsewhere. It is time, then, to disrupt the 'successful exploitation' of creativity as expressed by Cox, to decode its diversion into aggregates underpinning massifications of power and control, and offer ways in which such organisation can dissolve and reform in ways more conducive to the distribution of such power and control.[19] Easy to say, maybe, but some tips for action have already been mentioned. Look for who holds the whip, or who controls the flows through various points of blockage. Find the places where leakages or resistances occur, or where feedback flows in, and ask whether these can impress new expressions. Poised Designing or Innovating Machines are those whose BwOs are uncovered and unleashed, whose conditions of exploitation are decoded and expressed particularly at each instantiation of the workings of the machines. For these poised BwOs of designing and innovating the affective relations between elements come to the fore, and when using these as trajectories that replace those of exploitation, designing and innovating may make different creative impacts.

A philosophy of innovation/design becomes an innovative/designed philosophy, and in this becoming philosophy, design and innovation are released on their own, ever-dynamic journeys. There is an immanence of thought and act in all of this that responds to contingencies at the same time as creating them anew: between order and chaos, critically complex, where the catalysts of the emergence of the new have their future catalytic properties reinvigorated by such emergence. This is where the becoming each other of designing and innovating need to operate to be successful, creative and impactful. Where they resist being pinned down, always curious and experimental: becoming poised and complex.

Acknowledgements

Thanks to: Joanna Brassett (Studio INTO), Lucy Kimbell (Saïd Business School, University of Oxford), John O'Reilly and, of course, Betti Marenko, for valuable feedback on versions of this piece that helped me immeasurably. Derek Hales for discussions and feedback on these topics. Colleagues and students on MA Innovation Management whose insights and creative challenging have taught me much. Roy Sandbach for sharing thoughts and experiences of innovation management. Anisha Peplinski, organiser of *TEDxCentralSaintMartins*, 'Emergence' (London, 2012), for providing me with the opportunity to test-drive the prototype forms of some of these thoughts. The organisers, reviewers and participants at the following conferences where some of these concepts had an outing: 'Scenarios and Design', Oxford Futures Forum (Oxford, UK, 2014); IEEE-Tsinghua International Design Management Symposium (Shenzhen, China, 2013); 'the territory in-between', The 6th International Deleuze Studies Conference (Lisbon, Portugal, 2013); 'Creative Assemblages', First Annual Deleuze Studies in Asia Conference (Taipei, Taiwan, 2013); Design Studies Forum Panel, College Arts Association Annual Conference (New York City, USA, 2013). To Hochschule für Wirtschaft und Recht, Berlin, who without any fuss allowed me to use their facilities when finishing this piece. And to my family whose support has known no bounds.

Notes

1. Jean-François Lyotard (1993) notes the 'tyranny of the Sign'; and Deleuze's position on meaning can be summed up here: 'The only question is how anything works, with its intensities, flows, processes, partial objects – none of which *mean* anything' (1995: 22; original emphasis). The recent promotion of 'meaning-centred design' influenced by Verganti's work might do well to take note of the power and control conditions any prioritisation of meaning might bring. A research hub called 'meaning-centred design' exists at the University of Leeds, UK; and the excellent London-based strategic design company Precipice (www. precipice-design.com) speak well on this subject.
2. This is, of course, not only true for design, where complexity as a systems theory has been impacting for a while, highlighting ways to engage with such fluidity (see particularly, for example, Johnson et al. 2005; Johnson 2008; Alexiou and Zamenopoulos 2008; Alexiou, Besussi and Zamenopoulos 2008; Zamenopoulos 2012; Zamenopoulos and Alexiou 2012). Similar arguments are made in a wide range of disciplines and practices. I note the following as they impact innovation and design directly: organisation theory (Simon 1962; Cooper 1986; Chia 1998, 1999; Tsoukas 1998; Tsoukas and Chia 2002); innovation management (Oster 2010); politics and economics (Page 2010, 2012).
3. This is a vast area of study. Some of the key texts are: Berger 2009; Brown 2009; Martin 2009; Neumeier 2009; and Lockwood 2010. For the best critiques, see note 4 below.
4. See the best of this by Kimbell 2011, 2012; Tonkinwise 2011, 2014; Johansson-Sköldberg et al. 2013.
5. The most 'classic' definition is Schumpeter's and covers: (1) the introduction of a new good; (2) the introduction of a new method of production; (3) the opening of a new market; (4) the conquest of a new source of supply of raw materials or half-manufactured goods; (5) the carrying out of the new organisation of any industry (1934: 66). Another is from the OECD's *Oslo Manual*: 'An innovation is the implementation of a new or significantly improved product (good or service), or process, a new marketing method, or a new organizational method in business practices, workplace organization or external relations' (2005: 46).
6. Askland et al. (2010) examine the many ways in which the concept of creativity has been approached in relation to design in their excellent paper 'Changing Conceptualisations of Creativity in Design'. They, too, highlight the fluidity of design definitions, adding one that brings it close to Cox on innovation, as well

as acknowledging the complexity of the issue. See also – regarding innovation, organisations and creativity – Mumford and Hunter (2005).

7. In '10,000 BC: The Geology of Morals', in *A Thousand Plateaus*, Deleuze and Guattari unpack 'overcoding' as follows: it is characterised by 'phenomena of centering, unification, totalization, integration, hierarchization, and finalization' (1987: 41).

8. There are many other instances of the same processes and issues having importance throughout their work: most notably in the discussion on space in *A Thousand Plateaus*.

9. Kauffman's use of 'sub-' and 'supra-' to prefix 'critical' is interesting as these give senses, respectively, of spatially below and above, and temporally before and after. This highlights the inadequacy of thinking of order-complex-chaos in simplistic regional or linear temporal ways, and that their mixture is, itself, much more complex.

10. Political scientist and economist Scott Page defines complexity under two broad categories: 'BOAR. Complexity lies between order and randomness. DEEP. Complexity cannot be easily described, evolved, engineered, or predicted' (2012: 7; see also Page 2010). Though he says that these two characterisations have many moments of infiltration into and from each other.

11. This essay is rich with detail on the geographic, spatial, voyaging and cartographic concepts that find expression throughout Deleuze and Guattari's work (singly and together). I have spent some years working on these topics too (see Brassett 1992 and 1994), but in relation to the issues of design and innovation and complexity see Brassett 2013a, 2013b, 2014. See also O'Reilly in this volume encountering milieu and design.

12. *Autopoiesis* – self-creating – has an interesting lineage across philosophy and science. John Deck (1967) uses it to describe the nature of the One as put forward by the Neoplatonist Plotinus (c. CE 205–70) in the *Enneads*. Humberto Maturana and Francisco Varela coined the term in biology and neurophenomenology to describe a dynamic, but closed, process of an organism's self-production (Maturana and Varela 1980: xvii; Varela 1996).

13. To highlight the complex nature of the BwO that Deleuze and Guattari recreate, these 'miserable territorialities' have other, more consistent and beneficial attributes for the BwO. In *A Thousand Plateaus* they write: 'You have to keep enough of the organism for it to reform each dawn; and you have to keep small supplies of signifiance and subjectification, if only to turn them against their own systems when the circumstances demand it, when things, persons, even situations force you to; and you have to keep small rations of subjectivity in sufficient quantity to enable you to respond to the dominant reality' (1987: 160). (Note: 'signifiance' is the translator, Brian Massumi's choice. His note explains: 'I have followed the increasingly common practice of importing *signifiance* . . . into English without modification' (Deleuze and Guattari 1987: xviii); it refers to the syntagmatic, signifying capacity of regimes of signs.)

14. I have mentioned elsewhere (Brassett 2013a, 2014), when discussing Deleuze and Guattari, design and innovation, the importance of strategy thought topologically (see also Serres, 'Lucretius: Science and Religion' (1982: 98–124)). For an excellent account of the value of a topological account of culture in terms that intersect with concepts mobilised in this chapter, see Lury et al. 2012, and the special issue of the journal *Theory, Culture and Society* that their essay introduces.

15. See Chesbrough 2003 for a good discussion of this. My critique of Chesbrough's position can be found in Brassett 2013a, in relation to some of the concepts found in the current chapter.

16. 'A line of becoming', Deleuze and Guattari write, 'is not defined by points that it connects, or by points that compose it; on the contrary, it passes between points, it comes up through the middle' (1987: 293).
17. The plateau '587 BC–AD 70: On Several Regimes of Signs' of *A Thousand Plateaus* offers a clear expression of Deleuze and Guattari's pragmatic philosophy with generative, transformational, diagrammatic and machinic components. Their activist, pragmatic philosophy will try 'to make maps of regimes of signs: we can turn them around or retain selected coordinates or dimensions, and depending on the case we will be dealing with a social formation, a pathological delusion, a historical event' (1987: 119).
18. 'Design digestion' was practised a year after its first theorisation on a project for a baby food manufacturer. Brassett and Booth (2009) described the findings.
19. This is the political project also of others inspired by Deleuze and Guattari and interested in developing new ways of considering materialism today (for example: Massumi 2002, 2011; DeLanda 2006; Bennett 2010; Braidotti 2010; Connolly 2011). See also Hroch in this volume, as well as the 'design activism' work of Julier (2013a, 2013b) and the contributors to the special edition of the journal *Design and Culture*, for which Julier (2013a) provides the introduction.

References

Agamben, G. [2006] (2009), 'What is an Apparatus?', in G. Agamben, *What is an Apparatus? And Other Essays*, trans. D. Kishik and S. Pedatella, Stanford: Stanford University Press, pp. 1–14.

Alexiou, K. and T. Zamenopoulos (2008), 'Design as a Social Process: A Complex Systems Perspective', *Futures*, Special Issue: 'Design out of Complexity', 40:6, pp. 586–95.

Alexiou, K., E. Besussi and T. Zamenopoulos (eds) (2008), *Futures*, Special Issue: 'Design out of Complexity', 40:6.

Askland, H., M. Ostwald and A. Williams (2010), 'Changing Conceptualisations of Creativity in Design', *Proceedings DESIRE '10* (16–17 August), Aarhus, Denmark, pp. 4–11.

Bennett, Jane (2010), *Vibrant Matter: A Political Ecology of Things*, Durham, NC and London: Duke University Press.

Berger, Warren (2009), *Glimmer: How Design Can Transform Your Business, Your Life, and Maybe Even the World*, London: Random House.

Braidotti, R. (2010), 'The Politics of "Life itself" and New Ways of Dying', in D. Coole and S. Frost (eds), *New Materialisms: Ontology, Agency, and Politics*, Durham, NC: Duke University Press, pp. 201–18.

Brassett, J. (2014), 'Restless Innovation: Connecting Philosophy, Design and Innovation', Interreg conference. Global Culture and Creativity: From Design to Innovation and Enterprise? Winchester, UK.

Brassett, J. (2013a), 'Networks: Open, Closed or Complex. Connecting Philosophy, Design and Innovation', in J. Cai, T. Lockwood, C. Wang, G. Tong and J. Liu (eds), *Design-Driven Business Innovation. 2013 IEEE-Tsinghua International Design Management Symposium Proceedings*, Beijing, IEEE, pp. 1–11.

Brassett, J. (2013b), 'Smooth Space Alone Won't Save Us. Mapping Order, Creativity and Chaos', 'the territory in-between', 6th International Deleuze Studies Conference (8–10 July), Lisbon, Portugal.

Brassett, J. (2012), 'At the Edge of Chaos: Emergence, Self-Organisation and Innovation', *Emergence: TEDxCentralSaintMartins* (March), London, UK.

Brassett, J. (1994), 'Space, Postmodernism and Cartographies', in S. Earnshaw (ed.), *Postmodern Surroundings*, Amsterdam: Rodopi, pp. 7–22.

Brassett, Jamie (1992), *Cartographies of Subjectification*, unpublished PhD Thesis, University of Warwick.

Brassett, J. and P. Booth (2009), 'Using Design Digestion. Opportunities for Innovation', 3rd International Design Principles and Practices Conference, (15–17 February), Technical University Berlin, Germany.

Brassett, J. and P. Booth (2008), 'Design Digestion. Work in Progress', *Design Principles and Practices. An International Journal*, 2:3, pp. 75–82.

Brown, Tim (2009), *Change by Design: How Design Thinking Transforms Organizations and Inspires Innovation*, New York: HarperCollins Publishers.

Chesbrough, Henry (2003), *Open Innovation*, Boston: Harvard Business School Press.

Chia, R. (1999), 'A "Rhizomic" Model of Organizational Change and Transformation: Perspective from a Metaphysics of Change', *British Journal of Management*, 10, pp. 209–27.

Chia, R. (1998), 'From Complexity Science to Complex Thinking: Organization as Simple Location', *Organization*, 5:3, pp. 341–69.

Christensen, Clayton (1997), *The Innovator's Dilemma: When New Technologies Cause Great Firms to Fail*, Cambridge, MA: Harvard Business Review Press.

Connolly, William E. (2011), *A World of Becoming*, Durham, NC and London: Duke University Press.

Cooper, R. (1986), 'Organisation/Disorganisation', *Social Science Information*, 26:3, pp. 299–335.

Cox, Sir George (2005), *Cox Review of Creativity in Business: Building on the UK's Strengths*, Norwich: Her Majesty's Stationery Office.

Deck, John (1967), *Nature, Contemplation, and the One: A Study in the Philosophy of Plotinus*, Toronto: University of Toronto Press.

DeLanda, Manuel (2006), *A New Philosophy of Society: Assemblage Theory and Social Complexity*, London: Athlone.

DeLanda, Manuel (1997), *A Thousand Years of Nonlinear History*, New York: Zone Books.

Deleuze, Gilles [1993] (1998), *Essays Clinical and Critical*, trans. D. W. Smith and M. A. Greco, London: Verso.

Deleuze, Gilles [1990] (1995), *Negotiations 1972–1990*, trans. M. Joughin, New York: Columbia University Press.

Deleuze, Gilles [1968] (1990), *Expressionism in Philosophy: Spinoza*, trans. M. Joughin, New York: Zone Books.

Deleuze, Gilles [1970] (1988), *Spinoza: Practical Philosophy*, trans. R. Hurley, San Francisco: City Lights Books.

Deleuze, Gilles and F. Guattari [1991] (1994), *What is Philosophy?* trans. G. Burchell and H. Tomlinson, London: Verso Books.

Deleuze, Gilles and F. Guattari [1980] (1987), *A Thousand Plateaus. Capitalism and Schizophrenia 2*, trans. B. Massumi, London: Athlone.

Deleuze, Gilles and F. Guattari [1972] (1984), *Anti-Oedipus. Capitalism and Schizophrenia 1*, trans. R. Hurley, M. Seem and H. Lane, London: Athlone.

Dong, A. (2014), 'Design x Innovation: Perspective or Evidence-based Practices', *International Journal of Design Creativity and Innovation*, pp. 1–16, DOI: 10.1080/21650349.2014.943294.

Eames, C. and R. Eames (2005), *The Films of Charles and Ray Eames*, film, dir. Charles and Ray Eames. USA: Image Entertainment, 2005.

Findeli, A. and R. Bousbaci (2005), 'L'Eclipse de l'objet dans les théories du projet en design', *The Design Journal*, 8:3, pp. 35–49.

Flynn, F. J. and J. A. Chatman [2001] (2004), 'Strong Cultures and Innovation: Oxymoron or Opportunity?', in M. L. Tushman and P. Anderson (eds), *Managing Strategic Innovation and Change: A Collection of Readings*, 2nd edition, Oxford: Oxford University Press, pp. 234–51.

Fulton Suri, J. (2003), 'The Experience Evolution: Developments in Design Practice', *The Design Journal*, 6:2, pp. 39–48.

Johansson-Sköldberg, U., J. Woodilla and M. Çetinkaya (2013), 'Design Thinking: Past, Present and Possible Futures', *Creativity and Innovation Management*, 22:2, pp. 121–46.

Johnson, J. (2008), 'Science and Policy in Designing Complex Futures', *Futures*, Special Issue: 'Design out of Complexity', 40:6, pp. 520–36.

Johnson, John, T. Zamenopoulos and K. Alexiou (eds) (2005), *Proceedings of the ECCS 2005 Satellite Workshop: Embracing Complexity in Design*, Milton Keynes: The Open University.

Julier, G. (2013a), 'Design Activism: Introduction. Material Preference and Design Activism', *Design and Culture*, Special Issue: 'Design Activism', 5:2, pp. 145–50.

Julier, G. (2013b), 'From Design Culture to Design Activism', *Design and Culture*, Special Issue: 'Design Activism', 5:2, pp. 215–36.

Julier, Guy (2013c), *The Culture of Design*, 3rd edition, Oxford: Sage.

Kauffman, Stuart A. (2008), *Reinventing the Sacred*, New York: Basic Books.

Kauffman, Stuart A. (1993), *The Origins of Order: Self-organization and Selection in Evolution*, New York and Oxford: Oxford University Press.

Kearnes, M. (2006), 'Chaos and Control: Nanotechnology and the Politics of Emergence', *Paragraph*, 29:2, pp. 57–80.

Kimbell, L. (2012), 'Rethinking Design Thinking: Part II', *Design and Culture*, 4:2, pp. 129–48.

Kimbell, L. (2011), 'Rethinking Design Thinking: Part I', *Design and Culture*, 3:3, pp. 285–306.

Latour, B. (2008), 'A Cautious Prometheus? A Few Steps Toward a Philosophy of Design (with special attention to Peter Sloterdijk)', in F. Hackney, J. Glynne and V. Minto (eds), *Proceedings of the 2008 Annual International Conference of the Design History Society*, Falmouth (3–6 September 2008), e-books, Universal Publishers, pp. 2–10.

Lockwood, Thomas (ed.) (2010), *Design Thinking: Integrating Innovation, Customer Experience and Brand Value*, New York: Allworth Press.

Lury, C., L. Parisi and T. Terranova (2012), 'Introduction: The Becoming Topological of Culture', *Theory, Culture and Society*, 29:4–5, pp. 3–35.

Lyotard, Jean-François [1974] (1993), *Libidinal Economy*, trans. I. H. Grant, London: Athlone.

Martin, Roger (2009), *The Design of Business: Why Design Thinking is the Next Competitive Advantage*, Boston: Harvard Business Press.

Massumi, Brian (2011), *Semblance and Event: Activist Philosophy and the Occurrent Arts*, Cambridge, MA and London: The MIT Press.

Massumi, Brian (2002), *Parables of the Virtual: Movement, Affect, Sensation*, Durham, NC and London: Duke University Press.

Maturana, Humberto and F. Varela [1972] (1980), *Autopoiesis and Cognition: The Realization of the Living*, Boston Studies in the Philosophy of Science, ed. R. S. Cohen and M. W. Wartofsky, Dordrecht: D. Reidel Publishing Co.

Mezzadra, S. and B. Neilson (2012), 'Between Inclusion and Exclusion: On the Topology of Global Space and Borders', *Theory, Culture and Society*, 29:4–5, pp. 58–75.

Mumford, M. D. and S. T. Hunter (2005), 'Innovation in Organizations: A

Multi-level Perspective on Creativity', in F. Dansereau and F. J. Yammarino (eds), *Multi-Level Issues in Strategy and Methods (Research in Multi Level Issues, Volume 4)*, Bingley: Emerald Group Publishing, pp. 9–73.

Neumeier, Martin (2009), *The Designful Company: How to Build a Culture of Nonstop Innovation*, Berkeley: New Riders.

OECD (2005), *Oslo Manual: Guidelines for Collecting and Interpreting Innovation Data*, 3rd edition, Paris, OECD/Eurostat.

Oster, G. (2010), Characteristics of emergent innovation, *Journal of Management Development*, 29:6, pp. 565–74.

Page, S. E. (2012), 'A Complexity Perspective on Institutional Design', *Politics, Philosophy and Economics*, 11:1, pp. 5–25.

Page, Scott E. (2010), *Diversity and Complexity*, Princeton: Princeton University Press.

Plotinus (1930), *The Enneads*, trans. S. MacKenna, 2nd edition, revisions by B. S. Page, London: Faber and Faber.

Porter, Michael (1990), *The Competitive Advantage of Nations*, New York: The Free Press.

Porter, Michael (1985), *Competitive Advantage: Creating and Sustaining Superior Performance*, New York: The Free Press.

Prigogine, Ilya (1980), *From Being to Becoming: Time and Complexity in the Physical Sciences*, San Francisco: W. H. Freeman and Company.

Prigogine, Ilya and I. Stengers (1984), *Order Out of Chaos: Man's New Dialogue with Nature*, London: Flamingo.

Schumpeter, Joseph A. [1911] (1934), *The Theory of Economic Development: An Inquiry into Profits, Capital, Credit, Interest and the Business Cycle*, Cambridge, MA: Harvard University Press.

Serres, M. (1982), *Hermes: Literature, Science, Philosophy*, ed. J. V. Harari and D. F. Bell, London and Baltimore: Johns Hopkins University Press.

Shove, Elizabeth, M. Watson, M. Hand and J. Ingram (2007), *The Design of Everyday Things*, Oxford and New York: Berg.

Simon, H.A. (1962), 'The Architecture of Complexity', *Proceedings of the American Philosophical Society*, 106:6 (December), pp. 467–82.

Spinoza, Baruch [1677] (1955), *The Ethics*, in B. Spinoza, *On the Improvement of the Understanding. The Ethics. Correspondence*, trans. R. H. M. Elwes, New York: Dover Publications Inc., pp. 45–271.

Stengers, Isabelle [2002] (2011), *Thinking with Whitehead: A Free and Wild Creation of Concepts*, trans. M. Chase, Cambridge, MA and London: Harvard University Press.

The Design Council (2005), *Eleven Lessons: Managing Design in Eleven Global Brands. A Study of the Design Process*, London: The Design Council.

Thorpe, A. and L. Gamman (2011), 'Design with Society: Why Socially Responsive Design is Good Enough', *CoDesign: International Journal of CoCreation in Design and the Arts*, 7:3–4, pp. 217–30.

Tonkinwise, C. (2014), 'Design Studies – What is it Good For?', *Design and Culture*, 6:1, pp. 5–44.

Tonkinwise, C. (2011), 'A Taste for Practices: Unrepressing Style in Design Thinking', *Design Studies*, 32:6, pp. 533–45.

Tsoukas, H. (1998), 'Chaos, Complexity, and Organization Theory', *Organization*, 5:3, pp. 291–313.

Tsoukas, H. and R. Chia (2002), 'On Organizational Becoming: Rethinking Organizational Change', *Organization Science*, 13:2, pp. 567–82.

Tushman, M. L. and C. O'Reilly III [1996] (2004), 'The Ambidextrous Organization: Managing Evolutionary and Revolutionary Change', in M. L. Tushman and

P. Anderson (eds), *Managing Strategic Innovation and Change. A collection of Readings*, 2nd edition, Oxford: Oxford University Press, pp. 276–91.

Varela, F. (1996), 'The Early Days of Autopoiesis: Heinz and Chile', *Systems Research*, 13:3, pp. 407–16.

Verganti, Roberto (2009), *Design-Driven Innovation*, Boston: Harvard Business Press.

Zamenopoulos, T. (2012), 'A Complexity Theory of Design Intentionality', *Artificial Intelligence for Engineering Design, Analysis and Manufacturing*, 26:1, pp. 63–83.

Zamenopoulos, T. and K. Alexiou, (2012), 'Complexity: What Designers Need to Know', in S. Garner and C. Evans (eds), *Design and Designing: A Critical Introduction*, London: Berg, pp. 411–28.

Chapter 2

Design in Guattari's Ecosophy

Manola Antonioli
Translated by Stephanie Daneels

For a Singular Design

There are many points of convergence between Félix Guattari's eco-sophic project and contemporary design issues, which explains why he began to develop an interest for the field of design just before his death.[1] For Guattari, the phenomena of ecological imbalance that threaten life on the planet can never be separated from its increasingly noticeable deterioration, which affects, in parallel, intelligence and sensitivity, as well as modes of individual and collective life. Guattari defines ecosophy in *The Three Ecologies* as a philosophic articulation 'between the three ecological registers (the environment, social relations and human subjectivity)' (Guattari 1989: 28).

A purely technocratic approach to ecological problems (an approach which today is continually found in speeches and guidelines for 'sustainable development') is therefore radically insufficient, since what is at stake is rather a comprehensive reorientation of production goals for both tangible and intangible assets. The objects and technical devices which populate our daily lives are never simple, inert 'tools', but essential components of the 'production of subjectivity' (both individual and collective), like acting and relational entities, which are not exclusive to the industrial or merchant domain but, above all, affect the 'molecular' domains of sensitivity, intelligence and desire.

In 'Aphorisms on Eco-design' – a letter sent in response to an invitation to participate in the catalogue of the second edition of the design quadrennial *Caravelles*, published in 1991[2] – Guattari states that the role of designers can neither be reduced to that of 'specialists in formal packaging' nor to the demands of marketing and mass production. If the designer can be defined as 'a professional in the ways of seeing', we must remember that the look 'is worked' just as one works scales in music or styles in literature.

While industrial design, associated with marketing, has become during the second half of the twentieth century a place of 'generalized desingularisation' through a 'disenchantment of forms', one can imagine the invention of a 'design of singularity', which 'would have the merit of vibrating the virtual at the heart of the usual interface – the chair, the table, can opener, electric razor' (Guattari 1991a: 46). Objects would therefore never be simple 'inanimate objects', but always relational interfaces, forms of 'proto-otherness', knowing that otherness (as well as subjectivity) is never a given for Guattari, but is instead a place of material and immaterial 'production':

> This is a way to produce the other as other, to desire otherness, an otherness in its consistency of otherness, hence in its ethical, specifically existential, dimension. This is something that is very much against a political consensus but which goes in the direction of a culture of *dissent*. (Guattari 1991b: 4; original emphasis)

The Role of the Designer

The *Caravelles 2* catalogue also includes a long interview with Félix Guattari, invited by Jean-Claude Conésa and Vincent Lemarchands to express his views on 'machine design'. In design Guattari perceives an essential ambiguity between the dynamics of desingularisation and trends of resingularisation: on the one hand, the activity of the designer belongs to market relations, it produces a vision of things and products which is 'serialised' and standardised; on the other hand, it can become a place of resingularisation, a subjective reconfiguration of the existential territories of each. It is not a question of choosing between industrial 'seriality' and radical resingularisation, but of rethinking the interweaving between these two dimensions. Located in a prospective dimension, Guattari speculates that the new opportunities for production afforded by advanced technologies and computing could enable the evolution towards a 'post-design era', conceived in a similar way to the general context of a 'post-media' era, characterised by increasingly miniaturised, 'light' and nomadic computer and technological devices.

'Post-media' devices designate, according to Guattari, a multiplicity, a rhizome of 'small media' that could offer to individual subjectivities or groups the opportunity to express themselves outside of mass media and the standardised models of subjectivity that they offer. The contemporary 'mecanosphere', which now offers the technical possibilities to make this project a reality, is likely to generate new forms of ownership and creativity for everyone, without the obligation of passing through the major communication culture industry circuits. In Guattari's eyes, the future of design is situated in 'a kind of junction between mass production and creation, which could be found adjacent to a creation aesthetic' (Conésa and Lemarchands 1991: 52), in the eminent ecosophic creation of singular environments that would be opposed to any kind of generalised seriality. That which is being called into question is equally the function of the designer: destined to make things more complex in order to evolve from the state of a 'unique' interface of mediation between production and consumption, to that of a multiplicity of interfaces. Far from being a mere intermediary between a manufactured object and a consumer, the designer must also produce 'dynamic modules of composition', to open up the range of possibilities available to consumers. Technological evolution calls into question (in the field of design as in others), the role of the isolated creative professional in order to make way for 'amateur creators'. The 'professional' creator is indeed constrained by subjective formations that are not under his control, and is trapped by the same imaginary and symbolic constraints to which other consumers are subjected. Furthermore, in the worst case and for commercial reasons, the 'professional' creator tries to put him- or herself in line with these constraints.

More generally, for Guattari, the case of design and the designer have become emblematic of a global reorganisation of the production of individual and collective subjectivity, as well as modes and forms of production of objects and services, of a new function of creation, and of the forms of production in which the duties of creation and innovation are no longer reserved for specialists and professionals, but have spread more and more into society. Well before MP3 players and the widespread availability of the internet, Guattari anticipated, for example, the birth of a world of differentiated music usage: current possibilities of creation in an aural environment that are not necessarily incompatible with the attention given to creation, and which cannot be reduced to a simple form of consumption of standardised products. Guattari opposes the passivity of a consumer in relationship to 'intellectual objects' or 'creative objects', forms of 're-appropriation of sensitive, intellectual and emotional modules'.

A 'Minor' Design

This interview also touches upon the contradiction existing at the heart of design between, on the one hand, the necessity to submit to the demands of profitability that passes through notions of form/function/standard/series to a dimension of standardisation defined in the interview by Jean-Claude Conésa as 'the adaptation of products and their image to the ideology of conquering' of the market, and on the other, the desire to escape from the logic of serial objects and from products marked by function. Design fits into a market where finalities are, for the moment, neither ethical nor ecological, but exclusively economic and which also include, more and more often, a market of taste and sensitivity to which the designer and artists are subject. Guattari does not advocate for a utopian exit from market rules: design is inserted into the machines of production and, while trying to develop a 'processuality' of its own, is not intrinsically a means to change the modes of production which would be wholly independent of economic constraints, of production systems, and of a technological evolution.

There is not just one kind of power of emancipation of the object and of the creative act, which would be completely autonomous and independent of market rules. The question of the designer's 'responsibility' must not be broken down into a kind of 'culpability', but in the capacity to operate from singular choices, to anticipate the evolution of machinic processes, to 'play all of the virtual cards' rather than to passively adapt to the demands of an ethical, political and economic context as well as the pre-existing culture. In the search for a 'minor' design, Guattari also proposes resorting to 'neoarchaisms', a registration or re-enrolment in the cultural or aesthetic territories that the ideals of modernity have simply wanted to eradicate. Any repertoire of forms, sensitivities, or traditional know-how specific to each culture is therefore susceptible to being exploited in artistic production and creation, without falling inevitably into folkloric reterritorialisation. Guattari calls for the invention of forms of production of subjectivity that can be combined with regionalised refrains [*ritournelles*] while exploiting the resources of the most advanced technologies. He gives as an example the evolution of African music, which is constantly capable of borrowing new instruments, and feeding off music from around the world while fertilising them in return. Thus it is never a matter of opposing archaic 'territorialities' (destined to be erased forever by technological processes and modernity) to processes and procedures wholly 'deterritorialised', inscribed in a purely industrial and standardised logic, but of envisaging new forms of alliance between tradition and the most advanced technologies, and (in the domain of design) between manual and artisanal expertise and the virtualities opened up by the new technological devices [*dispositifs*] of the other.

The other proposed path for thinking about how to get out of standardisation is to research in the direction of a redefinition of design, which now goes far beyond the simple production of objects. If the designer works exclusively on an object's form the critical function of design becomes considerably reduced, if not impossible: a series of definitions and constraints (for example, in the conception of streamlining an airplane or car) in the end completely elude him.

Just as Guattari proposes a definition of the machine as an 'abstract machine' – the diagram of the workings of a machine (technical, theoretical, aesthetic, or desiring) – he also proposes the concept of an 'abstract' or 'conceptual' design, which extends the scope of intervention of design from the conception of daily objects to the definition or redefinition of complex spaces (up to those of chemical compounds [*molécules chimiques*] or 'cognitive scripts' [epistemological models that inform how we think and understand the world – Eds.]). Rather than having 'his nose glued to the object', the designer has therefore to work with forms as essential components of the production of subjectivity.

Far from being 'universal', forms (visual, aural and emotional) – which are in Guattari's eyes a sort of manipulation, inventiveness, DIY [*bricolage*] – place design in an 'ethico-pragmatic' dimension essential to the ecosophic project as a whole. Thus the reinvention of design is a weapon (among others) in the fight against 'the constitution of a global capitalist economic market that lays waste to existential territories' (Conésa and Lemarchands 1991: 61) in all their dimensions (simultaneously environmental, social, mental, political, technical and aesthetic).

Technosphere

The ecosophic approach allows us to envisage design and perspectives on eco-design beyond a simple logic of nature 'preservation', towards a reinvention or a 're-fabrication' of exchanges between nature, culture and the environment.

Starting from *Anti-Oedipus*, Deleuze and Guattari propose to get out of the artificial opposition between men gifted with morality, intelligence and language, and the inert nature of instruments aimed at specific, man-made goals. They conceive a multiple and heterogeneous layout, a 'machinic' function, in which some elements are human, others are technical, while others still are natural (revealing that we can no longer understand nature outside of the intervention of man and technology).

It is necessary to think about a very complex interaction between humans and non-humans, where technical objects are a part of us as much as we are a part of them. In this perspective, nature can no longer be understood either as the world well known by science, ruled by its laws, or as a spontaneous source and the origin of life and meaning, but as a differentiated rhizomatically fragmented ensemble that has always been implicated in the becomings of technology, culture and society.

Reflections on the 'technosphere' or 'mechanosphere' are subsequently of primary interest in Guattari's thinking (even above and beyond his collaboration with Deleuze), in constant reference to Gilbert Simondon and his work *On the mode of existence of technical objects* (in which he finds philosophical expression of his own desire to raise awareness of the 'meaning of technical objects'). Like Guattari, Simondon's interest in technology does not reside in automatism but at the level of indetermination, in the 'opening' that the technological tool can and must remain: 'The machine with superior technicality is an open machine, and the ensemble of open machines assumes man as permanent organizer and as a living interpreter of the inter-relationships of machines' (Simondon 1980: 13). Man is therefore neither the master nor slave of machines; he is *among* the machines. The more the complexity of technological machines increases, the more man is able to become a coordinator and a permanent inventor of the machines that surround him.

In Simondon, Guattari finds equally an interest in the genesis of a technical object, for the definition of different lines of technological objects (for the 'phylogenetic evolution of mechanisation' in Guattari's language). The emergence of new families or technical 'lines' still depends on the procedures put into place and the choices that we make to produce or impose them. The technical object possesses a historicity of its own, making it irreducible it to a simple pile of inert matter. Its evolution supposes an awareness of the dual relationship that each object maintains with the technical milieu, the natural milieu and the human actions associated with it: 'The technical object stands at the point where two environments [*deux milieux, technique et géographique*] come together, and must be integrated into both these environments at the same time' (Simondon 1980: 46). Technology/ technique is always recorded in a natural environment, which it radically transforms and which allows it to survive and to develop further; it deeply modifies not only physical geography and natural environments, but human geography also: notably the individual and collective perception of time, speed, space, and the recording of territories. A philosophy of 'machines' and technical objects is therefore always necessarily and paradoxically an idea of nature and earth, but also a cartography and ecology of spirit.

Design, in its 'machinic' and ecosophical dimension, must therefore aspire to produce resingularised and resingularising 'artefact-interfaces', places of heterogenesis connecting natural, cultural, subjective and technical elements. Once it gets out of its 'Paleolithic Era', design can then become a 'major art' of ecosophy, where 'the form, the envelope, the way of doing things will no longer be that of non-biodegradable trash, but will become the heart of the productive project' (Conésa and Lemarchands 1991: 46–7).

Notes

The French version of this article, *'Design et écosophie. Pour un design de la singularité'*, first appeared in *Multitudes*, 53 (Autumn 2013), pp. 173–8.

1. For a discussion of design in an ecosophic perspective, see the work of physicist and philosopher Nicolas Prignot (2010).
2. This text was published for the first time in the catalogue for which it was intended, *Caravelles 2. 2ème quadriennale internationale de design*. A manuscript version was subsequently reproduced in the review, *De(s)générations. Le devenir révolutionnaire*, 4 (October 2007), with commentary from Jean-Claude Conésa. [Editors' note: It also appeared in *Multitudes*, 53 (Autumn 2013), pp. 214–16.] My thanks to Jean-Claude Conésa for informing me of the existence of these publications.

References

Conésa, J.-C. (2007), *'Le machino du singulier* [The Machinist of the Singular]', in *De(s)générations. Le devenir révolutionnaire*, 4, pp. 63–7.
Conésa, J.-C. and V. Lemarchands (1991), *'Entretien avec Félix Guattari* [Conversation with Félix Guattari]', in V. Lemarchands (ed.), *Caravelles 2. 2ème quadriennale internationale de design*, Lyon: Caravelles.
Deleuze, Gilles and F. Guattari [1972] (1984), *Anti-Oedipus. Capitalism and Schizophrenia 1*, trans. R. Hurley, M. Seem and H. Lane, London: Athlone.
Guattari, F. (1991a), *'Aphorismes sur l'éco-design* [Aphorisms on Eco-design]', in *Caravelles 2. 2ème quadriennale internationale de design*, Lyon: Caravelles, pp. 45–7.
Guattari, F. (1991b), *'Produire une culture du dissensus: hétérogenèse et paradigme esthétique* [To Produce a Culture of Dissent: Heterogenesis and Aesthetic Paradigm]'; available at http://www.cip-idf.org/spip.php?page=imprimer&id_article=5613 (last accessed 8 September 2014).
Guattari, Félix (1989), *Les Trois ecologies*, Paris: Galilée.
Prignot, N. (2010), 'Retour sur les trois écologies de Guattari [Return to Guattari's *The Three Ecologies*]', in B. Lechat, C. Derenne, I. Durant and P. Lamberts (eds), *Etopia – Revue d'écologie politique*, 7, pp. 157–83.
Simondon, Gilbert (1980), *On the Mode of Existence of Technical Objects*, trans. N. Mellamphy, London, ON: University of Western Ontario.
Simondon, Gilbert (1958), *Du Mode d'existence des objets techniques*, Paris: Aubier-Montaigne.

Chapter 3

Design Machines and Art Machines

Anne Sauvagnargues
Translated by Ruth Clarke and Jamie Brassett

Design 'in-signs' (Deleuze and Guattari 1987: 75) merchandise and provides art with a pertinent reminder that it has only recently lost its own utilitarian status. Since it fully established itself in the nineteenth century, design has raised a critical issue which has shaken up our entire art machine: the slow-moving story of the individuation of art in the west, supported by the compelling effort that has been made since the Renaissance to separate utility from beauty. With this art machine taking the dominant role, design registered a protest against its brother-becoming-enemy – Art with a capital A – mirroring the protest which led the autonomy of art in the Renaissance to differentiate 'fine' arts from technology.[1]

But design is not content to assert for the functional or utilitarian the same legitimacy and validity that are claimed by art. It also criticises industrialisation, judging it to be a social and ecological disaster. This deviation from the conditions of ordinary technical production, at the same time as reiterating the protest registered by the arts with regard to technologies, demonstrates the efforts to free workers from dominant capitalist production methods. This sets out, as Marx would say, to shorten the distance between the workers-producers and their products, to influence the divisions of labour of which we feel the full impact in a capitalist system. These also determine both our work and domestic environments, unified by a regime of production that integrates distribution, communication and consumption circuits at the outset, to create a single industrial production of subjectivity. A burst of political emancipation from the structures of power and production/distribution/consumption circuits – in short, from the modes of contemporary capitalist subjectification – sings a slightly offbeat refrain amidst our otherwise repetitive social routines. On the one hand, there are concerns that it does not simply reassure consumers by singularising

them: therefore it is possible to go on consuming, all the while hoping
to escape the social control of consumption. On the other hand, this
critique can be made within the industrial process, or at the margin – the
space where art emancipated itself by seeking to distance itself fully from
the utilitarian – showing the complicity between industrialisation and
the western art machine.

Art Machine

The eventful history of the relationship between art and technology in
the west is most clearly seen in the case of design. It can be summarised
using the formula '*ars* (Latin) = *techne* (Greek)'. Fine arts, a sector spe-
cialising in producing beauty, sets itself apart from the other 'arts' and
artificial products, that is to say technical/technological products. This
process, often taken to be the empowerment of art, I call 'art machine'
because talking about empowerment assumes there is a type of art
before its individuation – which would naturally be distinguished by the
advancement of civilisation – when it is precisely this individuation that
we need to explain.

It was only at the beginning of the nineteenth century that people
started to concern themselves with recognising this new distinction by
using the Greek word, thereby reserving the term technique/technology
for physical production, professional manufacturing that did not call
for this extra touch of soul. The terms *ars* (Latin) and *techne* (Greek)
strictly speaking cover the same scope and indiscriminately mix artisanal
production, the production of art, and technical skill. The Roman writer
Pliny the Elder,[2] when drawing up one of the first histories of Greek art
for posterity, arranged the complex chronologies of artists and genres
in his *Natural History* (1991 [AD 77]) by categorising them by material:
stone or metal, powder or paste. This approach in no way prevented
him from assessing exceptional products, but meant that he did so not
by indexing them according to the particular individual who created
them (although he does list the artists according their merits and give
their names); where he gives us information about painters and sculptors
– and, sometimes, enthusiastic descriptions of works – it is as part of
a natural history of the materials. The last five books of his *Natural
History* are dedicated to: gold and silver (book 33), bronze (book 34),
earth (book 35), marble and other stone (book 36) and finally precious
stones (book 37). It is in these books that he includes information about
sculptors (book 34 and 36) and painters (book 35). Whatever admira-
tion Pliny has for Greek art, whose marvels he inventories in minute

detail, he sticks to an epistemology of materials, and shows no concern whatsoever for art in the sense that we understand it. His *Natural History* remains a history of materials, stones, earth and metals. From this Roman point of view, art and design are strictly equivalent. All that counts is technical innovation and precision of execution, a set of functional criteria where what constitutes our usual distinction between aesthetic and utilitarian is of no relevance. The artificial is defined according to its material and the work that goes into shaping it: from this point of view, there is no distinction between art and design, or art and technology.

For design to be able to set itself apart on all sides, and appear different from both ordinary technical production and art considered as non-utilitarian, it had to overcome a number of hurdles that we now take for granted, and which obscure the debate around design. The emancipation of artists and their social elevation from the mechanical sphere (laborious and servile) towards the liberal arts was not achieved in a day. This shift from manual work, from worker (who works with their hands), to artist, creator, was made through a complex semiotic involving twisting values and statuses, flows of raw material, capital, and production networks, which the sociology of art has highlighted. We must add to this the components of nascent capitalism's industrialisation, and the discourses, status, institutions and other collective structures that guarantee art this relative independence under the cover of independent beauty.

Sociologically speaking, humanism's social ladder takes in a certain class of workers outside the degraded sphere of physical work, and gradually frees them from their servile condition. This is not the case for all, however, just for a few rare privileged makers of art: artists held up as examples on the grounds of their fame, success, protectors and clientele, and soon their art market. Meanwhile the multitude of small producers continue to live out a difficult existence as artisans, sign painters, clothes manufacturers, carpenters, or entrepreneurs in construction (applied arts), then as proletarians of culture (artists who are not famous, not listed on the market). Belonging to one or other of these classes is purely performative. Success is determined by the protection of the Greats, an opening on the market, entry into a museum collection, in short, the sale of merchandise.

The differentiation of design proceeds along exactly the same dividing line, but on a slightly different level of the art-technology continuum. The specific legitimacy it claims places it at the peak of ordinary technical production, the point where technology meets art. However, and even with regard to architecture and products clearly assumed to be part of the art field (like the Bauhaus), it would not be possible simply to integrate design into art, as this risks dissolving design's characteristic traits and the critical virtue of its position, both of which transform our notions of art and technology.

In short, at the level on which it concerns the mass production of utilitarian objects, design repeats the specific loop that in a similar glorifying process had taken the art out of manufacturing. In this, design summarises and abridges the process of the art machine. We will also see that it displaces it, and draws from this a claim for elevated status recognised by a single process: *artialisation*. Alain Roger[3] proposed this term (1978) to define the appearance of landscape, gradually establishing its own identity in painting until it set itself apart as a specific genre, constructing visible territories in turn, transforming mountains and forests, oceans and fields before our eyes, making them 'picturesque' (worthy of being painted). This same 'artialisation' is produced in the industrial production system, 'artialising' the bottle opener and the table, the lowly wheel, and all utilitarian artefacts, which will now be shrouded in historic or aesthetic value, or escaping ordinary production by adding a supplement of art. When we consider fame, criticism, talent or circulation as definite criteria for establishing what constitutes, and what does not, design or art, we forget to take into account the relevant social organisation that makes this distinction possible.

Similarly, the alleged autonomy of art makes us blind to the actual subjugation of people working in art, something they have in common with designers and anyone involved in production. Beethoven was one of the first court musicians to feel he was on an equal footing with the aristocracy who employed him. Instead of assuming this subjugation of practitioners from the Middle Ages to modern times (people working at every stage: from temporary entertainment workers, luckless poets, Sunday painters, to great artists and great designers making a living from their art, and the multitude of situations in between), any discussion about art or design will always reference the fiction of an exceptional figure (Picasso, Duchamp, Warhol; Frank Lloyd Wright, Gropius), an avant-garde movement (Bauhaus, de Stijl), or modern reincarnations of supreme genius (Michelangelo). This dispenses with the need to explain the specific status afforded to this fictional product.

The divide between those rare, well-known artists and designers on the one hand, and the proletariat producing artefacts on the other, is still most commonly defined according to a naive idealism of evident beauty, value or success, dazzling in and of themselves. This is taken to be a natural distinction, which distinguishes the work of genius from popular, batch, or mass production. The grey areas where technical works and batch-produced works of art merge completely do not bother anyone. The entire scene is lit from above, by the harsh glare of beauty.

It is because they understand how to handle their status as mere artisans (a social minority) that certain painters (Cennino Cennini,[4] Vasari[5]), sculptors (Ghiberti[6]) and architects (Alberti[7]) adopt the enviable position of humanism, picking up a quill and using it to invent a new type of discourse about art, a definite link between practice and erudite commentary. Which at the same time launches the history of art as a literary genre, as a discipline required to guarantee its own criteria, and art. This history of art produces both a theory of art and a history of its development, based on the cultural ideals of beauty as a natural thing, embedded in the ancient past, which Europe constructed, prospectively, as its origin. Certain practitioners, like Alberti, covet the enviable status of the liberal arts, and set about writing up their practice, to claim their status as learned and knowledgeable humanists, with a grasp of writing and Latin, not just a chisel and a paintbrush. They contributed to shaping this independence in art (that philosophers accept as something that goes beyond them) on the basis of a universality of (European) reason first envisaged by the Greeks. In reality the sudden burst of humanism amongst Renaissance painters was accompanied by a twist now so engrained in our thinking that we do not even notice it, and which violently drags western history back to the fifteenth century, an antiquity experienced as present and rediscovered . . . as renascent.

It does not even come as a shock that the intervening period should be classed as the 'Middle Ages': the age of the milieu, a simple interlude and transition between two cultural high points, antiquity and its renaissance, which reflect each other. Art historians however, have ceaselessly stressed multiple, diverse relationships with the Roman past and distant memories of the Greeks. The steamroller of Beauty smoothes the way for a Europe that has inherited the Greek miracle; a Europe founded by practitioners, stonemasons and ironmongers, powder grinders and carpenters who, aspiring to a more enviable social status, changed the frame of reference for the production of art.

The art machine does not only imply the pragmatic element of social demand, but also the emergence of a new discourse on beauty, history and European identity. This process is supported by the fiction of art's ancient origins, tagging the visual arts, painting, sculpture, architecture, on to art forms which had already been intellectualised: literature and music. Literature and music had already had the chance to benefit from the significant backing of *logos*, writing and mathematics, practice of Latin and harmony. The devaluation of mechanical work in Greece and the marked class distinction between theorists and practitioners on the sociological scale, explains that the affirmation of the specificity of fine arts paradoxically took the form of a radical separation from technique. All of which increases the value of artistic work and its subject matter. It simply cannot have entered their thinking that language and writing can themselves be considered in terms of body-technics and the technological transformation of the social machine.

This claim of ideality for the arts of beauty together with the breakdown of the frame of reference gave Europe a clear identity, albeit one seen as a reflection of the history of antiquity. Giotto, Alberti, Brunelleschi, Ghiberti – Florentine production's primary neoclassical burst – consciously transformed style inherited through apprenticeship. They no longer tacked their profession onto those of previous generations but, through creative discontinuity, onto those they fictionalised as representing ideal beauty. The antique is more modern than the present and the ancient already out-dated. So the antique is thought of as the spiritual origin of art, as its nature, to the extent that mediaeval artistic production (which was not seeking to distance itself from technique) is no longer considered artistic. This formula for the renascent art machine is built on a new rule: a rule that considers art's nature to be its essence, whereas it should be sought in the history of a past civilisation (archaeological excavations, art separated from technique, political history of civilisations); a rule that, in forming its components, places art on this temperature curve of progress. Antiquity, the birthplace of beauty, capital of art, is the root of tension, where Europe – with the warring differences between its national identities, and the shared sense of certainty that comes from sitting at the peak of a united civilisation – stabilised and defended itself as the white unity of western reason. This means that there is a privileged position for Greece, set up as the birthplace of universality, democracy and mathematics, art and philosophy, in the entire white rationale. Although it should be said that Plato thought himself Egyptian![8]

Is there any need to specify here that the adventure of art is consolidated by colonial pretensions and successfully universalised, and that in so doing is globalised, technically and pragmatically, by boats and guns, commerce and military action, which supplied Europe as much with precious raw materials and labour as with works of art: legacies of civilisations which Europe arranges and displays in its museums? While the news – that art is universal, that it is a human privilege, that it is an anthropological marker, that all people use it, even if Europeans were the first to sense its true power for affirming their independence, and marking their progress on the curve of civilisation – spreads slowly with palaeontology's chronological expansion at the end of the nineteenth century.

The discourses on art and design that do not take the art machine into account in any way, and take art or the formal beauty of design to be timeless (from Panofsky to Merleau-Ponty, from Heidegger to Michael Fried), drive home this idealistic heightened status of matter, together with a claim of Europe's very real domination over production in different cultures not party to the European emancipation of art from technique/technology.

The Art Machine and Packaging Design

Design is able to take alternative modes from the standardisation of industrial production, but the very term *design*, with its history, clearly demonstrates the ambiguity of its complicity with the idealistic division of production that characterises the art machine. This complicity is now noticeable, as we are living in a system of art that is no longer that of Art with a capital A, but one where art is indistinguishable from technique/technology. After the modernist split, we no longer perceive art as a unitary standard, protected by its affiliation with antiquity, under the dual varieties of the *mimesis* of nature (Greek) and the *imitatio* (Roman) of the Ancients. Our system is one of art after art: ready-made, Pop Art, installations, scrap and obsolete objects. We have stopped relating exclusively to the antique or the beautiful. Duchamp and African art have cured us once and for all of the separation between art and technology, as with photography and cinema, even though they have taken a long time to establish themselves as whole and separate art forms, not just industrial reproduction technology and mass entertainment. The idealistic certainty that art and technology have a different nature, which defined the birth of aesthetics and the philosophy of art from the eighteenth century, from Kant to Heidegger, is rendered utterly void with design.

There is nothing surprising, either, in the fact that design took shape around the middle of the nineteenth century, as a reaction against triumphant industrialisation, establishing a division between minor (standard production) and major (spiritualised utilitarian objects). Design revitalises the technical domain, by cloaking it in a romantic idea of old-fashioned handicraft, along with the revolutionary utopia of transforming industrial working conditions, and the socialist demand for re-establishing the producer's mastery of their product (for example, Arts and Crafts). The very choice of the term 'design' shows this complicity with the art machine. Discussed by Shaftesbury in his 1712 *Letter Concerning the Art or Science of Design*, it originated with the painter, sculptor and architect, Vasari, who produced the first history of art in Renaissance Florence.

Disegno – design – in Italian strikes a chord with the line of graphic design: an ideal line for Vasari. There we see the first act in the Florentine birth of the history of art, but also the social project of extracting the artisan from the indignity of manual work by prioritising the abstract element, the ideal of design. Alberti began his *De pictura* by bringing painting back to a formalism inspired by Euclid, even though he specifies that the painter, unlike the mathematician, is inspired by a 'fat Minerva': Minerva the goddess of wisdom, not reduced to the emaciated, ideal skeleton of *eidos*, but developing the jolly portliness of empirical forms. When, in sixteenth-century Florence, Vasari (probably a collective) established a paper museum to classify, rank and protect the production of art dating back to the *Trecento*,[9] he claimed new status as a practitioner of the mind: by writing, by adding the work of the mind to his practice (still considered artisanal) of painting, architecture and sculpture. The unity of art production, its social value – moving away from colour corporations, powder merchants and mediaeval ironmongers, to win the right to sit alongside the other humanists on the terraces of intellectual culture – is all assured by *disegno*, the father, as Vasari would have it, of painting, sculpture, architecture, ideal design, and form.[10]

With its double meaning in Italian, of drawing and design, *disegno* firmly assigns manual work the status of creation informed by an idea. The fact that, in this role, the idolised form comes in the shape of the father, a common matrix, with the operating idea serving to free form from matter, should come as no surprise: the developmental power of the element of *cosa mentale*[11] informs matter and, from the mind, develops the coloured surface, the sculptural volume, and then the space it inhabits. It is a somewhat popularised *eidos,* a fat Minerva, as Alberti put it, but the operation sets out to bring production, in terms of this ideal, knowledgeable, mental line, back from the *belle forme*, while at the same time protecting artistic production from its own working-class indignity. In this way Vasari shelters art from its own history, its idealised history, in a paper frame which would soon unfold into a stone museum (the Uffizi Gallery in Florence was built by his very hand).

At the other end of the chain, the second chance given to the applied arts in the nineteenth century by the Arts and Crafts movement (Morris, Ruskin, etc.) signals the irate, slightly technophobic reaction to mass production and the standardisation of merchandise, but implies just as much of a jolt backwards into the old fashioned world of artisanal handicrafts, bathed in the golden light of a return to primitivism, sharing the hope held by the Nazarenes and other pre-Raphaelites of finding extra meaning in the history of production, the good workman mastering his craft. This reaction against industrial capitalism and its standardised production methods, does however tie in with the idealistic division of art and technique, and the prestige awarded to old-fashioned artisanal production. In the birth of design, there is a certain role for assessing the added cultural, aesthetic and financial gains of an overvalued technical object 'saved' from its technical indignity. The ordinary concept of design, as an exception in technical mass production, drives home this divide between matter and form. In the system of artefacts, all objects for everyday or industrial use – transport equipment, household utensils, household motors, scientific robots – all technical machines recognise the same asymmetry. A silver spoon and a plastic spoon, a bottom of the range car and a Ferrari generate the same discrepancy in value in their own field.

This idealisation is a reflection of the idealisation that led the Renaissance to privilege antiquity, which led Morris and the Romantics to value the Middle Ages, primitive paintings predating Raphael, just as Alberti relied on antiquity as a reaction against the Byzantine mediaeval norm that came immediately before him. The Arts and Crafts movement showed the same archaeological passion for progress that art theory is still suffering from today. Whenever we declare something to be avant-garde – a colonial understanding of the transformation of value – we define an identity based on the nature of art. The dreary succession of avant-gardes in the twentieth century, relying on the same reactionary passion as the first, which can be found in African art, palaeontology, or the latest trendy artist or designer, resembles the succession of products the industry uses tirelessly to revive consumption. This frantic dash towards progress seeks to establish itself on an origin thought of as nature, as value that is timeless and yet well chosen in history. But neither art nor design can claim to have its origin in the past. It is this idealistic vision of the art machine that is challenged by freeing production from the protection of a supposedly joint standard; while in each era, with whatever models it dreams up, art and technology propose a method of techno-aesthetic subjectification, a social ecology.

Chic design (pure aestheticism) and industrial design (concerned with profiting from its surface attraction) participate in this concept of the ideal, exterior form that nourishes a kind of packaging design. Both of these types of design accentuate the naked form: the first idealising it with elitism, the second reducing the product to its external form, an exchange membrane calculated as a snare, intended to take over consumers' sensory-motor circuits. These two seemingly contradictory attitudes fully overlap in their concept of form, neither of them paying attention to the materiality of form, to the individuation of the product within its milieu of individuation.[12] The poet Lucian made fun of people who revered bronze statues, ignorant of the technical processes that went into producing them, limiting the form to the external casing. While a bronze God, 'Poseidon with his trident, Zeus with his thunderbolt, all ivory and gold', if we study the interior, 'is one tangle of bars, bolts, nails . . . not to mention a possible colony of rats or mice' (Lucian 1905: 105). Form is not an external cast; it is, as Simondon said, a modulation between forces and matter. Instead of thinking of form as the ideal principle which imposes itself on inert matter – masculine design which shapes a passive material – modulation places itself in the middle of the operating chain: the slightest technical operation, for example casting bricks, already consists of a meeting between a material mould (the 'form') and a prepared material (the clay), in a way that shows all form is matter, and all matter is formed. Rather than the inert opposition between form and matter, which leads design to privilege only the packaging, with no concern for the production process itself, we should prefer the interaction between materials and forces: an operational design.

Design Modulation

This is a shift from packaging design to operational design, which takes a completely different view of the relationships between form and matter, recognising the materiality of form, and the forming of matter. Rather than coating the outside of insignificant content, material form is produced by the interaction of forces and matter. It takes on a form, and any form comes from the relationship between forces acting on the materials. In this sense design has never been decorative; it has always been functional. Or rather, critics of decorative art have always based their arguments on precisely the division between form and matter that I have set out to challenge: if we take decoration to be an unnecessary extra, as it is seen by Loos and Gropius, we continue both to give form an essential function and to consider decoration as hypertelic[13] matter, excess fat. These are two different formal propositions. Claiming that the highly ornamental and the abstract are different things is all well and good, but not that they oppose one another: this point of view would be mistaken when it comes to form, taking it to be a minimal framework (osteology) rather than considering it at the same time as a proliferation network (nervous system). Lalique and Gaudi, Mies van der Rohe and Le Corbusier draw up two very different maps of affects,[14] with different senses of proliferation and different ecological content – vegetable and mineral. Both of these equally regulate material form but not through the partial imposition of an exclusive rule.

What comes into play in design is actually the political status of form, as a reaction, but also tangled up with industrial capitalism and mass production. This means there are two related movements we can identify: first, design counteracting industrial derealisation, which is an ecological safeguard for humans and technology, but which, in making a reactionary refusal, risks seeking refuge in the past instead of transforming neocapitalist production relationships. Second, an industrial world chasing after design, and monopolising it entirely so that it can take advantage of its extra meaning, its consumer-friendly[15] aspect, its well-thought-out ecological reputation, and its classification as art. Industry has certainly made the most of the social power of the subjectification of design and has already established the strict equivalence of production, communication and consumption. Marketing, market research, reducing consumers to streams of statistics on compulsive purchasing, debt, the planned obsolescence of products and advertising are a fundamental part of the industrial production of goods, in the cognitive and emotional as well as material senses. On the one hand it is a design of escape, on the other, design of redundancy. But we must not allow ourselves to be confined to this disillusioned alternative. There is a third way to be explored: design as a mode of existence for technical objects. But to approach this, we have to rid design of the ambiguities in its packaging, and stop reducing it to a covering layer, perceived as a membrane for exchange and harnessing, industrially formatted to the highest level by multinationals capable of producing their own ideal consumer: the smoker, the brand lover, standardised equipment, leisurewear, Coca-Cola, Nikes and blockbusters that abound from Greenland to southern Africa.

Design certainly assumes a demarcating role, and separates the ordinary from the remarkable, the banal from the disconcerting. It would, however, be a mistake to identify this separation as the reproduction of dominant social relationships, as though design were condemned to maintaining an aristocratic exception reserved for the most culturally endowed: those with noble taste, financial clout, an alternative spirit, resourcefulness or civic awareness. Social divisions do not automatically imply fitting redundancy into dominant circuits of established hierarchies. Design is not only a matter of purchase price, rarity, excellence and ethics, but also the transformation of production. This transformation implies a new conception not only of form, and of biopolitical, ecological and technological modes of subjectification, but also of the utilitarian. The entire field of what is known as 'material culture' in anthropology also changes status: from body rhythms to the apparatuses of capture that equip our socialised bodies; the collective machinery of power, from road maps to information highways, from agribusiness to the supermarket; in short, all our social and domestic routines.

Resingularisation of Production

Thinking about design as the packaging of exception or the production of excellence leaves the art machine and its complicity with capitalist production methods untouched, while the emergence of the new status of the material technological world raises new issues.

It was Simondon who brought to light the individuation of technical objects as a mode of existence. By giving technical objects a form of individuation sufficient to merit the term 'modes of existence' (which he borrows from Souriau[16]) Simondon approaches them with his own consistency, which is enough to consider them *phylums*: axes of development, but also of taking shape, of gradients of consistency, like evolutionary taxonomy in biology. Just like living species, technical/technological lines have their own consistency, their own axiology, but without indexing them according either to universal genus, or to a unitary line of development that ensures the progress of civilisations. However, it is by allowing himself to consider art as the exception in the utilitarian production system, that Simondon is able to make this transformation. After the appearance of his supplementary thesis *On the Mode of Existence of Technical Objects* in 1958 he returns frequently to this complicity. He specifies that he coins the term 'technical object' – used the way we use 'sacred object' or 'art object' – to draw attention to the lack of attention suffered by the technical field (due to the art machine), and to reintegrate it into culture.

In France Leroi-Gourhan[17] had studied the genesis of utility objects and production techniques. In perceiving technology as a mode of existence, Simondon is insisting on the autonomy and autoconsistency of technical objects, and thus opens up new scope for developing the technical/technological field, which had until then been divided by the two symmetrically reductive approaches of Marx and Heidegger. Philosophers, prisoners of the art machine, blinded by the idealism of the transcendent origin of art, and technophobes, like Heidegger, reduce the technological to the useful, and frown upon instrumentality,[18] as though any work, from a Greek temple to replaying a piece of music on the radio or internet, were independent of its technical/technological moment. Marx, on the other hand, was only interested in the technical object from the point of view of working conditions and social production methods, with regard to a political analysis of the economic relationships of domination. His analysis of goods does, however, give way to a materialistic psychiatry of fetishism and concerns itself with the material aspect of biosocial production of subjectivity. Simondon, as well as Leroi-Gourhan, benefits from the anthropology and works of Marcel Mauss[19] on material culture: the most insignificant artefact is raised to the dignified level of a material archive symbolic of the social fact, and all artefacts share the same historical and scientific value as a monument to human culture, whatever assessment can be made of their technical level. The technical fact is always well rounded and fully socialised.

But Simondon's take on this is new: he is not only interested in the technical operation, but also the objects produced as a result of these operations, in their own consistency, detachable from their operators, pursuing their own independent, social existence, and above all, providing feedback on their producers and users, meaning that technique achieves its own mode of existence, which must be taken in the strongest, Spinozist sense, as a degree of individuation which is just as important as the individuation of art or other spiritual products, science or philosophy. Thus Simondon proposes a psycho-sociology of technology[20] which, today, we should not only apply to design,[21] in its narrow sense – forms of production which make a claim for the distinctive status of design, luxury design, and its enemy-brothers (poor design, or ecological design) – but also to design as the resingularisation of the entire field and use of production.

This implies three propositions that renew the very status of the object, as well as that of technology and art. First of all, it is not sufficient to consider existent objects according to their usage, or their historical or aesthetic nature (their form, their design in a narrow sense), but according to their underlying structure of technicity. With Simondon, technical functionality comes to the fore. It is a commendable moment of rehabilitation, but a provisional one, as it also has the disadvantage of closing the technical object in on itself, on its own functionality, by giving it autonomy and a closure comparable to that claimed by the art object. Transforming this art machine means no longer considering autonomy as closure, identity and a closing in on itself; it is understood, finally, as an autopoietic process: opened transversally to the modes of social subjectification that it starts and on which it develops.[22]

Secondly, it means considering technical objects as actual objects with which we exist symbiotically, and not just as motionless prostheses. I would therefore like to open up the object not only to its internal functionality, but also to its ecological area of expression. By which I mean that the function of the object is never reduced to its internal functionality, even if this is what determines its form. This is like reducing an organism to its anatomy, without taking into account the ecological environment in which it lives and which it transforms in return. Any object is an effector and is sensory: sensory-motor. Each object clears a small area of functionality, from a chair to a cork, from an ashtray to a window. It is what I call the ecological area of the object, which is not an addition to the amorphous human body but in fact a becoming-technical/technological of socialised human beings. This means that any object is at the same time both motor and sensory. Even a chair has motive force: as a device for bearing weight, giving new mobility to the arms, head and legs. Not only does furniture capture or immobilise, relieve or expand bodies as a prosthetic, but it is also a veritable ecological field of expression. As well as having motive force, the object is also sensory: a chair is effective and sensory, as much as a car or a hammer. The utilitarian does not fulfil any great, supposedly timeless, organic function (relieving weight; bearing heavy loads without getting tired), without which we would be required again to separate the technical from the bodily and give ourselves a human nature in place of proposing an ecology of social production. This is what is implied by Guattari's term 'machine'. Not only does the technical object return to a technical universe that is first of all social, but it must also be perceived as a related ecological milieu through which we transform our modes of living, our refrains. This is how 'subjectivity can be manufactured just like electricity or aluminium' (Guattari and Rolnik 2007: 49).

It seems to me, thirdly, that from this point of view we reduce the distance between art and technology as much as possible: a tram creates an image, as does any mode of transport. If it is true for a window, a car windscreen, a computer screen, a rocket, or an aeroplane, it applies to all technical ecologies, from the most basic cart or canoe to walking. Perspective systems in reality only make us choose a point of capture, focusing our gaze. From the Renaissance perspective this is the space in front of the easel, the chair in front of the window. In the current digital age it is electronic scanning and transparency, connection of and equivalence between the interior and the exterior.

In his analysis of technical phyla, Simondon comes close to such an ecopolitical perception of technique/technology. Instead of aligning technique/technology with the historical curve of the linear progress of civilisations (stone age, metal industry, capitalist industry, digital neocapitalism), he concerns himself, as Deleuze and Guattari do in *A Thousand Plateaus*, with the different semiotics of the technical/technological: sign language used by sedentary communities; the jewels and weapons of the nomads; or other typologies yet to be invented. In this multiple history, there are cracks and twists, relics and recoveries, and art never fails to cross paths with technology. A phylum which seems to have no future finds itself the bearer of new connections and links; a branch that appeared to be dead is suddenly brought back to life. William Kentridge, who gives a new lease of life to devices cast aside by the technical tradition of cinematographic equipment, uses them to produce previously unseen effects, both artistic and technical, and shows the implied sensory nature of obsolete technology. These are not worth more than the most recent technology: what counts is making sure they are implemented. The next step would be to apply an analysis such as Simondon's to both the history of art and the history of design in terms of discontinuous phyla and ecological potential.

In any case, design makes an exemplary case for a materialistic approach to art: as an ecological formalism which affirms the indiscernibility of art and technique/technology against such widespread notions that place art in the pantheon of good taste, bourgeois culture and fat wallets, leaving the poor to worry about trips to the supermarket to get their fill of mass production and mass consumption.

One of the major issues for design comes back to shaking off this idealistic layer which separates art from technique/technology in the western system, and which is clumsily communicated when we set about defining it exclusively as an exception to ordinary production, driving home the elitist duality of the addition of soul, the added value that had secured art's path out of the technical, material production system. To talk about the art machine is at the same time to affirm the functionality of art and the integration of technical processes into modes of subjectification.

Notes

The translators thank Anne Sauvagnargues for her patient and insightful comments that helped us improve this translation.

1. [Trans. The word Sauvagnargues uses here, and often throughout the chapter, is *technique*. This encompasses technique (as used in English), technology and technical. We have tried to make a choice where the context seems to favour one particular sense, however in some places we have rendered *technique* with 'technology/technique' or 'technological/technical'. While somewhat inelegant, we felt this construction to be justified in those contexts where the dynamism or tension between the different meanings is pertinent. We are aware too of the Simondon-related 'technic' that is relevant in some cases: this is used where appropriate.]
2. [Trans. Pliny the Elder, Gaius Plinius Secundus (AD 23–79).]
3. [Trans. Alain Roger is a philosopher and landscape theorist whose concept of '*artialisation*', developed from Montaigne, highlighted the mediation between the earth, people and their artistic expressions of the earth. He was a student of Deleuze's.]
4. Cennino Cennini [trans. artist and writer, c. 1370–c. 1440] (born in the Florence area, moved to Padua around 1389).
5. [Trans. Giorgio Vasari (1511–74), Florentine painter, architect and writer.]
6. Lorenzo Ghiberti (1378–1438) [trans. Florentine sculptor].
7. Leon Battista Alberti (1404–72) [trans. important theorist of the Early Renaissance].
8. Europeans believe rationality is Greek (Greece being a part of a White identity, a sort a pre-European world); but Plato thought of himself as being Egyptian (Egypt was for Greece what Greece is for Europe). Therefore, there is no Greek miracle: only European colonialism. The Greeks thought about themselves as part of a South-Mediterranean community – including Egypt, Persia – places that never received the status of founders in European discourses (from the eighteenth to twentieth centuries) because of colonialism (see Saïd 1977). [Trans. See also Deleuze and Guattari 1994.]
9. [Trans. This is an Italian abbreviation for the thirteen hundreds, but is used mainly to identify fourteenth-century proto-Renaissance art.]
10. In Florence in 1562, according to the specific *Quattrocento* [trans. fifteenth century] model for literary academies, Vasari established the first Academy, *l'Accademia del Disegno* (Academy of Design), where painters and sculptors were officially emancipated from their corporation in 1571. Florence was clearly at the head of this movement. By comparison, Paris's Royal Academy of Painting and Sculpture was only established in 1648. This establishes the clear dominance of *disegno*, design, which Vasari, in the 'Introduction' to *Lives of the Artists*, cites as the common root of painting, sculpture and architecture.
11. [Trans. '*Il disegno è una cosa mentale*' – design/drawing is a mental thing – is a phrase attributed to Leonardo da Vinci, though sometimes it is rendered as '*pittura è una cosa mentale*': painting is a mental thing.]
12. [Trans. The concept of 'individuation' is one that is key in the work of Gilbert Simondon – on whose work Sauvagnargues is also expert – which also influences Deleuze and Guattari. Jean-Hughes Barthélémy defines Simondon's use as follows: 'individuation as genesis founds and encompasses the differentiation between individuals, which only becomes fully meaningful in the case of the living individual and its individuation. This is continuous' (2012: 214). For

Deleuze and Guattari the concept is linked to Simondon's critique of hylomorphism (discussed in the present volume by Marenko and Crawford), especially in so far as it relates to haecceities and singularities (Deleuze and Guattari 1987: 408–10), and technology. They write: 'to the form-matter schema, Simondon opposes a dynamic schema, that of matter endowed with singularities-forces, or the energetic conditions at the basis of a system. The result is an entirely different conception of the relations between science and technology' (1987: 555 n. 33). For one of the few books in English to examine Simondon's work – and in which Sauvagnargues has a chapter – see De Boever et al. 2012.]

13. [Trans. Hypertelos happens when the concentration upon/of the *telos* of a thing has led to its hyper-specialisation. A thing so constructed has pushed beyond any simple functional *telos* into an evolutionary niche whereby the hyper-identified *telos* becomes dominant, leading to a thing's fragility. Simondon uses this word in *On the Mode of Existence of Technical Objects* (1980: Chapter 2).]

14. [Trans. Sauvagnargues uses the phrase *'cartes d'affects'* here. Deleuze uses this when discussing Spinoza. In *The Ethics* Spinoza urges us to consider bodies not in terms of form, function or substance but in terms of the speeds and slownesses of its particles, and its capacities for affecting/being affected. Commenting on this in 'Spinoza and Us' (Deleuze 1988: 124), Deleuze says that we can make a list of all the affective capacities of a dray horse and it will map closer to an ox than a racehorse: its form and matter tell us less about the animal than the affective capacities and the speeds/slownesses of its particles. Furthermore, as Sauvagnargues says here, material forms itself as an expression of these affective capacities and speeds/slownesses.]

15. [Trans. 'friendly' in English in the original.]

16. [Trans. Étienne Souriau (1892–1979), philosopher famed for his work on aesthetics, wrote *Les Différents modes d'existence* [The Different Modes of Existence], which influenced Simondon. There is little of his work in English, however Bruno Latour has written on Souriau (2011), and with Isabelle Stengers provided the introduction to Presses Universitaires de France's (2009) edition of *Les Différents modes d'existence*.]

17. [Trans. André Leroi-Gourhan (1911–86) was an influential French anthropologist and archaeologist, who specialised in pre-history. Deleuze and Guattari discuss his work favourably in both *Anti-Oedipus* and *A Thousand Plateaus*, especially in terms of the relationships between hand, tool, speech and mark-making. The technologies, techniques and technics of these relationships are also of importance to Simondon.]

18. [Trans. Sauvagnargue's word *'l'utensilité'* is the usual French translation of Heidegger's *'Zeughaftigkeit'*, most often given as 'instrumentality', sometimes 'equipmentality', in English.]

19. [Trans. The French sociologist and anthropologist Marcel Mauss – famous for his (1925) book *The Gift* and his examination of *potlatch*, an extreme form of gift giving as conspicuous waste demanding excessive reciprocation (see Bataille 1985: 121–5) – was Leroi-Gourhan's PhD thesis supervisor.]

20. See Simondon 2014, 'Psychosociology of Technology, 1960–1961'.

21. See the works of Vincent Beaubois, who is currently writing a thesis on *Simondon and Design* at the Université Paris Ouest Nanterre. [Trans. Beaubois has a chapter in this volume.]

22. In my view Guattari and Donna Haraway's work on this is definitive.

References

Alberti, Leon B. [1568] (2013), *On Sculpture*, trans. J. Arkle, Florence: Jason Arkles Publisher.

Alberti, Leon B. [1444] (2007), *The Delineation of the City of Rome*, Tempe: MRTS.

Alberti, Leon B. [1450] (1991), *On Painting*, trans. C. Grayson, Harmondsworth: Penguin.

Alberti, Leon B. [1485] (1987), *The Ten Books on Architecture*, New York: Dover.

Barthélémy, Jean-Hughes (2012), 'Fifty Key Terms in the Works of Gilbert Simondon', in De Boever et al. (eds), *Gilbert Simondon: Being and Technology*, Edinburgh: Edinburgh University Press, pp. 203–31.

Bataille, Georges (1985), *Visions of Excess: Selected Writings, 1927–1939*, trans. A. Stoekl, C. Lovitt and D. Leslie Jr., Minneapolis: University of Minnesota Press.

Cennini, Cennino [fourteenth century] (1960), *The Craftsman's Handbook*, trans. D.V. Thompson, New York: Dover.

De Boever, Arne, A. Murray, J. Roffe and A. Woodward (eds) (2012), *Gilbert Simondon: Being and Technology*, Edinburgh: Edinburgh University Press.

Deleuze, Gilles [1970] (1988), *Spinoza: Practical Philosophy*, trans. R. Hurley, San Francisco: City Lights Books.

Deleuze, Gilles and F. Guattari [1991] (1994), *What is Philosophy?* trans. G. Burchell and H. Tomlinson, London: Verso Books.

Deleuze, Gilles and F. Guattari [1980] (1987), *A Thousand Plateaus. Capitalism and Schizophrenia 2*, trans. B. Massumi, Minneapolis: University of Minnesota Press.

Deleuze, Gilles and F. Guattari [1972] (1984), *Anti-Oedipus. Capitalism and Schizophrenia 1*, trans. R. Hurley, M. Seem and H. Lane, London: Athlone.

Ghiberti, Lorenzo (1948), *The Commentaries of Lorenzo Ghiberti*, with J. R. von Schlosser, London: Courtauld Institute of Art.

Guattari, Félix and Rolnik, S. [1986] (2007), *Micropolitiques*, Les Empêcheurs de penser en rond, Paris: Le Seuil.

Latour, B. (2011), 'Reflections on Etienne Souriau's *Les différents modes d'existence*', trans. S. Muecke, in L. Bryant, N. Srnicek and G. Harman, *The Speculative Turn*, Melbourne: re.press, pp. 304–33.

Lucian (1905), 'Alectryon, the Cock', in *The Works of Lucian of Samosata*, trans. H. W. Fowler and F. G. Fowler, Oxford: The Clarendon Press.

Mauss, Marcel (1967), *The Gift: Forms and Functions of Exchange in Archaic Societies*, trans. I. Cunnison, New York: Norton.

Pliny the Elder [AD 77] (1991), *Natural History: A Selection*, Harmondsworth: Penguin.

Roger, Alain (1978), *Nus et paysages: essai sur la fonction de l'art*, Paris: Aubier.

Saïd, Edward (1977), *Orientalism*, Harmondsworth: Penguin.

Shaftesbury (1712), "Letter Concerning the Art or Science of Design".

Simondon, Gilbert (2014), 'Psychosociologie de la Technicité 1960–1961 [Psychosociology of Technology]', in G. Simondon, *Sur la technique, 1953–1983*, Paris: Presses Universitaires de France.

Simondon, Gilbert [1958] (1980), *On the Mode of Existence of Technical Objects*, trans. N. Mellamphy, London, ON: University of Western Ontario; available at https://english.duke.edu/uploads/assets/Simondon_MEOT_part_1.pdf (last accessed 4 September 2014).

Souriau, Étienne [1943] (2009), *Les Différents modes d'existence*, Paris: Presses Universitaires de France.

Spinoza, Baruch [1677] (1955), 'The Ethics', in B. Spinoza, *On the Improvement of the Understanding. The Ethics. Correspondence*, trans. R. H. M. Elwes, New York: Dover, pp. 45–271.

Vasari, Giorgio [1550, 1568] (2008), *Lives of the Artists*, trans. J. Conaway Bondanella and P. Bondanella, Oxford: Oxford University Press.

Chapter 4

Thinking Hot: Risk, Prehension and Sympathy in Design

T. Hugh Crawford

> They were friends, as only a craftsman can be, with timber and iron. The grain of wood told secrets to them.
>
> George Sturt, *The Wheelwright's Shop*

In just a few pages of her magisterial *Thinking with Whitehead*, Isabelle Stengers introduces most of the concepts necessary to develop a Deleuzian concept of design. In the chapter 'Entry into Metaphysics', she wrestles with Whitehead's notion of 'eternal objects' as articulated in *Science and the Modern World*. She notes that once Whitehead gets to *Process and Reality* and develops a full-blown theory of prehension, his philosophy no longer depends on eternal objects. Nevertheless, Stengers argues they are fundamental to the development of his thought and are best understood through a perspective provided by Deleuze's concept of the virtual. She distinguishes the realisation of the possible from the virtual:

> Realization is therefore the selection of the one that will be realized. Of the virtual, in contrast, one must say that it is not actualized without changing 'in nature' (taking on a different 'mode of existence'), a thesis Deleuze took over from Bergson. This implies, first of all, that it cannot be conceived in the image of its actualization, and that the latter can [by] no means be assimilated to a simple selection. (Stengers 2011a: 214)

From this perspective, eternal objects cannot be known as objects, but instead can enter into configurations with other eternal objects into an (often novel) actualisation that is in no way determined, nor are the selections within the process obvious or absolute. In the actualisation of the work, objects take on a different mode of existence. The position Stengers is laying out applies directly to an understanding of design as process, as making, or what I would like to call, following the blacksmithing practice of designing in the heat of forging, 'thinking hot'. It is significant that at this moment, when she is deep into the abstractions of Whitehead's unfolding metaphysics, she turns to Deleuze and to Étienne Souriau: 'More precisely, [realisation] will participate in the mode of existence that Deleuze, here following no longer Bergson but the philosopher Étienne Souriau, confers upon the virtual: that of a problem to be solved or a work to be accomplished' (Stengers 2011a: 214). Her linking of the virtual to practice, to work to be done, is here fundamental as many of the existents figuring in the work being accomplished are multiple, active, variable and not all human.

What I propose to do in this essay is work through several design theorists who emphasise design as making, but also to examine the recent work of Lars Spuybroek, a practising architect and theorist, in order to trace his affinities with elements of Deleuze as read through the lens of Stengers and, to a lesser extent, Gilbert Simondon and Étienne Souriau. In *The Sympathy of Things*, Spuybroek develops his 'Gothic ontology' to articulate a twenty-first-century design practice based on a Ruskinian concept of beauty. He argues for 'design without designers' enabled through understanding how the 'sympathy' of things works towards beauty. However he dismisses Deleuze's notion of assemblage as an externalist figure that neglects what he sees as the internal sympathy of things – their ability to feel relations non-cognitively. He argues that affect is not sufficient to explain what actually holds things together. Within the frame of his argument, Spuybroek's point is well founded; however, his focus is primarily on the notion of the machinic assemblage and, in many ways, the assemblage theory articulated by Manuel DeLanda (2006). From another perspective (the one I would like to explore), Deleuze creates a place for a notion of design very much in sympathy with Spuybroek's 'entanglement theory' through his articulation of Whitehead's 'prehension' in *The Fold*, the 'ambulant smith' detailed in 'Nomadology', and in the 'pure immanence' envisioned in his final essay.

Risk

Stengers's turn to Souriau draws the virtual away from the heady abstractions to which it is sometimes subjected and brings it right back to the floor of the designer's workshop (which is where I hope to remain for most of this essay). She quotes his *Du mode d'existence de l'oeuvre a faire*: '*I insist on this idea that as long as the work is in the workshop, the work is in danger. At each moment, each one of the artist's actions, or rather* from *each of the artist's actions, it may live or die*' (Stengers 2011a: 215; original emphasis). One could see this as an idealist position – the work as envisioned by the artist or designer is doomed by the imperfect abilities of the craftsmen in the workshop – but by no means is that Souriau's (or Stengers's) point. Instead, the work *is* danger, it *is* risk. From the perspective I hope to develop through these thinkers, 'work to be accomplished' is not a designed object but instead is risky process; the designer is not The Maker but instead is an accident-prone part of a not-always 'agile choreography' (Stengers 2011a: 215). Above all else, a workmanship of risk is a fundamental principle of design.

Stengers then expands the Deleuzian implications she draws from Souriau. Work to be done, that which invokes the virtual, is a problem, but it is a problem (to use one of Stengers's favourite words) of 'wonder' (Stengers 2011c), not of a scripted process. The work to be done demands of the designer and his or her materials and tools a form of 'negative capability', which, as Keats so clearly explains, is 'when man is capable of being in uncertainties, mysteries, doubts, without any irritable reaching after fact and reason' (Colvin 1921: 48). Stengers draws from Souriau a similar lesson, but brings with it something more than passive acceptance. Risk drives the process:

> The insistence of the problem does not implicitly contain the means for its solution; the work's 'idea' is not an ideal from which the artist takes inspiration. It exists only through the risk it brings into existence, by the fact that at every step artists know they are exposed to the risk of betrayal, particularly when, through laziness, ease, impatience, or fear, they believe they can decide on the path, instead of capturing, step by step, the question posed to them at that step. (Stengers 2011a: 216)

The risk is not that of impending chaos or collapse. Instead, her risk is workmanship, a slow deliberate practice that revels in the anexact, in that very uncertainty.[1] Not to give in to chance, but to cooperate with all those forces: the grain of the wood, the sharpness of the axe, the aching of muscles, sweat-blurred vision, the sweet smell of sap. Stengers summarises her and Deleuze's appropriation of Souriau thus:

> Unlike the mythical Sphinx, the sphinx of Étienne Souriau does not know the answer to the riddle. The 'deficiency' of envisagement is then no longer a lack, but designates Deleuzian difference in nature between the virtual and the potential, connoted by a risk and a wait. A risk has no determinate identity or stake before it is actually taken. A wait is a wait for what will answer, not for such-and-such an answer. (Stengers 2011a: 216)

Fig. 4.1 Shutter Dog © Hugh Crawford 2011

Identity is indetermined or is not pre-determined. In the workshop the 'wait' is a process that cannot point to predetermined outcomes, but instead is an opening out to possibilities revealed in time. A 'risk and a wait' bring both the virtual and the temporal back into design/making practices as a function of the practice rather than that which must be overcome in production.

   This notion of a 'risk and a wait' is fundamental to design as 'thinking hot', a blacksmith's term that occupies the nether ground between practical imperative and professional pride. Iron and steel can be shaped in a number of ways, and decisions during a forging process are inflected by a broad range of imperatives including technical exigency, economic considerations, physical capabilities, available tools and material, and of course a profound, historically articulated sense of how things should be done (Keller and Keller 1996: 130). For example (Fig. 4.1), on completion of forging the curves of this shutter dog (a device mounted perpendicularly on a shaft so as to pivot and hold an exterior shutter open), a blacksmith can simply cold-bore a hole with a drill press to attach the dog to the spike, or he could reheat the dog, risking both shape and temper of the object he has just forged, and hot-punch that hole. In the case of this fabrication, the smith opted to cold bore for the sake of time and uniformity, but he, like many smiths, prefers to think hot, forging all shapes at the anvil, striking while the iron is hot.

Such an attitude is closely related to what David Pye (designer and woodworker) calls 'a workmanship of risk'. In *The Nature and Art of Workmanship* (1968), he articulates an opposition between what he calls 'workmanship of certainty' and that of risk. He does not make this opposition to glorify a free-form version of design, but instead to call attention to the varying degrees of regulation workmanship functions under in order to understand better the complexity and multiplicity of design *in* practice. Briefly, a workmanship of certainty generally operates with highly uniform materials and significantly regulated tools (and workers), whereas a workmanship of risk must grapple with divergent possibilities enabled and demanded by material, tools and skills. An example from woodworking (Pye's favoured practice): one can square a timber using a table saw equipped with a rip fence. If the lumber is fairly uniform, the power of the saw will overwhelm knots and twists, and the fence will produce an evenly dimensioned 90-degree cut. This would be well within the workmanship of certainty. Moving along the scale, one could use a handheld circular saw equipped with a rip fence and achieve nearly the same results. The same tool cutting on a drawn line will vary a bit, as would cutting to a line with a hand saw. Moving further towards a workmanship of risk, one could square the timber with a broad-axe, a somewhat regulated tool as it has a bevelled edge that enables a skilled worker to cut relatively flat surfaces (Fig. 4.2). Finally, one could try to square the timber with a regular axe, but such an endeavour would require remarkable skill, and very close, deliberate attention to detail: a refined sense of the grain and density of the wood, the sharpness of the axe, and a well-developed sense of the perpendicular would all be fundamental to success.

Pye is not celebrating risk over certainty, but he helps demonstrate that, in the early stages of the design process (prior to the regulation brought on by scaling production), a workmanship of risk often figures prominently. This opposition bears a strong resemblance to Deleuze and Guattari's notion of the smooth and the striated, and the workmanship of risk is directly linked to the 'ambulant smiths' and their nomadic science. *A Thousand Plateaus* sharpens these concepts and provides a far-reaching vocabulary. In 'Nomadology' they link directly the broadly articulated notion of 'smooth space' specifically

Fig 4.2 Using a Broad Axe © Hugh Crawford 2011

to metallurgy and the action of smithing. Smooth space is the place of 'thinking hot':

> It has no homogeneity, except between infinitely proximate points, and the linking of proximities is effected independently of any determined path. It is a space of contact, of small tactile or manual actions of contact, rather than a visual space like Euclid's striated space. (Deleuze and Guattari 1987: 371)

The hylomorphic is geometric and depends on a mould that is the physical manifestation of a duplicatory idealism; it is an idea snared in Euclidian dimensionality. In contrast, the smithed smooth is that very place of continuous variation lacking precise determination, points of continuous extension lead to next points, uncountable, non-discrete continuous variation on the molecular level. In smithing, multiple heating drives off carbon variously, hammer blows hit smooth but not homogeneous material that pushes back. Thinking hot is material community.

Deleuze and Guattari continue:

> It would be useless to say that metallurgy is a science because it discovers constant laws, for example, the melting point of a metal at all times and in all places. For metallurgy is inseparable from several lines of variation:

variation between meteorites and indigenous metals; variation between ores and proportions of metal; variation between alloys, natural and artificial; variation between the operations performed upon a metal; variation between the qualities that make a given operation possible, or that result from a given operation. (Deleuze and Guattari 1987: 405–6)

Deleuze and Guattari recognise both the singularities and the intensities involved in the work to be done. A nomadic science, an ambulatory or itinerate technology, is set up against hylomorphism through such variables as heterogeneous material, temporal fluxions and the singularities of the immediately passing moment. The ambulant smiths do not design with form and matter, rather they recalibrate goals and evolving shapes in the heat of the moment:

All of these variables can be grouped under two overall rubrics: *singularities or spatiotemporal haecceities* of different orders, and the operations associated with them as processes of deformation or transformation; *affective qualities or traits of expression* of different levels, corresponding to these singularities and operations (hardness, weight, color, etc.). (Deleuze and Guattari 1987: 406)

In a traditional design perspective, focus remains on the traits of expression: how the object can express. Deleuze and Guattari use as an example a cast iron sword which expresses by piercing (among its many affective traits), but their insistence on including temporal-materiality (or material-time) and the granularity of process as fundamental to nomadic science reframes the design question, putting us right back on the workshop floor, with its risky productions.

Deleuze and Guattari turn to Simondon for assistance in this critique of hylomorphism and another way to articulate these haecceities:

Simondon exposes the technological insufficiency of the matter-form model, in that it assumes a fixed form and a matter deemed homogeneous. It is the idea of the law that assures the model's coherence, since laws are what submit matter to this or that form, and conversely, realize in matter a given property deduced from the form. But Simondon demonstrates that the hylomorphic model leaves many things, active and affective, by the wayside. On the one hand, to the formed or formable matter we must add an entire energetic materiality in movement, carrying singularities or haecceities that are already like implicit forms that are topological, rather than geometrical, and that combine with processes of deformation: for example, the variable undulations and torsions of the fibers guiding the operation of splitting wood. (Deleuze and Guattari 1987: 408)[2]

Fig 4.3 Affective Surfaces © Hugh Crawford 2011

Woodworking is perhaps the best choice to break open the failures of hylomorphism. Moulding depends on uniform pourable substance and, while today's oriented strand board approaches that in both its dimensionality and uniformity, wood qua wood – in the round – is inflected by rays, checks, knots and occlusions which the designer must accommodate. Indeed, the practice is helpful in unpacking the too-easy binary conscious/affective by undercutting judgements by the mind with judgements by the hand, or the smells brought out in cutting, splitting, or planing, not to mention telling vibrations recognised by the elbow (Fig. 4.3). Woodworkers know that their practice unfolds between conscious imaging and tactile manipulation. Singularities emerge in the space in between image and execution. Such singularities are topological rather than geometrical, but that science of surfaces is one of affect: topology is the study of felt surface, not measured depth.

Set up against nomadic practice is 'Royal science', a place of law without the wood's torsional fibres, promulgating principles of design and a workmanship of certainty; it is rectitude writ large. Royal science is a modular, discrete practice, building up from completely articulated, homogeneous units, precisely what nomad science avoids and even wards off. With articulated homogeneity, the material world becomes a play space where the masterful designer can push things around, tell them what to do, exert control, live autonomously. Royal science is masterful, powerful, but does not hear what the variable material has to say, cannot learn what it has to teach:

> what becomes apparent in the rivalry between the two models is that the ambulant or nomad sciences do not destine science to take on an autonomous power, or even to have an autonomous development. They do not have the means for that because they subordinate all their operations to the sensible conditions of intuition and construction befollowing the flow of matter, drawing and linking up smooth space. (Deleuze and Guattari 1987: 373)

The Royal Science of, for example, Euclid, with its rigid striations, denies processual variation and the emergence of zones of intensity: its absolute uniformity is atemporal and non-singular. The ambulatory smith restores time as action by following, drawing, linking, by responding in real time because the 'zone of fluctuation . . . is coextensive with reality itself' (Deleuze and Guattari 1987: 373). The action of the smith is to 'draw, upset, and weld' (Lasansky 1980): all terms specific to the practice but also pointing towards its dynamism. The very term 'upset', which means to thicken at the anvil through heat and hammer (the opposite of 'draw' which is to thin or draw out through similar practice: Fig. 4.4), marks the risk of production. To upset iron, then, is to disrupt in the hope of producing a satisfactory bulge across 'spatio-temporal haecceities of different order' (Deleuze and Guattari 1987: 405).

The nomadic sciences restore time to design by acknowledging the temporality articulated in the grammar of the phrase 'work to be done'. This brings concomitant questions of how time inflects autonomy and the hylomorphic, and what that means for ideation and for knowledge in general. In *Cognition and Tool Use*, Keller and Keller examine these questions in some detail, noting that 'An initial design is an orientation towards production of an artifact that the blacksmith anticipates will acquire an increasingly specific character as work proceeds' (Keller and Keller 1996: 118). The original idea, perhaps embodied in carefully detailed isometric drawings, remains provisional as the work emerges from the assemblage that is steel, heat, weight, skill, economics and time. The blacksmith's anticipation is often accompanied by a sense of wonder; not wonder as a sense of arrest, but instead wonder at shaping,

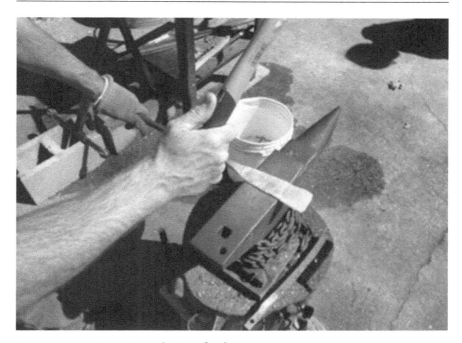

Fig. 4.4 Upsetting © Hugh Crawford 2011

wondering about emergence. Equally important are the orienting capacities of design practice: not just ideation but also material, embodied and processual. Design and knowledge are products of specific orientations – the bilateral symmetry of the human body coupled with binocular vision, otoliths in the cochlea that provide both a sense of gravity and spatial orientation. As famous woodworker Roy Underhill claims, a chair maker must have a 'well-developed sense of the vertical' (1981: 75). Indeed, current philosophical discourse taking place under the rubric 'Object Oriented Ontology' constantly moves back and forth between the terms Object and Ontology without lingering on the fundamental middle term, one that calls attention to how positions must be articulated through 'objects' (and ontologies) that produce specific orientations. Paying attention to objects in practice attunes both subjects and objects to possibilities of interaction, but, at the same time, to orientation. Objects and subjects can be grasped only in certain ways. These assemblages make specific worlds and work possible, and, at the same time, orient all the actors to various possibilities. Understanding what a body can do depends on a range of orienting capacities and affordances.

Time in design restores to knowledge not stability or completion, but instead an awareness of its dynamic unfolding as a result of the orientation of its actors. Keller and Keller explain: 'Knowledge and action are continually in revision and development; we must understand them as mutually constructed and equally dynamic entities' (1996: 109). What is key to their work is not just this simple but profound conclusion, but also their patient articulation of the mutual participation (both corporeal and noncorporeal) of dynamic entities: variable carbon in steel through multiple heatings, desires of the client, tools available for project, sense of history, strength of arm, as well as pride in particular forms of practice. The work to be done remains in flux, is always at risk, not a risk of being spoiled but instead as one of the fundamental elements of practice.

Prehension

Even after acknowledging the temporal in thinking hot, we must grapple with the emergence not just of singularities but also of the individual; in this case, the thing designed, the work that has been done. Here once again, Stengers's articulation of Deleuze and Whitehead points the way. In a remarkable chapter in *The Fold*, his book on Leibniz, Deleuze turns to Whitehead and the notion of individuals and prehension. Whitehead is particularly useful for a discussion of design on the floor of the workshop because for him the individual *is* creativity (Deleuze 1992: 77). Deleuze explains Whitehead's terminology:

> The individual is a 'concrescence' of elements. This is something other than a connection or a conjunction. It is, rather, a *prehension*: an element is the given, the *datum* of another element that prehends it. Prehension is individual unity. Everything prehends its antecedents and its concomitants, and, by degrees, prehends a world. (Deleuze 1992: 78; original emphasis)[3]

Through his notion of prehension, Whitehead helps frame an understanding of the orientation of materials and the possibilities they afford. Once again blacksmithing provides an example, in this case to glimpse the relation between Deleuze's notion of singularity and the individual. In nomad science, singularities are part of the smooth space of flowing matter. They do not map out or determine a state of affairs; instead they participate in its direction: they orient the work to be done. The individual then is the concrescence of elements that prehend each other and prehend the subject. Today most smiths work with mild steel, which has something of a crystalline structure and therefore tends to orient work in a certain way. In contrast, wrought iron – the pre-1900 traditional material of smithing – has grain that can be compared to wood: long crystalline fibres that direct the work of drawing, upsetting and welding in fairly specific ways. The smith acting in tune with their materials feels this grain, learns where it wants to go and the kinds of shapes it will accept. The smith does not cut and weld the wrought bar, but instead heats and folds, following the grain of this fibrous material. Wrought iron prehends production (in its many singularities) in particular ways, so the concrescence of the individual results from a capture of those tendencies, an expression of their desires.

Such a formulation raises questions about the agency of material, a question increasingly pressed by many thinkers today (for example: Jones and Cloke 2002; Malafouris 2008; Bennett 2010). Malafouris puts it elegantly in his discussion of human-clay interactions in pottery:

> If human agency is then material agency *is*, there is no way that human and material agency can be disentangled. Or else, *while agency and intentionality may not be properties of things, they are not properties of humans either: they are the properties of material engagement, that is, of the grey zone where brain, body and culture conflate.* (Malafouris 2008: 22; original emphasis)

This shift is particularly important for design theorists. Commonly, designers are thought to act consciously while the material world, however active, merely behaves in a mechanical, chemical or biologically determined fashion. Deleuze begins to unwind this via Whitehead's notion of prehension: 'The vector of prehension moves from the world to the subject, from the prehended datum to a prehending one' (Deleuze 1992: 78). Deleuze's prehensive vector moves *from* the world, prehensive desire precedes subjective cognition and plans. Given the multiplicity of prehensions, they do not determine but rather orient the subject, and of course the subject can, as another actor in the world, also be a prehensive vector in yet another concrescence. Whitehead explains this in *Science and the Modern World*:

> The word *perceive* is, in our common usage, shot through and through with the notion of cognitive apprehension. So is the word *apprehension*, even with the adjective *cognitive* omitted. I will use the word *prehension* for *uncognitive apprehension*: by this I mean *apprehension* which may or may not be cognitive. (Whitehead 2011: 69; original emphasis)

With this Whitehead sidesteps the problem of vitalism or at least the attribution of cognitive structures to nonorganic entities, but he leaves the door open for an understanding of something called 'uncognitive apprehension', prehension as a much more active force than simple material tendency.

Before moving on to things prehensive, it is helpful to linger on cognition and the workshop for yet another moment, specifically with the question of conceptualisation as a way of modelling or as a form of orientation. Once again, Keller and Keller raise the issue in a fairly direct fashion: 'We will argue that this nonverbal component of mental activity constitutes an essential dimension of conceptual thought. Conceptualisation, then, is the characteristically human capacity to integrate diverse forms of information in active reasoning' (1996: 130). Working just outside the level of language, the Kellers look for a deeper understanding of the non-verbal as conceptual thought fundamental to design. As we saw earlier (Fig. 4.1), there is the graphic figure – the ever-present chalk marks on the floor – that participates in the emerging design/production of a shutter dog, but the Kellers are pressing a bit harder here and may be clearing a space for uncognitive apprehension. The chalk drawing functions alternately as gesture, concept and template which provides only an approximation of what was initially only an approximation. The space of thinking hot (with the emphasis here on thinking) is displaced slightly outside the realm of representation and into the world of material prehension – a place at some distance from the hylomorphic model and Royal science.

A way to illustrate this point is through an observation by Humberto Maturana in 'The Biology of Cognition'. There he discusses the function of language in cognition, setting up the notion of language as connotative and denotative, reserving for denotative the idea of representational adequacy. Then he notes,

> Conversely, if it is recognized that language is connotative and not denotative and that its function is to orient the orientee within his cognitive domain, and not to point to independent entities, it becomes apparent that learned orienting interactions embody a function of non-linguistic origin that, under a selective pressure for recursive application, can originate through evolution the system of cooperative consensual interactions between organisms that is natural language. (Maturana 1980: 130–1)

Maturana makes this claim in the middle of a discussion about the emergence of natural language and leaves some of the implications of his claims unexamined, but, when teased out, these claims are significant for understanding noncorporeal prehension. If language's primary (or even largely secondary) function is to orient behaviour, then even the practice most seemingly distant from the workshop – that of abstract representation – is actually just one more orienting tool not significantly different from the height of the anvil or a well-developed sense of the vertical.

Michael Pollan provides an anecdote that helps illustrate this point. Although primarily known as a critic of industrial food production, Pollan describes in *A Place of My Own* his sometimes-fumbling attempts to build a writing house in the back yard of his rural Connecticut home. As an editor, he rarely questions his representational capacities, but this book is a compendium of his doubts about his ability in the world of wood, hammers and nails. Late in the project, after Pollan begins to feel more confident with his own material skills, the carpenter he has hired to help him is injured and unable to supervise. Faced with waiting for the man's recovery or continuing on his own, Pollan embraces the latter and attempts to trim out his windows (cut and nail the mouldings and sills that surround the windows on the interior). Although he does not comment on the implications of his actions, the scene he describes is telling. He lays out his materials on the floor, measures, cuts to length, all the while talking to himself in what he recognises as the hushed voice of a television commentator for a golf tournament. Pollan's self-effacing humour aside, this is a clear example of the claim Maturana was making: in the scene, his use of language is connotative. Pollan is oriented towards his work because of the bilateral symmetry of his body, the disposition of the material on the floor, the highly regulated chop saw, the length and weight of his hammer, the gauge of the nails, *and* the words he uses to talk himself through the work to be done. Of course language is not exhausted of its denotative or representational function, as Pollan is successful in presenting this scene through words printed in a book. Nevertheless, the point that should not be lost is that uncognitive apprehension, or prehension, takes place across a broad register of corporeal and noncorporeal relations; that the carefully planned, hylomorphic model ignores the uncognitive orienting performed not just by the grain of the wood, but also the connotative capacities of such rarified abstractions as words, diagrams and other representational systems.

Sympathy

Cognitive and even uncognitive models still re-inscribe a bifurcation – for example, between human designer and the process of production – but prehension begins to provide a different model, one that functions through the sympathy things have for each other. For Spuybroek, design is ecological, not wilful: 'I have become the most radical advocate of the design argument: I believe in design without a designer' (2011: 271). He sets himself up against the design tradition which design theorist Richard Buchanan defines as 'the human power of conceiving, planning, and making products that serve human beings in the accomplishment of any individual or collective purpose' (2001: 191). Buchanan's position is clearly human(istically) centred as opposed to the more scientific version offered by Herbert Simon in *The Sciences of the Artificial*: 'Everyone designs who devises courses of action aimed at changing existing situations into preferred ones' (1996: 111).[4] While maintaining a focus on process and temporality, Spuybroek turns our attention to the prehensive moment, the point where 'things' hook onto each other in some form of sympathy:

> The main issue in design is the choice between cruelty and tenderness; there is no other. And if we want to begin to conceive what I would call an ecology of design, I think there is only one option, and that is the one for tenderness, or sympathy: a fundamental reaching out of things to things. (Spuybroek 2011: 132)

This extends Pye's discussion of a workmanship of certainty and a workmanship of risk by creating a different set of distinctions. While the term 'tenderness' with its direct connection to 'sympathy' is an interesting concept, Spuybroek's use of the term 'cruelty' needs some unpacking. In the context of Pye's terminology, one could claim that a workmanship of certainty can practice both cruelty and tenderness, while a successful workmanship of risk must be framed as tenderness. Returning to the blacksmith's workshop for a moment in search of an example of what I think Spuybroek points towards with the notion of cruelty, let us imagine our smith making a set of shutter dogs for an entire house. Today, instead of drawing out his iron at the forge, he can draw out a CAD sketch, purchase pure mild steel in 3/8ths of an inch thickness, and cut dozens out with a water jet followed by an automated cold bore and powder coating. This is, of course, how such production regularly takes place, and to call it 'cruelty' in a traditional sense is absurd, but Spuybroek sets out tenderness and sympathy as a form of practice acutely attuned to the variations of materials, tools and skills. The sympathy of things is their ability (and desire) to enter into specific, often complicated assemblages. Sympathetic design both allows and helps these assemblages to occur. Within the workmanship of certainty, the sheer uniformity of material and the brute force brought to bear on shaping it neglects the complexities of the reaching out of things to things. One could think of cruelty as the intentional neglect of human responsibility to or care for other humans, so extending the notion of cruelty to things is only coherent in a situation where one acknowledges prehension or sympathetic connection – the orientation of things to other things – that is neglected or simply ignored in both the design process and in scaling production.[5]

Successful workmanship of risk takes the opposite approach: tenderness and sympathy in recognizing how prehension actually works. Indeed, if proper attention is paid to this sympathy, the design will be successful. Ultimately Spuybroek's position is grounded in affect: 'All relations are felt relations. The transitions are felt, and the substances connected to us by feeling become known to us' (2011: 152). But affects are between nonorganic things as much as they are between human designers and their materials. In Spuybroek's world, one simply cannot work with tenderness and not produce something that both works and is therefore beautiful (Spuybroek's criterion for successful design): it holds together prehensively.

Sympathy and tenderness imply care, a taking into account that demands circumspection and attention to detail. The examples I have chosen tend to celebrate careful handwork. Blacksmithing and woodworking demand slowness and strong awareness of the capacities and aptitudes of the actors, and as illustrations, they are simple. Recognizing the sympathy of things is perhaps a form of slowness, if we remember Deleuze and Guattari's careful distinction between slow and rapid: '*Slow and rapid are not quantitative degrees of movement but rather two types of qualified movement*, whatever the speed of the former or the tardiness of the latter' (1987: 371; original emphasis). Getting in tune with the sympathy of things does not require a quantitative slowing down, but rather a qualitative alteration of speed based on the limiting factors of prehension. Stengers raises precisely this point in her figure of the idiot and her more recent plea for 'slow science' (Stengers 2005; 2011b). Royal science might be ponderous, but the speed of ambulant practices is not pure quickness. Rather it is keyed to the temporality of the actors involved. The blacksmith must both wait for the object to heat and strike while the iron is hot.

Spuybroek is careful to distinguish his position from many other thinkers including Whitehead, Simondon and Deleuze, but it is his relation to Deleuze that is perhaps most interesting. He claims, 'In the Deleuzian fold system, continuity always precedes singularity, while in the rib system, entities precede continuity: Gothic things are thing-actions' (2011: 66). This is a fair distinction and can be generally construed as an accurate representation of much of Deleuze's work. It is significant that Spuybroek focuses on the fold here as it brings along Whitehead (and perhaps Stengers) as part of the critique. He is, at this point, in close alignment with those arguing for an Object Oriented Ontology (particularly Graham Harman[6]) which privileges the ever-withdrawn object over some form of processual, relational unfolding, but as many of the above quotations make clear, Spuybroek's focus remains on the relations those entities are capable of forming and is not that worried about their ontology. By emphasising the Gothic rib system – the very stones that form the Gothic line – Spuybroek is able to draw out thing-action. It is telling that Deleuze's focus on metallurgy (although of course he has much to say about the Gothic line himself) does privilege flow over entity, but, as we learned above, singularities are very much a part of the smooth space of our itinerant smiths. They may be avoiding the striations of Royal science, but their smooth world is hardly homogeneous. Their iron is fibrous, it has singularities, and those very singularities that may or may not precede continuities are also thing-actions. Temporal processes are fundamental for any theory of design, but all processes start in the middle. The designer does not begin with a set of separate entities that predate the work; rather he or she is always already caught up in other processes. Singularities and flows co-emerge in design. Worrying over which comes first ignores this fundamental circumstance.

Deleuze and Guattari address this specifically in '1227: Treatise on Nomadology – The War Machine' where they note:

> artisans are obliged to follow in another way as well, in other words, to go find the wood where it lies, and to find the wood with the right kind of fibers. Otherwise, they must have it brought to them: it is only because merchants take care of one segment of the journey in reverse that the artisans can avoid making the trip themselves . . . We will therefore define the artisan as one who is determined in such a way as to follow a flow of matter, a machinic phylum. The artisan is the itinerant, the ambulant. To follow the flow of matter is to itinerate, to ambulate. (Deleuze and Guattari 1987: 409)

An artisan following the flow of matter fits well Deleuze and Guattari's nomadic concept, but it is important to see how material flows across human and non-human assemblages, with human and non-human singularities making at strategic points transverse cuts that alter or turn turbulent that very flow. As Deleuze's contemporary, the philosopher of science Michel Serres (1982) makes clear, turbulences are not chaotic but instead are highly complex systems: a rock, water current assemblage, or the puddled crystalline vortices of pig iron are all examples of complex 'turbulences' of matter. Spuybroek is right to pay particular attention to the singular entity, particularly in how its desires must be accommodated in a sympathetic manner (even as the thing itself shows its own sympathies), but Deleuze is equally right in having his artisan follow the flow, because flow/singularity are of a piece. One can argue the ontology of the withdrawn object, but why bother?

If there is a corollary to Spuybroek's sympathy in Deleuze, it would have to be desire, and it is there that Spuybroek's quarrel with Deleuze is further articulated. As claimed in *A Thousand Plateaus*:

> Assemblages are passional, they are compositions of desire. Desire has nothing to do with a natural or spontaneous determination; there is no desire but assembling, assembled, desire. The rationality, the efficiency, of an assemblage does not exist without the passions the assemblage brings into play, without the desires that constitute it as much as it constitutes them. (Deleuze and Guattari 1987: 399)

This is very much in line with Spuybroek's emphasis on the affective at the expense of the rational, but here Deleuze does not turn to the desire of things to be *in* the assemblage. The main line of this affective desire is that assemblages are not the product of an antecedent desire, but rather are productive *of* desire. What is missing in Deleuze's formulation are the micro-desires of all the entities that compose the assemblage. Spuybroek gets us to step back a moment in this formulation to see the desires of all the actors that must be called on to make the machine work, and it is in this calling that the sympathy of things emerges for the human designer. She can come to see her utter dependence on those little desiring machines, those pulsing haecceities.

This draws us closer to an understanding of Spuybroek's celebration of design without designers, his displacement of the principles of design to account for, or at least acknowledge, all the entities that participate in the design. This displacement questions the very notion of a designer's creativity and brings us back to Stengers. In *Thinking with Whitehead* she takes up the term, inflected by her articulation of Souriau:

> Every decision is thus explained by its reasons, and as such it exemplifies creativity, the way in which 'the many become one.' Creativity has then nothing to do with a form of 'supplement of soul', of 'subjective evaluation' of what is given, adding a touch of originality to what already holds together. It is presupposed by this very 'holding together'. (Stengers 2011a: 263)

Although she does not use the term 'beauty', nor does she appeal here to the affective, this can be seen as a restatement of the notion of thinking hot, and a different articulation of Spuybroek's principle of sympathy. Running against romantic notions of genius and the visionary maker, Stengers's designers are not blessed with a 'supplement of the soul'. Stengers instead give us, via Souriau, creativity through that which 'already holds together', those beautiful, sympathetic, prehensive entities that exemplify Deleuzian Design.

Immanence

Spuybroek's embrace of design without designers figures nicely as a counter to evangelical Christians' embrace of intelligent design, the argument that the world is too complex not to have been designed by an intelligent creator. Spuybroek is not proposing a Darwinian, evolutionary concept of design, but his decentring of consciousness, wilfulness and plans in favour of temporality and sympathy, opens the door for a (brief) examination of 'Immanence: A Life', Deleuze's last published essay. He opens with this question and answer:

> What is a transcendental field? It can be distinguished from experience in that it doesn't refer to an object or belong to a subject (empirical representation). It appears therefore as a pure stream of a-subjective consciousness, a qualitative duration of consciousness without a self. (Deleuze 2001: 25)

The transcendental field precedes subject/object differentiation, exists prior to modern philosophy, but it is also rooted in a pure stream of a-subjective consciousness. This is where thinking Deleuzian design is most productive because it folds back on itself. Thinking hot, as a material practice, is the embodiment of the transcendental field. It is not that there is design without designers resulting from the sympathy of discrete things. Rather, Deleuzian design irrupts in the pre-objective (and pre-subjective) moment – right there where the work is done. Deleuze continues, 'There is something wild and powerful in this transcendental empiricism that is of course not the element of simple sensation (simple empiricism), for sensation is only a break within the flow of absolute consciousness' (2001: 25). This passage directly echoes another of his late works, *What is Philosophy?* where, in a discussion of Whitehead, Deleuze and Guattari praise Whitehead's 'free and wild creation of concepts' (1994: 105): a phrase Stengers uses as a subtitle for *Thinking with Whitehead*. It seems we have come full circle, with a return to

Stengers's Whitehead whose wild and powerful philosophy takes us out of the bifurcation of nature, out of subjects and objects, and directly into non-cognitive apprehension of temporal process. This sensation is a break from thinking hot, a sometimes-necessary pause or bending of the moment to pull the singularity back into smoothness (without homogenisation). This freedom and wildness can be figured in the abstractions of metaphysics, or can be found in the workshop transactions of everyday work. As Deleuze famously appropriated from Whitehead: 'the abstract does not explain, but must itself be explained' (Deleuze and Parnet 1987: vii).

But what then of judgement? Traditional notions of design demand it: the 'yes' or 'no' of good practice and functionality. Spuybroek produces non-cognitive judgement through the sympathy of things: if materiality (and immateriality) come together sympathetically, the design will be beautiful (and good). Beauty and sympathy for and of things are of a piece. Deleuze famously wanted to 'have done with judgment' (1998: 126–35), and instead offers pure immanence: 'It is a haecceity no longer of individuation but of singularization: a life of pure immanence, neutral, beyond good and evil, for it was only the subject that incarnated it in the midst of things that made it good or bad' (2001: 29). This is a step away from Spuybroek whose beauty depends on sympathy between discrete things, but very close to the Stengers passages on Souriau and Whitehead that open this essay. The 'beyond good and evil' framed by haecceities referenced above is a repudiation of *arrestive* judgement in the design process. It is a critique of the subject – the judge – whose ideas about the affordances of the materials and bodies at hand define the good and the bad. Singularities, unlike individualities, are beyond good and evil because they cannot be cut out for judgement but instead must be accommodated in the process. The fibres in the iron are what *they* are.

Returning directly to the beginning, we must look to the conclusion of Deleuze's life's work and his final articulation of the virtual: that exceeding troubled and fraught term. 'What we call the virtual', he writes, 'is not something that lacks reality but something that is engaged in a process of actualization following the plane that gives it its particular reality. The immanent event is actualized in a state of things and of the lived that make it happen' (2001: 31). Deleuzian design is not mastery because it takes place in the transcendental field prior to subject/object distinctions. Instead he gives us work being done, emerging as risk, becoming immanent: A Life. There it is, now we are thinking hot.

Notes

1. Bruno Latour raises a similar point in his reading of Souriau: 'Obviously we would misinterpret Souriau if we took this to be a description of the movement between form and matter, with the ideal of the form moving progressively into reality, a potentiality that would simply become real through the medium of a more-or-less inspired artist. It is rather a case of instauration, a risk taken, a discovery, a total invention: But this growing existence is made, we can see, of a double modality that finally comes together, in the unity of a sole being progressively invented in the labouring process. Often there is no warning: up to a certain point the finished work is always a novelty, discovery, or surprise. So that's what I was looking for! That's what I was meant to make!' (2011: 310).
2. For an extended discussion of Simondon's critique of hylomorphism, see Combes 2012: 66–70.
3. Another way to address this question with a similar terminology is through Simondon. See for example Combes's discussion in the introduction to her book (2012) of the emergence of the individual from the pre-individual, rather than as a result of atomistic or hylomorphic construction.
4. For a detailed discussion of these figures and others, see Carl DiSalvo's *Adversarial Design* (2012).
5. Spuybroek's notion of cruelty differs somewhat from that articulated by Deleuze in *Coldness and Cruelty*. There Deleuze stresses the contractual nature of Masochism where cruelty is linked to suspension, to a wait. It is the contract – the rigidly procedural – that connects Masochistic cruelty to Royal science, but in Masoch, the suspension or the wait is marked as a form of cruelty rather than as an attentiveness that enables sympathetic or tender design.
6. See, for example, Harman, *The Quadruple Object* (2011), and the collection of essays titled *The Speculative Turn* (Bryant et al. 2011).

References

Bealer, Alex W. and C. McRaven (1976), *The Art of Blacksmithing*, New York: Funk and Wagnalls.
Bennett, Jane (2010), *Vibrant Matter: A Political Ecology of Things*, Durham, NC: Duke University Press.
Bryant, L., Srnicek, N., and Harman, G. (eds) (2011), *The Speculative Turn: Continental Materialism and Realism*, Melbourne: re.press.
Buchanan, R. (2001), 'Design and the New Rhetoric: Productive Arts in the Philosophy of Culture', *Philosophy and Rhetoric*, 34:3, pp. 183–206.
Colvin, S. (ed.) (1921), *Letters of John Keats to his Family and Friends*, London: Macmillan.
Combes, Muriel [1999] (2012), *Gilbert Simondon and the Philosophy of the Transindividual*, trans. T. Lamarre, Cambridge, MA and London: The MIT Press.
DeLanda, Manuel (2006), *A New Philosophy of Society: Assemblage Theory and Social Complexity*, London and New York: Continuum.
Deleuze, Gilles (2001), *Pure Immanence. Essays on A Life*, trans. A. Boyman New York: Zone Books.
Deleuze, Gilles [1993] (1998), 'On Philosophy', in G. Deleuze, *Essays Clinical and Critical*, trans. D. W. Smith and M. A. Greco, London: Verso.
Deleuze, Gilles [1988] (1992), *Fold: Leibniz and the Baroque*, trans. T. Conley, Minneapolis: University of Minnesota Press.

Deleuze, Gilles [1967] (1991), *Coldness and Cruelty*, trans. J. McNeil, New York: Zone Books.

Deleuze, Gilles, and F. Guattari [1991] (1996), *What is Philosophy?* trans. G. Burchill and H. Tomlinson, New York: Columbia University Press.

Deleuze, Gilles and F. Guattari [1980] (1987), *A Thousand Plateaus. Capitalism and Schizophrenia 2*, trans. B. Massumi, London: Athlone.

Deleuze, Gilles and C. Parnet [1977] (1987), *Dialogues*, London: Athlone.

DiSalvo, Carl (2012), *Adversarial Design*, Cambridge, MA and London: The MIT Press.

Harman, Graham (2011), *The Quadruple Object*, Ropely: Zero Books.

Harman, Graham (2010), *Towards Speculative Realism: Essays and Lectures*, Ropely: Zero Books.

Jones, Owain and P. Cloke (2002), *Tree Cultures: The Place of Trees and Trees in Their Place*, Oxford and New York: Berg.

Keller, Charles M., and J. D. Keller (1996), *Cognition and Tool Use: The Blacksmith at Work*, Cambridge: Cambridge University Press.

Lasansky, Jeannette (1980), *To Draw, Upset, and Weld: The Work of the Pennsylvania Rural Blacksmith, 1742–1935*, Oral Traditions Project of the Union County Historical Society, University Park, PA: Penn State University Press.

Latour, B. (2011), 'Reflections on Etienne Souriau's *Les différents modes d'existence*', in L. Bryant, N. Srnicek and G. Harman (eds), *The Speculative Turn: Continental Materialism and Realism*, Melbourne: re.press, pp. 304–33.

Malafouris, L. (2008), 'At the Potter's Wheel: An Argument for Material Agency', in C. Knappett and L. Malafouris (eds), *Material Agency: Towards a Non-Anthropocentric Approach*, Vienna: Springer-Verlag, pp. 19–36.

Maturana, H. R. [1970] (1980), 'The Biology of Cognition', in H. R. Maturana and F. J. Varela, *Autopoiesis and Cognition: The Realization of the Living*, Dordrecht: D. Riedel Publishing Company, pp. 5–58.

Meyer, S. (2005), 'Introduction', *Configurations*, 13:1, pp. 1–33.

Pollan, Michael (1997), *A Place of my Own: The Education of an Amateur Builder*, London and New York: Bloomsbury.

Pye, David (1978), *The Nature and Aesthetics of Design*, London: Barrie and Jenkins.

Pye, David (1968), *The Nature and Art of Workmanship*, Cambridge: Cambridge University Press.

Serres, Michel (1982), *Hermes: Literature, Science, Philosophy*, ed. J. V. Harari, and D. F. Bell, Baltimore: Johns Hopkins University Press.

Simon, Herbert A. (1996), *The Sciences of the Artificial*, 3rd edition, Cambridge, MA and London: The MIT Press.

Simondon, Gilbert [1958] (2001), *Du Mode d'existence des objets techniques*, Paris: Aubier-Montaigne.

Souriau, Étienne [1943] (2009), *Les Différents modes d'existence: suivi de Du mode d'existence de l'oeuvre à faire*, Paris: Presses Universitaires de France.

Spuybroek, Lars (2011), *The Sympathy of Things: Ruskin and the Ecology of Design*, Rotterdam: V2_Publishing.

Stengers, Isabelle [2002] (2011a), *Thinking with Whitehead: A Free and Wild Creation of Concepts*, Boston: Harvard University Press.

Stengers, I. (2011b), '"Another Science is Possible!" A Plea for Slow Science', Lecture, 13 December 2011, Faculté de Philosophie et Lettres, Université Libre de Bruxelles.

Stengers, I. (2011c), 'Wondering About Materialism', in L. Bryant, Srnicek, N., and Harman, G. (eds), *The Speculative Turn: Continental Materialism and Realism*, Melbourne: re.press, pp. 368–80.

Stengers, I. (2005), 'The Cosmopolitical Proposal', in B. Latour and P. Weibel (eds), *Making Things Public: Atmospheres of Democracy*, pp. 994–1003.

Sturt, George (1963), *The Wheelwright's Shop*, Cambridge: Cambridge University Press.

Underhill, Roy (1981), *The Woodwright's Shop: A Practical Guide to Traditional Woodcraft*, Chapel Hill, NC: University of North Carolina Press.

Watson, Aldren A. (2000), *The Blacksmith: Ironworker and Farrier*, New York and London: W. W. Norton and Company.

Whitehead, Alfred N. (2011), *Science and the Modern World*, Cambridge: Cambridge University Press.

Chapter 5

Digital Materiality, Morphogenesis and the Intelligence of the Technodigital Object

Betti Marenko

> There can only be a simultaneous genesis of matter and intelligence.
> Gilles Deleuze, *Bergsonism*

> The robot does not exist.
> Gilbert Simondon, *On the Mode of Existence of Technical Objects*

We have entered a new object landscape. We now inhabit an object*scape* populated by intelligent things made of carbon and silicon, databytes and neurons, where the mineral, the technical and the social intermix.[1] Our interaction with digital devices prompts questions about the boundary between organic nervous systems and electronic circuits, between the born and the manufactured, between the organic and the inorganic. Equally under question are the boundaries of the technodigital object *per se*. I refer to any of the hand-held devices we engage with daily: all the smartphones, tablets and PDAs that have become our companions. Taken together these devices generate a pulsating object*scape* with no fixed borders where new forms of intelligence emerge and new types of agency are performed. An entity gone blurry by velocity, the digitally distributed, open-ended technodigital object merges any distinction still standing between hardware, software and interaction.[2] It does so by becoming whatever it is running (an app, a program, a stream of data) at any given moment. The convergence of hardware, software and interaction engenders a kind of highly immersive, sensory and somatic experience: a new assemblage of multiple material intelligences, not necessarily and not exclusively human.

This chapter investigates these new assemblages from the specific viewpoint of their materiality. It suggests that the status of contemporary technodigital objects should be rethought on grounds of their materiality and the forms of intelligence this materiality expresses. Some key concepts – from Gilles Deleuze's own work and from his collaboration with Félix Guattari – are deployed to unpack the argument of the materiality of the technodigital object: the transition from object to *objectile*; a morphogenetic account of matter; and the implications of a radical material vitalism for the way design approaches technodigital objects. Particular relevance is given to Deleuze and Guattari's thought that matter is to be apprehended via intuitive and inquisitive forms of knowledge. This serves as a springboard to suggest a new research frame for design based around problem finding, rather than problem solving. The insights gathered are then utilised to investigate the silicon-based materiality of the technodigital object.

Key to an understanding and reframing of our relationship with the current incarnation of the technodigital object is what Deleuze wrote in *The Fold* concerning the transition from object to *objectile*. It was between the late 1980s and the early 1990s, when Deleuze was occupied with these ideas, that the World Wide Web and the programme of mass digitalisation as we now know them were taking hold globally. Since then, our relationship with intelligent machines has become more complicated, our entanglement with this wondrous techno-landscape posing more and more questions about what counts as human in the digital era. A full discussion of such an entanglement is beyond the scope of this chapter. Instead, its focus is upon a specific aspect of the technodigital object: the intelligence of its materiality at once processual and designed, and how to design for this material intelligence.

Indeed, important implications of the changes in the status of the object concern design. As objects mutate, then the process of design must be rethought to account for such changes. Design is defined here as a process that is *simultaneously* of thing-making and of meaning-making. This process always concerns the near future, what has not happened yet, but *might* happen. A model of material variability based on morphogenesis is proposed to make sense of this process and its outcomes, to unfold design's innate propensity into the 'not yet', its own material becomings. Thus, it is argued that design should be rethought *morphogenetically*. According to this perspective form emerges from the continuous variability of matter, rather than being imposed on it by an external agency: this is the morphogenetic model. Morphogenesis is understood as the key theory that explains the emergence not just of individuated form but of thoughts and practices too, specifically those circulating around the technodigital object. This is to say that thoughts and practices, like form, emerge by the interplay of continuity and variability, rather than being imposed by a blueprint.

This chapter contends that Deleuze and Guattari's creative, immanent and practical philosophy and radical, vital, molecular materialism that takes matter as self-organising and emergent, must impact on some of the discourses currently circulating within the theory and practice of design. A morphogenetic perspective on matter forces design to question how objects actually come to exist, and in broader terms, design's own relationship with materiality. By rethinking design *through* Deleuze, the chapter shows how some of this philosophical corpus might steer design into rethinking some of the key principles it takes for granted. For instance, a morphogenetic perspective, by questioning the hylomorphic form-matter coupling, takes apart the convention of the relationship between form and function. The transition from object to objectile reframes the notion of object, and consequently the role of the user-subject. Here an investigation of the technodigital object may reveal how design's insistence on the centrality of the user needs a reappraisal.[3] As the object becomes an open-ended, relational, intelligent event, so the user-subject is shifting accordingly.

Thus, the proposed conceptual framework for design research is based on an argument against both the hylomorphism and the teleological fixation with form and function that still intoxicate ways of thinking about – and consequently of practising – design and technology. For instance, a matter-based understanding of the technodigital object casts a new light on the discourses on dematerialisation. It questions the dichotomy between the tangible and the intangible that often supports them. Dematerialisation's double claim for invisibility and immediacy obscures the indisputable material reality of the complex and messy infrastructure any digital performance depends upon. As sociologist Jennifer Gabrys points out, digital technology is framed by the twin technoscientific 'spectres of virtuality and dematerialization' (2011: 4), with the result that the materiality of our always-on status is seldom, if ever, acknowledged. The paradigm of dematerialisation is thus not only highly problematic, but also misleading. By disregarding the materiality of the digital – the circuit boards, copper wires, optic fibres, cables, radio masts, servers warehouses, minerals and, fundamentally, the silicon – that collectively makes possible our increasingly naturalised digital experiences, the paradigm of dematerialisation culturally dominates by means of invisibility. A morphogenetic perspective, on the other hand, leads us straight into the core of the materiality upon which our digital world is based.

Design must confront these questions by taking on board and examining in their discourses, practices and processes what radical materialist philosophies have to offer. My argument suggests that in order to rethink the design processes that enable the existence of technodigital objects, their performance, efficiency and their effects of subjectivity, we must begin from a morphogenetic understanding of their materiality. This position allows a deeper understanding of the affective and somatic investments at stake in the programmable and computational devices we currently engage with.

Some of the questions this chapter addresses are: What is the contribution of Deleuze to an assessment of the technodigital object? What does it mean for design to take into account, practically and experimentally, a morphogenetic perspective and matter's own capacity to spontaneously self-organise? How does this impact on, and affect, the way the technodigital object is designed?

The chapter is divided in two parts. The first part draws on Deleuze's *objectile* and uses the shift from object to event it portrays to analyse the status of the technodigital object. The argument is that for this shift to be understood in its currency, a morphogenetic model must be made explicit, with its embedded critique of hylomorphism. Deleuze and Guattari's distinction between Royal and nomadic science is drawn upon to reinforce this critique. They write that if matter is a flow, then it can only be followed. To follow matter is to apprehend material variability via intuition. Intuition, it is argued, is what can allow design to put morphogenesis at its core and to shift its remit from problem solving to problem finding. This means for design to be engaging with a complexification – rather than a reduction – of the existent, in other words, to move away from the conventions of problem solving.[4] The extent to which material variability affects processes of form-making cannot but impact profoundly on the way design is conceptualised.

The second part of the chapter takes a different approach. The technodigital object is examined through Deleuze's image of a sieve or a membrane that, stretched over chaos, makes possible the emergence of individuation (Deleuze 1993). I take this individuated outcome as an appropriate description of an open-ended relational object in its technodigital form, namely the interface. The ontological status of the technodigital object is then examined by investigating its silicon-based materiality. The argument positions the technodigital object as a material intelligence developing and unfolding morphogenetically, thus contesting the cultural discourse of dematerialisation. It then looks at the ways hand-held digital mobile devices are reshaping what constitutes a designed object and, as a consequence, what constitutes a user or subject. Digital devices are taken here as the tangible encounter between different forms of intelligence, human and non-human.

By 'following' the paths of materiality and metallurgy (Deleuze and Guattari 1988: 451) we plunge into the main constituent of the microchip: silicon. Silicon is investigated as the main constituent of our digital assemblages and the essential component of our digital world. Deleuze's prophetic 'revenge of the silicon' (2006: 178) is drawn upon to chart the rise and dominance of this material in our era. Silicon's supremacy is beginning to be questioned, however, by a new breed of microchips that emulate neural activity: *neuromorphic* chips (Simonite 2013; Talbot 2013; Hof 2014; Monroe 2014). Neuromorphic chips bypass the distinction between carbon and silicon, and articulate new forms of material intelligence. This convergence of silicon and carbon, of organic and inorganic, is brought back to a philosophical examination through a concluding assessment of Deleuze's concept of nonorganic life (Deleuze 2001). Concepts harvested from the work of design theorist Benjamin Bratton (2002, 2008, 2009, 2013), architecture theorist Sanford Kwinter (1992, 1998, 2001, 2007), and philosopher Manuel DeLanda (2004, 2009) further populate these reflections.

Part 1

From object to event

The object, writes Deleuze, has a new status. No longer confined within the mould that has created it, it has become an event continually modulated in time. 'This new object we can call *objectile*', Deleuze states in *The Fold*, continuing:

> As Bernard Cache has demonstrated, this is a very modern conception of the technological object: it refers neither to the beginnings of the industrial era nor to the idea of the standard that still upheld a semblance of essence and imposed a law of constancy ('the object produced by and for the masses'), but to our current state of things, where fluctuation of the norm replaces the permanence of the law; where the object assumes a place in a continuum by variation; where industrial automation or serial machineries replace stamped forms. The new status of the object no longer refers its condition to a spatial mold – in other words, to a relation of form-matter – but to a temporal modulation that implies as much the beginnings of a continuous variation of matter as a continuous development of form. (Deleuze 1993: 19)

Deleuze refers here to the evolution of the technical object. He also, to an extent that is perhaps not always fully appreciated, addresses design as an historical process. He does so by singling out moulding, the traditional design technique of form-making, and by projecting it into temporalities of perception where it disaggregates and recomposes into the pulsating intensities of pure modulation. The designed, man-made object is positioned on a fractured timeline, where what counts is no longer a 'spatial mold' (form-matter), but a 'temporal modulation' (formation). As form becomes formation, object becomes event.

In our daily interaction with digital devices we no longer deal with objects but with events. This transition from object to event is framed historically as a shift from moulding to modulation. It takes place when the object is no longer withdrawn from the mould that forms it, but expresses the continuous variation of a morphing and mobile matter. The object ceases being the fixed representation of a relation between matter and form to become instead the temporal expression of an event-affect continuum, that is, the active and affective dynamism that permeates matter. The implications for the technodigital object are clear. The permanently connected, programmed and plugged-in environment we inhabit through our interaction with technodigital objects takes shape through a process of continuous modulation. Although we may call it 'environment', this is not a space. As Kwinter (2007) points out this is not where but *when* our attention is captured and held. This experience is evoked by Bratton (2009) when he describes the inertial mobility of the archetypal Los Angeles event of being stuck in gridlocked traffic whilst simultaneously being connected, and sucked in by an absorbing else*when* made of checking, updating, emailing, browsing, scrolling.

Deleuze's insight offers a frame of analysis that will be deployed in the second part of the chapter. What need to be further investigated now are the implications of a morphogenetic model of matter for the technodigital object and for design.

Slices of intelligent matter

Variously defined as matter-flow, matter-movement and matter-energy, the 'unorganized, nonstratified, or destratified body and all its flows: subatomic and submolecular particles, pure intensities, prevital and prephysical free singularities' (Deleuze and Guattari 1988: 43), is what Deleuze and Guattari call 'the prodigious idea of *Nonorganic Life*' (1988: 411). Here 'the essential thing is no longer forms and matter, but forces, densities, intensities' (1988: 343). This self-organising, spontaneously shifting matter, traversed by flows of nonorganic intensities, has its philosophical roots in the thought of Baruch Spinoza. Spinoza's single substance, of which everything that exists is a modification, manifests itself actively in the world through its capacity of producing and being produced according to a non-hierarchical and un-mediated dynamics (Hardt 1993). It is a substance that does not precede its attributes, a cause that does not precede its effects, a whole that does not precede its parts. It is a process and production with no beginning or end. It is a process through which difference keeps on generating itself (Montag and Stolze 1997). With this singular and remarkable substance Spinoza shifts his philosophical project from metaphysics to physics. Everything that other philosophies invest in a variety of god(s), Spinoza locates in this inherent capacity of things to produce. Thus, Spinoza's is a 'metaphysics of the producing force' (Matheron 1998: 14), opposed to classic metaphysics that subordinates the productivity of things to a transcendent order. Intended in this way, matter possesses both the power of affecting and of being affected. Matter is therefore both production and sensibility. It has intelligence. Each and every body, each and every thing, organic or nonorganic, living or non-living, animated or inanimate is therefore, from this perspective, a slice of intelligent matter traversed by intensities.

Drawing on Spinoza, Deleuze and Guattari's materialism postulates that all things are formed through differentiation and individuation of the same substance, and that matter vibrates with the potential of its creative evolution and innovation.[5] Infinite permutations are seen through a relational world-view where the human and the non-human, the sub-personal and the molecular ceaselessly combine and recombine through a myriad of rhizomes, assemblages and machines. In this relationality what counts are relationships 'with neither object nor self' (Deleuze 2001: 26), the forms that matter might or might not take in its recombinations. Matter is a dense, non-subjective and affirming force. What counts, then, is not subject or object, form or matter, structure or attributes, but the 'silent dance' of forces, intensities and the most disparate things. In this dance 'a semiotic fragment rubs shoulders with a chemical interaction, an electron crashes into a language, a black hole captures a genetic message, a crystallization produces a passion, the wasp and the orchid cross a letter' (Deleuze and Guattari 1988: 77).

Deleuze and Guattari state repeatedly how on this plane of immanence 'peopled by anonymous matter, by infinite bits of impalpable matter entering into varying connections ... it is a question not of organisation but of composition: not of development or differentiation, but of movement and rest, speed and slowness' (1988: 282). These relations of movement and rest, speed and slownesses take place between unformed and unsubjectified elements, what Deleuze and

Guattari describe as 'haecceities, affects, subjectless individuations that constitute collective assemblages' (1988: 294). The inanimate and the animate, the natural and the artificial, the living and the non-living, the organic and the nonorganic are found here, no distinction among them. This is the 'unnatural participation' (1988: 267) that takes place in the making and unmaking of the plane of composition, where different things are all expressions of the same material substance in becoming. We are in the Spinozistic plane of immanence, a plane of proliferation and contagion where *haecceities*[6] predating any categorical determination keep on emerging, combining and dissolving. Here we also find the various assemblages of silicon and carbon into which this chapter will probe.

This radical materialism allows us to theorise the technodigital object and its transformations, while staying clear of the hylomorphic model. This is because one of the key implications of this radical materialism is that the categorical distinction between matter and form is uprooted. Instead, we move *beyond* matter-form: 'the *material-force* couple replaces the *matter-form* couple' (Deleuze 2006: 160). What is important for design is precisely this shift: how material variability offers a radical alternative to the hylomorphic model (DeLanda 2004, 2009). What is also important here is the extent to which this analysis can have an impact on how technodigital objects are designed and experienced. Before proceeding any further let us examine more closely what the hylomorphic model implies, and why it is necessary for design to move forward.

Beyond hylomorphism: for an intuition-driven nomadic design

The hylomorphic model assumes an external agency acting upon a matter seen as fundamentally passive and inert. It therefore presupposes homogeneity of matter and organisation of form. It also implies that matter is imbued with non-material properties. As Deleuze and Guattari remind us in *A Thousand Plateaus*, it is French philosopher Gilbert Simondon who 'exposes the technological insufficiency of the matter-form model, in that it assumes a fixed form and a matter deemed homogeneous' (Deleuze and Guattari 1988: 450). Simondon shows how the hylomorphic model, by assuming that form and matter are two distinct and separate entities, cannot adequately account for the active and affective dynamisms that permeate matter, the 'ambulant coupling *events-affects*' (1988: 450).

In an essay on morphogenesis, form-making and Umberto Boccioni's futurist paintings, Kwinter explains further the limitations of hylomorphism, which is unable to account for the genesis of form 'without recourse to metaphysical models' (1992: 53). For Kwinter, this 'perennial misunderstanding' has cast its shadow on the modern western scientific tradition 'because it lent itself well to reductionism and controlled quantitative modelling' (1992: 53).[7] It is only with topology that the qualitative transformations that a system undergoes can be captured and analysed as transformational events happening in time. From a topological perspective the relationship matter-form is postulated as an encounter of divergent forces. Form emerges from a process of morphogenesis, rather than being imposed by an external blueprint, ideal, or agency. Anthropologist Tim Ingold gives an example of this process by offering an alternative reading of the process of brick making. If brick making is usually seen as a typical example of the moulding process, Ingold thinks otherwise:

> The brick, with its characteristic rectangular outline, results not from the *im*position of form onto matter but from the *contra*position of equal and opposed forces immanent in both the clay and the mould. In the field of forces, the form emerges as a more or less transitory equilibration. (Ingold 2013: 25)

The idea of objects emerging as events produced by the encounter of different forces is underpinned by a consideration of matter as, and in, continuous variation. As matter coalesces and disaggregates, changes of states take place, thresholds of intensities are reached at various speeds, and forms unfold, not as fixed things, but as 'continuous metastable *events*'. 'Forms are always new and unpredictable unfoldings shaped by their adventures in time' writes Kwinter (Kwinter 1992: 59). Time releases the forms present in matter as virtualities yet to be actualised.[8] Matter is thought of in terms of events and processes, rather than things and objects.

This material vitalism, where all matter possesses an immanent power – a material 'esprit de corps' (Deleuze and Guattari 1988: 454) – sets free what the hylomorphic model conceals. It also paves the way for a reappraisal of objects through an equally radical material vitalism. The material combination of energy and movement, together with the intensities liberated in their topological deformations, constitute a flow of material variation that, as we shall see in the second part of this chapter, is particularly apt to describe the current technodigital object and its evolution. For the moment, it is worth quoting Deleuze and Guattari at length:

> On the one hand, to the formed or formable matter we must add an entire energetic materiality in movement, carrying *singularities* or *haecceities* that are already like implicit forms that are topological, rather than geometrical, and that combine with processes of deformation: for example, the variable undulations and torsions of the fibers guiding the operation of splitting wood. On the other hand, to the essential properties of matter deriving from the formal essence we must add *variable intensive affects*, now resulting from the operation, now on the contrary making possible: for example, wood that is more or less porous, more or less elastic and resistant. At any rate, it is a question of surrendering to the wood, then following where it leads by connecting operations to a materiality, instead of imposing a form upon a matter: what one addresses is less a matter submitted to laws than a materiality possessing a *nomos*. One addresses less a form capable of imposing properties upon a matter than material traits of expression constituting affects. (Deleuze and Guattari 1988: 450)

There are two important points to make here. First, the form-making process has to do with energy and movement. Drawing on Simondon, Deleuze and Guattari identify an intermediary zone of 'energetic molecular dimension' between form and matter, 'a space unto itself that deploys its materiality through matter, a number unto itself that propels its traits through form' (1988: 451). Again, this is where we find the 'ambulant coupling *events-affects*' which points us towards a new way of investigating the mobile intensities characteristic of our object*scape*.

Secondly, if matter is a flow, then it 'can only be followed' (1988: 451). The idea that matter can only be followed is one of the key implications of the morphogenetic model. It opens up to a resiliently matter-led approach to design.[9] But what does it mean to 'follow matter' in practice? Deleuze and Guattari are explicit on this point. To follow matter, they say, is 'intuition in action' (1988: 452). Their distinction between Royal and nomadic science is useful to establish this point. They write:

> Royal science is inseparable from a 'hylomorphic' model implying both a form that organizes matter and a matter prepared for the form; it has often been shown that this schema derives less from technology or life than from a society divided into governors and governed, and later, intellectuals and manual laborers. What characterizes it is that all matter is assigned to content, while all form passes into expression. It seems that nomad science is more immediately in tune with the connection between content and expression in themselves, each of these two terms encompassing both form and matter. Thus matter, in nomad science, is never prepared and therefore homogenized matter, but is essentially laden with singularities (which constitute a form of content). And neither is expression formal; it is inseparable

from pertinent traits (which constitute a matter of expression). (Deleuze and Guattari 1988: 407)

Royal science focuses on linear behaviour in states of equilibrium and is concerned with formal laws imposed on inert matter from the outside. While Royal science deals therefore with matter-form and consists chiefly in 'reproducing', nomadic science concerns material-forces and deals with 'following' (1988: 410). The 'reproducing' has to do with iteration; 'following' has to do with itineration. The distinction is clearly between Royal science's reproduction and permanence of an established viewpoint, and nomadic science's search for singularities and intensities through the practice of following.

It is important to note that this nomadic, following, itinerant mode through which material variability can be apprehended is 'inseparable from a sensible intuition of variation' (1988: 407). It is only through intuition that matter can be apprehended in all its variability (Deleuze 1991). Thus, intuition is the best possible way of knowing a matter populated by *vague and material* essences' that are 'vagabond, anexact and yet rigorous' (Deleuze and Guattari 1988: 449). What distinguish these vagabond essences from 'fixed, metric and formal' ones are the two qualities of *vagueness* and *fuzziness* (1988: 449). Again, matter is revealed in its traits, which are neither formal nor formed, but indeterminate, vague, fuzzy. Intuition operates precisely via this indeterminacy, by its coupling with the vagueness of events through which individuation takes place. It is through this intuition-driven process that objects emerge. Objects come to exist not out of a predetermination, as a compound of matter and form, but as the outcome of the continuity and variation of matter captured as a specific type of individuation: the *event*.

Commenting upon Henri Bergson's notion of intuition, philosopher Elizabeth Grosz observes that intuition is a method for 'the discernment of differences' (2011: 50).[10] In Grosz's account, intuition is defined as:

a mode of 'sympathy' by which every characteristic of an object (process, quality, etc.) is brought together, none is left out, in a simple and immediate resonance of life's inner duration and the absolute specificity of its objects. It is an attuned, noncategorical empiricism, an empiricism that does not reduce its components and parts but expands them to connect this object to the very universe itself. (Grosz 2011: 48)

This notion of intuition as a mode of sympathy among objects suggests that intuition belongs to a cosmic way of apprehending the world whereby things resonate with each other and are grasped in ineffable ways.[11] This process works by establishing an approximate knowledge that is 'dependent upon sensitive and sensible evaluations that pose more problems that they solve' (Deleuze and Guattari 1988: 412).

Here we reach, via intuition, a key idea to deploy to rethink design. As intuition counteracts categories, embraces vagueness and can only proceed by following material variation, it produces a knowledge grounded in a sensitivity to posing problems, rather than in a drive to find solutions. This is an important theoretical point, as it puts forward a shift for design from problem solving to *problem finding*. It proposes to stop thinking about design as a process of finding the solution to a problem – a rational interpretation that evaluates design outcomes solely in term of efficiency and performance – to think instead about design as a problem-finding enterprise.

On the one hand, design as problem solving is a task-oriented, per-formance-measured, linear exercise that reduces uncertainty. It is based on a conventional view of design as a technology of affective capture that enforces and reproduces market ideologies (Marenko 2010). On the other hand, design as a problem finding activity has to do with an increase in complexity, a problematisation of the existent, and a devel-opment of a material sensitivity *via* design. As an agent of problemati-sation design becomes an intuitive, material, sensitive-rich enterprise, more akin to a *nomadic, minor* science than to a Royal science. It is a design that follows and produces minoritarian lines of creation and inventiveness: a *minor* design.

What Deleuze writes in *Bergsonism* is useful here: 'in philosophy and even elsewhere it is a question of *finding* the problem and consequently of *positing* it, even more than solving it' (1991: 15). For Deleuze positing a problem concerns invention rather than discovery. This is because dis-covery is always the unveiling of something that *already* exists. Invention concerns instead the creation of the terms by which a problem will be stated. To reposition design as a problem-finding activity means there-fore to embrace the idea that problems have no given solution. Instead, problems must generate their own solutions by a process through which what did not exist – what might never have happened – is invented. We are fully in the realm of the virtual (Marenko 2016b).

The relevance of these ideas for design is clear. By engaging with hylo-morphism design remains trapped in a matter-form paradigm, forced to reproduce the existent through a problem-solving apparatus based on retrofitting. On the other hand, by grasping matter from a morphoge-netic perspective, and by apprehending its variability through intuition, design is free to develop a new approach based on developing material sensitivity. Through intuitive apprehension it can develop new forms of inventive, creative and problematising knowledges that are minor and nomadic.

Part 2

Next I will examine another aspect of the dynamism inherent to matter. It concerns the ways in which the morphogenetic perspective articulates the material intelligence of the technodigital object. It looks at the encounter of different intelligences from the perspective of their materiality. It takes silicon as the entry point into the materiality of the technodigital object. Silicon is approached with a twofold perspective: first, by drawing on Deleuze's brief commentaries on the regime of silicon (Deleuze 1988b; 2006); then, by looking at the impending demise of silicon-based computation. New frontiers of computation beyond silicon such as neuromorphic chips are presented in order to speculate on the convergence of silicon and carbon. This section concludes by putting forward some insights on what this convergence may mean for the design of interactive, intelligent, increasingly alien, technodigital objects.

Interfaces, events and blending

Design theorist Benjamin Bratton (2002, 2013) takes the interface as the dominant material discourse of our times.[12] The interface is the object that visibly manifests the cloud-based surges of data streaming incessantly towards the user. The interface is the hinge of the user-device assemblage. By bringing together the human sensorium and electronic sensors, the interface mediates the encounter of two different intelligences: the human and the digital. This mediation between user and cloud engenders our contemporary experience of digital devices, where the omnipresent two-dimensional screen has become familiar to the point of naturalisation. However, far from being a benign or neutral technology of mere translation of information, the interface is a programmed *mode* of relating to technology. Design theorist Branden Hookway (2014) compares the interface to a mirror. In the same way in which we encounter our own mirror image always before encountering the mirror, similarly the interface is already there – a given threshold, quietly merging into the background – at the moment when interaction takes place. The naturalisation of the interface, which masquerades its agency under the double cloak of transparency and immediacy, generates a peculiar situation where the user is not fully aware of what is going on in terms of computation. Transparency and immediacy conceal the extent to which the user is being *designed* by this specific form of technology.

Hookway's use of the notion of *daimon* or *numen* to discuss the interface is useful here. In ancient Greek the *daimon* – and its Latin equivalent *numen* – was a divine being or spirit mediating the uncertain territory between spiritual and material worlds. The *daimon* has to do with 'the spiritual identity of a material thing, its proliferation or pro-creation, and the animation of inanimate things' (Hookway 2014: 82). *Daimons* reside in some objects and not others, especially in threshold objects, for instance household items charged with performing guardian duties. Hookway likens the interface to a locus inhabited by the *daimon* to stress the animation and indeterminacy of intelligent matter.

Similarly, in discussing the 'app', Bratton describes this particular interface as a 'thin membrane on top of a vast machine . . . the intersection point between two far more complex reservoirs of intelligence: the intentional user and the Cloud infrastructure upon which the little app is perched' (2013: n.p.). Bratton invites us to rethink what constitutes an app: a 'blended co-programming of space and software'. This 'blending' has become, says Bratton, the scope of design, now operating on this membrane/surface of mediation. Every time the material interface of our hand-held digital device is touched, clicked, tapped, stroked and swiped, its arrangement of icons 'melts, so it seems, into reality itself, and is perceived as an actual property of surfaces, things and events' (2013: n.p.). Crucially, this melting of computation and reality is what design engages with, shaping users, constructing lifeworlds, terraforming experiences.

The notion of the interface as a threshold where two different forms of material intelligence, not necessarily human, meet can be further explored by drawing on Deleuze's reply to the question '*What is an event?*' 'Events are produced in a chaos', says Deleuze, 'in a chaotic multiplicity, but only under the condition that *a sort of screen* intervenes' (1993: 76; emphasis added). The process by which the pure multiplicity (*Many*) of chaos becomes a certain singularity (*One*) happens because 'a great screen' is placed between them. Deleuze likens this screen to a sort of universal sieve that extracts differentials out of chaos's own 'universal giddiness' (1993: 77) and orders them into discrete perceptions. This universal sieve can be thought of as 'a formless elastic membrane' or an 'electromagnetic field'. Chaos is inseparable from this screen, but, says Deleuze, it is this screen that makes 'something – something rather than nothing – emerge from it' (1993: 76). It is therefore an event-producing screen.

I would like to take the interface as a historically located, culturally specific form of technology expressing Deleuze's event-producing screen.

As said, design has been shifting its operations towards this 'sort of screen', which has become the modulated and modulating object of design itself. This interface-based type of individuation cannot be reduced to a recognisable combination of form and matter. Instead, we have an individuation continually modulated in an incessant feedback loop of updating, access, data aggregation, reformatting of location and so on. Algorithm-driven objects collapse space and matter and make them indistinguishable, programmed remotely in a loop with instantaneous effects – effects both of reality and of subjectivity. Design is not only the process that constitutes the new technodigital object (the distributed, app-based *objectile*). It is also the process that programs the event. By designing the interface, design intervenes directly upon the screen that filters the giddiness of the chaos-cloud, and channels into programmed events. Through this process it also designs its users.

Taken as a sieve-membrane that filters the incoming chaos of data into an operational, tailor-made event, the interface can only be apprehended in conjunction with its own programmability. It is the design of the interface that makes possible the execution of a specific programme of action. The interface mediates between the physical and spatial sphere of action of the user, and the temporalities fabricated via cloud-based, platform-driven interventions. This mediation happens through a 'programmatic blending' of action and interaction. Design is the process of intervention on the threshold between chaos and event. The question is: how does design handle and manipulate the forms of intelligence circulating within this threshold? Let us investigate in more detail the characteristics of the technodigital object emerging at the encounter of human and non-human intelligences.

The open-ended technodigital object and its paradox

Rethinking the status of the designed object on the basis of morphogenetic dynamics, Kwinter argues that objects must be defined by the system of forces traversing them and by the practices of which they partake. Echoing biologist D'Arcy Thompson's notion that the form of any given portion of matter, and its changes, are designed by force – specifically that the form of an object is a 'diagram of forces' (Thompson 1961: 11), Kwinter suggests that the unity and coherence of the object would vanish into a field of micro and macro relations: the 'micro-architectures' that saturate the object and the 'macro-architectures' of which the object is part (2001: 14). A new paradigm for objecthood emerges: one that recognises the mutable, distributed, extensive relationality of objects. We no longer deal with a discrete, formal object, but with an object*scape* made of distributed materials, bodies, techniques and practices, some human, and some not. Again, this relational perspective on objecthood draws on Spinoza's notion that bodies are made up of relations of movement and rest, speed and slowness between the parts that compose them (Deleuze 1988a). This focus on the kinetics and dynamics of objects, rather than on a bounded, discrete, essential object-'unit', has important implications. There is a shift from a distinct object seen in terms of its form, functions and fundamental objecthood, to bodies considered in terms of their capacities of affecting and being affected. Objects are no longer watertight and self-contained wholes but are open-ended. They are made by their conjunctions, alliances and disruptions with their surroundings and through the pliable architectures of intensities and forces that traverse them. Formed by the multiplicity of their connections and capabilities, objects become a mixture of agencies distributed across analogue and digital territories.

In this sense, technodigital objects are blurry entities, conflating hardware and software. Their operational modalities are both intensive and extensive, and always highly mobile, morphing, meshing. At the same time, however, technodigital objects afford the instant capture of locative identities, temporalised by data circulation and propagation. They produce subjectivities programmed to be as liquid as the processual flow of data/code they are traversed by, always on the verge of further, entirely programmed and captured, modulation. This tension between the openness of the technodigital object and its utter programmability is accurately reflected in its formal standardisation.

In fact, the more the processing capabilities, speed of connectivity and miniaturisation turn the technodigital object into an un-bounded entity that translates the universal into the particular, the more its design slavishly submits to the global design orthodoxy of the hand-friendly rectangular design. The standardised, ubiquitous and instantly recognisable hand-held device, possessing a predictable and programmable range of capabilities, has become the digital equivalent of a *black box*. Not only does this refer to the formal qualities of the device (a rectangular box). It also alludes at the concept of 'black box' in science studies. As Bruno Latour explains, black boxing refers to 'the way scientific and technical work is made invisible by its own success. When a machine runs efficiently, when a matter of fact is settled, one need focus only on its inputs and outputs and not on its internal complexity' (1999: 304).

This could be easily taken as a paradox between material and immaterial. However, as Kwinter remarks, it would be absurd to oppose an allegedly material mechanical paradigm to an immaterial electronic one. Rather, the mechanical and the electronic are 'expressions of two continuous, interdependent historical-ontological *modalities*: those of Matter (substance) and Intelligence (order, shape)' (Kwinter 2007: 92). And yet, compared to mechanical processes, the electronic processes embodied in digital devices *appear* to possess a higher degree of material intelligence. Even more so, electronic processes 'appear to manifest the same magical qualities of *material intelligence* found in fundamental, free and unprocessed matter, a set of qualities that can summed up in the term, self-control' (2007: 93). There is, for Kwinter, an 'indeterminacy and magic of matter' (2007: 97) that opposes any electronic determinism and its entire disciplinary programme. To dismantle the illusion of autonomous control electronic mediation has accustomed us to, says Kwinter, we must follow the primitive and persistently morphogenetic path of matter.

Kwinter invites us to follow the '"minor", *archaic* path through the microchip' (2007: 97) and to fold back the digital object into pure metallurgy, that is, into the impersonal path of nonorganic life. This is an invitation to push further Deleuze and Guattari's claim that 'what metal and metallurgy bring to light is a life proper to matter, a vital state of matter as such, a material vitalism that doubtless exists everywhere but is ordinarily hidden or covered, rendered unrecognizable, dissociated by the hylomorphic model' (1988: 411).[13] By following matter beyond the interface we reach the very core of the digital-computational machine we are part of: the silicon-made microchip. By following the trail of silicon we can grasp what matter is capable of, the intensities it produces, its unfoldings, its intelligence, and how it becomes individuated in the historically specific form of the technodigital object.[14]

Silicon, the revenge

The microchip, an object made largely of silicon, is the essential component of our electronic world. Silicon is a crystal found mainly in common beach sand and dust. It is the most common element on earth after oxygen. The world of computation, the allegedly 'immaterial' world of data, our digitalised, manic connectivity: all hinge on crystals of sand and particles of dust.

In a 1980 interview with Catherine Clement, Deleuze discusses the 'life of modern machines'.[15] Here he succinctly considers the 'revenge of silicon'. He says:

> You know, it's curious, today we are witnessing the revenge of silicon. Biologists have often asked themselves why life was 'channelled' through carbon rather than silicon. But the life of modern machines, a genuine non-organic life, totally distinct from the organic life of carbon, is channelled through silicon. This is the sense in which we speak of a silicon-assemblage. (Deleuze 2006: 178)

With the second part of the twentieth century dominated by silicon, the silicon-assemblage Deleuze speaks of has become a reality. Deleuze makes further reference to the 'potential of silicon' in the appendix to his book on Foucault (Deleuze 1988b). In the same text he mentions also the enigmatic *Superfold*, which emerges from the forces mobilised by silicon: 'It would be neither the fold nor the unfold that would constitute the active mechanism, but something like the Superfold, as borne out by the foldings proper to the chains of the genetic code, and *the potential of silicon in third-generation machines*' (1988b: 131; emphasis added). Here Deleuze points out the coming impact of 'third-generation machines, cybernetics and information technologies' on processes of formation of subjectivity. The era of silicon gives tangible form to the vision of a new individual (a superman) described as neither god nor man, but as the assemblage of the forces existing within the human, together with the forces from the outside. The form this individual may take is the form of these new relations of forces. Deleuze writes:

> The forces within man enter into relation with forces from the outside, those of silicon which supersedes carbon, or genetic components which supersede the organism, or agrammaticalities which supersede the signifier. In each case we must study the operations of the superfold, of which the 'double helix' is the best-known example. What is the superman? It is the formal compound of the forces within man and these new forces. It is the form that results from a new relation between forces ... It is man in charge of the very rocks, or inorganic matter (*the domain of silicon*). (Deleuze 1988b: 131; emphasis added)

In analysing the new forces at play in the coming domain of silicon, Deleuze states that these forces 'would no longer involve raising to infinity or finitude but an unlimited finity, thereby evoking every situation of force in which a finite number of components yields a practically unlimited diversity of combinations' (1988b: 131). The 'practically unlimited diversity of combinations' reminds us of the incessant torrent of data streaming at us from our always-on interfaces and beckoning our attention with its mesmeric power.

Deleuze's vision of a superman in charge of rocks and inorganic matter brings to mind the researchers and tycoons of Silicon Valley and their predecessors who since the 1950s have laboured to harness the forces of silicon. It also brings to mind the technodigital assemblages humans take part in almost permanently where, as stated in the opening of the chapter, carbon and silicon collide and recompose. Deleuze's superman bears no resemblance to the 1990s trope of the cyborg *à la* Donna Haraway (1991) however. Deleuze is unconcerned with some of the rhetoric of hybridisation of the opposite poles of a dichotomy (nature and technology, human and machine, and so on), with its embedded presupposition of dualistic essences as characterised by some of those cyber-discourses. Instead, he evokes a co-evolving and co-producing technodigital assemblage, more indebted to Simondon's notion of technology.

Simondon's genesis of technical objects tells us that objects are always the temporary concrete expression of a morphological and spontaneous evolution, which depends neither on natural processes nor on human design (Simondon 1980; Chabot 2013). Rather, technical objects gain 'an intermediate position between natural object and scientific representation' (Simondon 1980: 46). Moreover, far from evolving in isolation, technical objects are the result of a process where internal parts converge and adapt 'according to a principle of internal resonance' (Simondon 1980: 13). This process (*concretisation*) describes a convergence of functions within a structural unit by which the object acquires an internal coherence that propels it beyond the intention of its inventor. Even though they are designed and made by human beings, technical objects *have a life of their own* (Schmidgen 2012).

Simondon's theory is relevant to my argument as it explains how technogenesis, whether concerning common artefacts, intelligent machines or digital devices, is fully integrated into both culture and nature. Technical objects are not to be considered as an extension of a pre-existing body. Rather, technology is something fully inherent to human life (Braun and Whatmore 2010). Humans are always already among machines. Likewise, technical objects are already among, and cooperating with, humans: the natural and the artificial, the animate and the inanimate become closer to each other.[16] Which brings me to a discussion of silicon-based computation, its impending demise and its material transformation.

Silicon, between materiality and dematerialisation

Deleuze's prophetic vision of a silicon domain also suggests that an understanding of the current electronic and computational regimes cannot exist without a full understanding of their materiality. However, as historians of technology Christopher Lécuyer and David Brock have pointed out in their 'materials centered approach to the history of micro-electronics' (Lécuyer and Brock 2006: 302), genealogies of technology have largely ignored the materiality of microelectronics and semiconductors. Instead, the history of computation has focused more on the design of devices rather than on their materiality. To counteract this under-materialisation, Lécuyer and Brock remind us that microchips, with us since the early 1960s, have transformed entire industries, the built environment and ultimately how humans and things interact. Microchips are integrated circuits made of silicon: 'postage-stamp-sized, thin slivers of silicon crystal that contain complex digital circuits' (Lécuyer and Brock 2012: 563). The basic component of a microchip is the transistor: 'a miniscule structure of chemically altered silicon and other materials that acts as an electrical switch. These tiny switches allow or prohibit the movement of electrical current through them, being either "on" or "off".' Transistors are the basis of all modern electronics; they produce 'the inaudible hum of the digital world' (2012: 563).

Silicon, the key component of the microchip, is a natural semiconductor. This means that it can be altered to conduct electric current or to block its passage. To make microchips, silicon is grown in vacuum chambers, and then stacked in ingots to be sliced into thin wafers. Today silicon microchips are everywhere. Our digital world depends on them and on their astonishing miniaturisation.

> In the early 1970s advanced microchips contained several thousand transistors, each roughly the size of a cloud droplet, measured in millionths of a meter. By 2007 leading-edge microchips contained over a billion transistors. These transistors were now each approximately the size of a virus, measured in billionths of a meter. (Lécuyer and Brock 2012: 563)

For example, in 2007 Intel's 45-nanometer (nm) technology produced transistors so small that 2 million of them would fit into the full stop at the end of this sentence.[17] In 2014 Intel released transistors made with 14-nm technology ($1nm = 10^{-9}$).[18]

Such feats of miniaturisation are troubling. If on the one hand they seem to point to an eventual disappearance of matter – of which more below – on the other they reveal materiality's persistence at the core of our digital world. Indeed, the more invisible matter becomes, the more firmly embedded it is within the computational paradigm: a paradigm that, as Kwinter observes, 'has nothing to do with computers' (2007: 53). Still, an obvious tension exists between materiality and immateriality.

Remarking on the paradox of this tension, Gabrys observes that the microchip is essentially, but also ambiguously, 'a miniature device that performs seemingly immaterial operations', while requiring 'a wealth of material inputs' (2011: 24). She also usefully reminds us that information is an *entirely material* process of on-off electrical signalling. Consequently:

> the transmission of information into bits, or binary units that correspond to electrical pulses, requires this composite of silicon, chemicals, metals, plastics, and energy. It would be impossible to separate the zeros and ones of information from the firing of these electrical pulses and the processed silicon through which they course. (Gabrys 2011: 24)

As Friedrich Kittler observed, there is no software, only hardware.

Gabrys makes another important point, drawing on philosophers Isabelle Stengers and Bernadette Bensaude-Vincent's (1996) notion of *informed materials*: information-rich and context-related materials that cannot be perceived outside of their environment. If we consider electronics as made of informed material, argues Gabrys, as silicon enables the flow of electricity, matter seems to disappear (2011: 85). In other words, a silicon-based understanding of computation reveals the *interdependence* of material systems and informational systems. This interdependence concerns also the way the human body itself participates in these processes chemically, electrically, affectively. In the same way in which the *bit* as a switching model (on-off) is coupled to the actual operations of electrical currents, our living, electrical body is made of cells ferrying ions in and out of electrical charges. Through the interface apparatuses of eyes, ears, nose, tongue and skin, these cells are chemically converting the undercharged outside world into currents that create a fusillade of spikes through our brains (Simonite 2013; Tingley 2013).

Post-silicon, towards the brain: neuromorphic chips

The convergence of digital and human points to a model of the technodigital assemblage that attends to the morphogenetic, growing capacities of the material in its bare components. There is a becoming-silicon in action through topological discontinuities that compute the assemblage human-technodigital by fragmenting identities and dissolving them into the endlessly replicable data swarms of manifold processes of subjectification. If the domain of silicon has to do also with infinite reproducibility – thus, with the absence of an original and the consequent disappearance of authenticity – what ensues is an anti-essentialism that sits comfortably with the idea that the regime of the Superfold points unequivocally *beyond* the domain of the silicon. As we have seen, for Deleuze the forces of silicon have superseded those of carbon. However, the relentless folding and unfolding of these forces (encapsulated by the Superfold) is now leading to a new phase in the lives of both machines and humans.

Some of the factors leading to this new phase have to do with the material capacities of silicon and the structural limits of the technology used to etch electronic circuits into silicon wafers (photolithography). The constant shrinking of silicon (silicon scaling) is pushing computers into the cul-de-sac predicted by Moore's Law, according to which the exponential increase in computation power is based on increasingly smaller and faster silicon transistors.[19] As said, Intel's latest chips are as small as 14nm. It is expected that by 2020 the size of these chips will be down to 5nm. Now, silicon ceases to exist as a crystalline solid once it has reached the threshold of 10nm, beyond which it becomes an amorphous material. The industry-led process of miniaturisation is shrinking silicon to its vanishing point (Winters 2003).[20] With silicon disappearing soon, what next?

Currently, the most promising area of research centres on neuromorphic chips (Hof 2014): microchips designed to emulate some aspects of brain behaviour. They attempt to model in silicon the way in which neurons (brain cells) behave, by changing how they connect to each other, and constantly learning and adapting though this process. Brains compute in parallel, with the neurons simultaneously connecting and influencing one another's electrical pulses via connections called synapses. As philosopher Catherine Malabou (2008) remarks, this process is called brain plasticity.[21] Each new input may cause a rearrangement of the synapses. The brain is, in other words, constantly in the process of being made, as a unique work. Neurons are more responsive to other neurons when their signalling activity is closely matched. This means that when groups of neurons work together in a constructive manner, their connections become stronger, while less useful connections may fall dormant (Simonite 2013). This is the process that underpins learning. In computing terms, it indicates a system that learns to reprogram itself.

Neuromorphic chips represent a new, alien form of intelligence (Simonite 2013). By learning through experience they constitute a leap from traditional chips. Devices powered by them will be able to learn and evolve by behaviour, rather than by program. Thus, neuromorphic chips shorten the distance between artificial and natural computation by blurring the boundary between silicon and biological systems (Monroe 2014). Inspired by the way the brain works, they are self-learning and therefore able to reprogram themselves through nonlinear and chaotic processes. Because they encode and transmit data in a way that replicates the electrical spikes[22] generated in the brain as it responds to sensory information, neuromorphic chips do not mimic, but try to *simulate* brain behaviour.

Thus, they will be used to detect and predict patterns in complex data rather than simply to execute complex calculations. Because of their propensity to learn, neuromorphic chips could transform smartphones and other mobile devices into cognitive companions that pay attention to users' actions and surroundings and learn their habits over time, understanding intentions and anticipating needs (Simonite 2013). The idea here is *not* to replicate the brain in complete detail (an impossible task), but to detect patterns that can be applied to industry use. Neuromorphic chips will be used to increase digital devices' environmental intelligence by turning them into better 'companions' able to read changes in the ambient and to act accordingly. For example, image analysis and voice recognition, which at present are still processed via a cloud, will be learned by adaptation rather than by program (Monroe 2014).[23]

There are two other examples worth mentioning that indicate a convergence of silicon and carbon, organic and inorganic. The first concerns carbon nanotubes. From the point of view of the history of materials, carbon may logically constitute the next platform for microelectronics (Castro Neto 2010). Carbon nanotubes are hollow cylindrical structures made from a sheet of carbon atoms. They are only 1 nanometre wide – less than a million of an inch – and require very little energy to move. Nanotube technology may have the capacity to design a computer working at a molecular level, that is, a computer *not* based on an on-off structure, but on the *movement of molecules* (Winters 2003; Hsu 2013; Simonite 2014).[24]

The second example concerns what is known as 'dark silicon' (Taylor 2013). Dark silicon is the expression used to indicate largely underused swaths of silicon in microchips. This is silicon that is either idle for long periods of time, or not used all the time, or not at full frequency, due to the difference between a microchip's growth of computational capabilities and its capacity to utilise effectively this benefit. What this points to is a paradigm shift from a model based on speed to a model based on energy efficiency. This is affecting the design of silicon chips and the theoretical model that underpins it, which needs to shift to an optimised energy-based paradigm, more akin to the nonlinear functioning of the brain. Indeed, the brain is already working in 'very dark operation' mode (Taylor 2013). While neurons fire at a maximum rate of approximately 1,000 switches per second, transistors toggle at 3 billion times per second. Thus, the 'most active neuron's activity is a millionth of that of a processing transistors in today's processors' (Taylor 2013: 17).

It is to the brain, its neurons and the pure movement of molecules, then, that digital science is looking, as it endeavours to rise to the challenge presented by the material morphogenesis signalled by the impending demise of silicon and by the emergence of new forms of intelligence that animate matter.

Concluding Remarks

To locate better the argument about the intelligence of matter, what follows are some thoughts on Deleuze's conception of nonorganic life (Deleuze 2001). Whatever it is that animates matter, it is neither about innate properties, nor about intentionality. Rather, it is relational, because it has to do with traversing intensities and flows affecting, influencing and colliding with other intensities, thus engendering material consequences in the world. Nonorganic life is matter seen as immanently creative. There is creativity and effervescence in matter, not dependent on organic form, but occurring *prior* to any determination of form. Everything is alive. This does not mean that there is an external vital principle infused in inert matter. This material vitalism should not be taken as a mystical life force, but as the abstract power of *a* Life. The indefinite article '*a*' signifies precisely this: a life, before any specification (Deleuze 2001: 8), an impersonal power that precedes any organised and lived experience.[25] Deleuze and Guattari stress the importance of distinguishing between two interpretations of vitalism: 'that of an idea that acts, but is not – that acts therefore only from the point of view of an external cerebral knowledge (from Kant to Claude Bernard); or that of a force that is but does not act – that is therefore a pure internal Awareness' (Deleuze and Guattari 1994: 213). Instead, material vitalism should be treated as a force pulsating in everything, making matter vibrate. As philosopher John Rajchman writes, this impersonal and yet singular life that has little in common with what we call self, demands a 'wilder sort of empiricism – a transcendental empiricism' (2001: 9). This wild empiricism points to how to experience materiality prior any formal determination. We are back to intuition as the experimental, experiential and affective apprehension of matter. Through this intuitive apprehension of material variation, we grasp how things come to exist, how things are made and what makes them. We grasp how to relate to them.

This is how Deleuze and Guattari's radical materialism can articulate our relationship with the technodigital object*scape*. It does so by providing an experimental, intuitive, material understanding of our interaction with, and experience of, digital objects, and by suggesting an ecology of the human and the non-human based on the crisscrossing and entanglement of silicon and carbon, and all their possible, wondrous becomings. Thus, the pertinence of Deleuze and Guattari's materialism to design should not be underestimated. Like design, it concerns the human and the non-human. As such, it prompts an argument in favour of an *anorganic* mode of expression and proliferation, where many diverse forces participate in the making of form. Design's task is to resist the hylomorphic convention of the form-matter coupling in favour of morphogenesis. As this chapter has argued throughout, morphogenesis offers ways of understanding the process by which objects come into being. This perspective also helps us to understand the complex demands posed by current technodigital objects. By posing their development as an evolution of different coexisting mutually affecting material intelligences, a morphogenetic perspective offers design new insights to rethink its response to the transformation of the technodigital object, and the issues this raises: the convergence of silicon and carbon; the increasingly independent life of objects and its impact on humans; how to move beyond the conventions dictated by the interface as the default form of interaction, and beyond the formalism of the black box.

The silicon-neural shift in the ways humans coalesce with the technodigital object demands a design paradigm that addresses our cohabitation with things and recognises the rapid transformations taking place within this cohabitation. Technodigital objects are never inanimate. The morphogenetic transformation of silicon heralds new forms of cognition – embodied, sensorial, contextual and distributed – that are quickly moving beyond ambient intelligence and leaning towards synaptic adaptation. The post-silicon, *neuromorphic* era, characterised by a breed of microchips that 'follow' neural activity, collapses the distinction between carbon and silicon, animate and inanimate matter, and works instead towards their convergence. New types of human-made things emerge, which are *simultaneously* animate and inanimate and are capable of expressing additive and adaptable intelligence, as well as learning through experience. What all this may imply for humans has to be neither feared nor embraced, but carefully considered.

This needs to inform the way design approaches technodigital objects. A morphogenetic model forces us to pay attention to the materiality of digital interaction, and the extent to which it is a key component of the technodigital assemblage we form with our devices. This is something that should concern design not only as the process of thing-making and meaning-making, but as the process of intervening upon that screen that separates and connects chaos and emergence. As I have argued elsewhere,[26] design must be alert to ideas circulating outside its most familiar domain. The approach suggested here assigns great relevance to an intuition-based following of matter, informed by Deleuze and Guattari's nomadic science. To think about design as a nomadic science – as opposed to the hylomorphic, iterative, retrofitting-prone, problem-solving, conventional view of design – means to regard it as a *minoritarian* line of creation, transformativity and becoming. To think about design as a nomadic science means to welcome non-human material agencies as key stakeholders in the process of design. These are the challenges to which design needs to rise.

If there is model for design research that Deleuze can inspire, it is most certainly within the boundless scope of a *nomadic, minoritarian* design, the rudimentary alliances of design with all its possible else*when*.

Acknowledgements

Thanks to Jamie. His rigorous philosophical reading coupled with generous and constructive feedback have prompted me to question a lot of my thinking. I have also received many helpful suggestions from colleagues at conferences and workshops where I have presented the thoughts and the ideas that went on to form this chapter. I am grateful to Maria Voyatzaki for the invitation to the *What's the Matter: Materiality and Materialism at the Age of Computation* conference at the Chamber of Architects, COAC, ETSAB, ETSAV (September 2014) in Barcelona. Also, ideas were road tested at the MIT Computational Making Workshop during the *Sixth International Conference on Design Computing and Cognition* (DCC 14), University College London (June 2014). Thanks to Terry Knight for creating a truly interdisciplinary event and to Theodora Vardouli for inspiring conversations. I am grateful to Marc Rolli for inviting me to the Political Aesthetics – Political Design Workshop at the Institute for Design Research (IDE), Zurich University of the Arts, in April 2014, and for initiating a network of thinkers and practitioners. Thanks to Sjoerd Van Tuinen, Monica Gaspar and Manola Antonioli. Thanks to Tom Fisher at Nottingham Trent University for inviting me to the Design Research Society *Good Things and Bad Things* symposium at Nottingham Contemporary in June 2013. The writing of this chapter was made possible by the Research Management and

Administration (RMA) of the University of the Arts London, who granted me a research sabbatical. It was also made possible by my daughter Joy, and her understanding of what drives me to write.

Notes

1. My use of 'we', 'our' and 'us' throughout the chapter refers not simply to the community of those who habitually use a digital device: a community that is likely to overlap with the readership of this book. It also, broadly, intends to make a point about the global implications of such objects, which affect everyone, users or not.
2. See media theorist Friedrich Kittler's seminal essay 'There Is No Software' (1995). Software is by necessity a material thing: 'without the correspondent electrical charges in silicon circuitry no computer program would ever run' (Kittler 1995: 4). Similarly, digital theorist Florian Cramer (2004) argues for the elimination of the dichotomy between software and hardware, while insisting on the unequivocal materiality that software possesses in its stored, coded form, as well as a cultural practice.
3. For a critique of user-centred design see the Introduction in this volume.
4. Although design seen as a tool of complexification of the existent implies a critical perspective, this view does not necessarily align with what is known as 'critical design'. For a useful taxonomy of critical practices in design and a critique of critical design see Malpass 2013.
5. Félix Guattari's contribution to this radical materialism should be remembered. Guattari's critique of structural semiotics is important. This critique brings back material intensities to the system of signification signifier/signified and the system of representation content/form. This semiotics of intensities draws on the work of Hjelmslev, '*the Danish Spinozist geologist*' (Deleuze and Guattari 1988: 43) who breaks the duality between expression and content by introducing matter in their distinction and paving the way for a non-hierarchic, nonlinear and non-representational distribution of content and expression.
6. Deleuze and Guattari use the term *haecceity* to define 'a mode of individuation very different from that of a person, subject, thing, or substance' (1988: 287). 'A season, a winter, a summer, an hour, a date have a perfect individuality lacking nothing, even though this individuality is different from that of a thing or subject. They are haecceities in the sense that they consist entirely of relations of movement and rest between molecules or particles, capacities to affect and be affected' (1988: 288).
7. 'Reductionism is the method by which one reduces complex phenomena to simpler isolated systems that can be fully controlled and understood. Quantitative methods, on the other hand, are related to reductionism, but they are more fundamental, because they dictate how far reductionism must go . . . this is, for example, the basis of the Cartesian grid system that underlies most modern models of form' (Kwinter 1992: 53).
8. 'Once time is introduced into this system, a form can gradually unfold on this surface *as a historically specific flow* of matter that actualizes (resolves, incarnates) the forces converging on the plane. These are the phenomenal forms that we conventionally associated with our living world. What we have generally failed to understand about them is that they exist, enfolded in a virtual space, but are actualized (unfolded) only *in time* as a suite of morphological events and differentiations ever-carving themselves into the epigenetic landscape' (Kwinter 1992: 63).

9. In a recent interview Italian designer Gaetano Pesce said: 'I believe that my time – *our* time – is liquid. I use resin, elastomers, like silicon and rubber, and all liquids, which I mix and cure to make them soft and pliable or rigid, depending on what I want. The materials I pick are both *from* my time and representative *of* my time. I find the dripping and pulling emotional. I don't impose my will on the material. I let the material do a lot of what it wants. It's fantastic when you allow liquid resin to move. It does things I couldn't have commanded. The results can be even richer than you imagined' (Groen 2014: 180).

10. Intuition is 'the attempt to make explicit the fine threads within and between objects (including living beings) that always make them more than themselves, always propel them in a mode of becoming. What intuition gives back to the real is precisely that virtuality which complicates the actual' (Grosz 2011: 51).

11. On the sympathy of things see Spuybroek 2011: 159–67.

12. Compare to media theorist Lev Manovich (2014) for whom *software*, taken as the key new media of our time, having superseded all other media technologies used to produce, store, disseminate and access cultural artefacts, is *the* interface between our imagination and the world. In this sense software constitutes an entirely new affective and material dimension.

13. As archaeologist Chantal Conneller (2011) has written in reference to metallurgy, what must be noted is that the vital principle pertains to metallurgy as a *process*: the assemblage of things and energies partaking in the entire process of production.

14. Bratton makes a similar point in his discussion of software. Software is not only 'a device-language with which we act upon space, it is also itself a material architecture' (2002: 13) made of glowing screens, copper and fibre wires.

15. 'Eight Years Later: 1980 Interview', in Deleuze 2006: 175–80.

16. As philosopher Thomas LaMarre reminds us, however, the ontological distinction between technical individuals and natural individuals is never blurred. For Simondon, the tendency to collapse this distinction is 'not merely a metaphysical error, but a form of moral panic as well, which ultimately serves to depoliticize the technical existence of humans' (LaMarre 2013: 91).

17. See Intel's website: http://www.intel.co.uk/content/www/uk/en/history/museum-story-of-intel-4004.html?wapkw (accessed 7 January 2015).

18. See Intel's article on this from 11 August 2014: http://www.intel.co.uk/content/www/uk/en/silicon-innovations/intel-14nm-technology.html?wapkw (accessed 7 January 2015).

19. Gordon Moore was one of the co-founders of Intel Corp. He predicted in 1965 that the density of transistors in a circuit would double every two years to allow for the rapid progress in electronics.

20. *Transient* electronics exploit this property. They are thin and malleable silicon circuits (100nm or less) that emulate bodily activity and dissolve within the body when their task is completed – silicon electronics as no longer inanimate otherness, but an increasingly integrated part of that thing we call 'us' (Rogers Research Group 2014, http://rogers.matse.illinois.edu).

21. Malabou explains the difference between plasticity and flexibility. Flexibility, she says is the 'the ideological avatar of plasticity . . . To be flexible is to receive a form or impression, to be able to fold oneself, to take the fold, not to give it. To be docile, to not explode. Indeed, what flexibility lacks is the resource of giving form, the power to create, to invent or even to erase an impression, the power to style. Flexibility is plasticity minus its genius' (2008: 12).

22. It is not a coincidence that the first neuromorphic chip developed in 2012 at the University of Heidelberg as part of the European Human Brain project is called

'Spikey' (Electronic Vision(s) Group 2014, http://www.kip.uni-heidelberg.de/cms/groups/vision).

23. 'Today's computers all use the so-called von Neumann architecture, which shuttles data back and forth between a central processor and memory chips in linear sequences of calculations. That method is great for crunching numbers and executing precisely written programs, but not for processing images or sound and making sense of it all. It's telling that in 2012, when Google demonstrated artificial intelligence software that learned to recognise cats in videos without being told what a cat was, it needed 16,000 processors to pull it off' (Hof 2014: 56).

24. This harks back to the origins of computational machines such as Charles Babbage's design for the Difference Engine where computation was based on the repetitive motion of moving parts, for example, a stack of toothed wheels (Winters 2003; Marenko 2016a). Winters also recalls Eric Drexler's seminal work on rod logic which would substitute transistors' controlled electrical pulses with arrays of minuscule rods, each knobbed at precise points. The extension of a rod would prevent another rod from moving, in a similar way to how electric current fed into a transistor can block another current in a circuit. These 'shuttling' movements of open and closed 'gates' would process data. For Drexler, 'arrays of such gates could create an entire computer processor *smaller than a bacterium*' (Winters 2003: 51; emphasis added).

25. One example that Deleuze uses is the 'obstinate, stubborn and indomitable will to live that differs from all organic life' of a new born baby 'who concentrates in its smallness the same energy that shatters paving stones' (Deleuze 1998: 133). This 'inorganic, germinal, and intensive' life is what Deleuze and Guattari also describe as the BwO traversed by powerful nonorganic vitality (Deleuze and Guattari 1988: 499).

26. See the Introduction to this volume; also Marenko 2014; 2016b.

References

Bensaude-Vincent, Bernadette and I. Stengers (1996), *A History of Chemistry*, Cambridge, MA and London: Harvard University Press.

Bratton, Benjamin (2013), 'On Apps and Elementary Forms of Interfacial Life: Object, Image, Superimposition'; available at http://www.bratton.info/projects/texts/on-apps-and-elementary-forms-of-interfacial-life (accessed 29 August 2014).

Bratton, Benjamin (2009), 'iPhone City', *Architectural Design*, 79:4, pp. 90–7.

Bratton, B. (2008), 'What Do We Mean By Program?', *Interactions: Experiences, People, Technology, The HCI Journal of the Association of Computing Machinery*, XV:3, pp. 20–6.

Bratton, B. (2002), 'Accounting for Pervasive Computing', *Afterimage*, 30:1, pp. 13–14.

Braun, Bruce and S. J. Whatmore (eds) (2010), *Political Matter: Technoscience, Democracy and Public Life*, Minneapolis: University of Minnesota Press.

Castro Neto, A. H. (2010), 'The Carbon New Age', *Materials Today*, 13:3, pp. 1–6.

Chabot, Pascal (2013), *The Philosophy of Simondon: Between Technology and Individuation*, London: Bloomsbury.

Conneller, Chantal (2011), *An Archeology of Materials: Substantial Transformations in Early Prehistoric Europe*, London and New York: Routledge.

Cramer, Florian (2004), *Words Made Flesh: Code, Culture, Imagination*, Media Design Research, Piet Zwart Institute Rotterdam; available at http://pzwart.wdka.hro.nl/mdr/research/fcramer/wordsmadeflesh (accessed 13 May 2014).

DeLanda, M. (2009), 'Material Evolvability and Variability', in L. Spuybroek (ed.), *The Architecture of Variation*, London: Thames and Hudson, pp. 10–17.

DeLanda, M. (2004), 'Material Complexity', in N. Leach, D. Turnbull and C. Williams (eds), *Digital Tectonics*, Chichester: Wiley, pp. 14–21.

Deleuze, Gilles (2006), *Two Regimes of Madness: Texts and Interviews 1975–1995*, New York: Semiotext(e).

Deleuze, Gilles (2001), *Pure Immanence: Essays on A Life*, trans. A. Boyman, New York: Zone Books.

Deleuze, Gilles [1993] (1998), *Essays Critical and Clinical*, trans. D. Smith and M. Greco, London and New York: Verso.

Deleuze, Gilles [1988] (1993), *Fold: Leibniz and the Baroque*, trans. Tom Conley, London: Athlone.

Deleuze, Gilles [1966] (1991), *Bergsonism*, trans. H. Tomlinson and B. Habberjam, New York: Zone Books.

Deleuze, Gilles [1970] (1988a), *Spinoza: Practical Philosophy*, trans. R. Hurley, San Francisco: City Lights Books.

Deleuze, Gilles [1986] (1988b), *Foucault*, trans. S. Hand, Minneapolis and London: University of Minnesota Press.

Deleuze, Gilles and F. Guattari [1991] (1994), *What is Philosophy?*, trans. G. Burchell and H. Tomlinson, New York: Columbia University Press.

Deleuze, Gilles and F. Guattari [1982] (1988), *A Thousand Plateaus. Capitalism and Schizophrenia 2*, trans. B. Massumi, London: Athlone.

Gabrys, Jennifer (2011), *Digital Rubbish: A Natural History of Electronics*, Ann Arbor, MI: University of Michigan Press.

Groen, T. (2014), 'King of Pop. Interview with Gaetano Pesce', *Frame*, 97, pp. 178–83.

Grosz, Elizabeth (2011), *Becoming Undone: Darwinian Reflections on Life, Politics, and Art*, Durham, NC: Duke University Press.

Haraway, Donna (1991), 'A Cyborg Manifesto. Science, Technology, and Socialist-Feminism in the Late Twentieth Century', in Donna Haraway, *Simians, Cyborgs and Women: The Reinvention of Nature*, New York: Routledge, pp. 149–81.

Hardt, Michael (1993), *Gilles Deleuze: An Apprenticeship in Philosophy*, Minneapolis: University of Minnesota Press.

Hof, R. D. (2014), 'Neuromorphic Chips', *MIT Technology* Review, 117:3, pp. 55–7.

Hookway, Brendan (2014), *Interface*, Cambridge, MA: The MIT Press.

Hsu, J. (2013), 'Carbon Nanotube Computer Hints at Future Beyond Silicon Semiconductors', *Scientific American*; available at http://www.scientificamerican.com/article/carbon-nanotube-computer-hints-at-future-beyond-silicon (accessed 29 August 2014).

Ingold, Tim (2013), *Making: Anthropology, Archaeology, Art and Architecture*, London: Routledge.

Kittler, F. (1995), 'There Is No Software', *CTheory.net*; available at www.ctheory.net/articles.aspx?id=74 (accessed 29 August 2014).

Kwinter, Sanford (2007), *Far From Equilibrium: Essays on Technology and Design Culture*, Barcelona and New York: Actar.

Kwinter, Sanford (2001), *Architectures of Time: Toward a Theory of the Event in Modernist Culture*, Cambridge, MA: The MIT Press.

Kwinter, Sanford (1998), 'Leap in the Void: A New Organon?', in C. C. Davidson (ed.), *Anyhow*, Cambridge, MA: The MIT Press, pp. 22–7.

Kwinter, Sanford (1992), 'Landscapes of Change: Boccioni's "Stati d'animo" as a General Theory of Models', *Assemblage*, 19, Cambridge, MA: The MIT Press, pp. 50–65.

LaMarre, Thomas (2013), 'Afterword: Humans and Machines', in M. Combes, *Gilbert Simondon and the Philosophy of the Transindividual*, Cambridge, MA: The MIT Press, pp. 79–108.

Latour, Bruno (1999), *Pandora's Hope: Essays on the Reality of Science Studies*, Cambridge, MA: Harvard University Press.

Lécuyer, C. and D. C. Brock (2012), 'Digital Foundations: The Making of Silicon-Gate Manufacturing Technology', *Technology and Culture*, 53, pp. 561–97.

Lécuyer, C. and D. C. Brock (2006), 'The Materiality of Microelectronics', *History and Technology*, 22, pp. 301–25.

Malabou, Catherine (2008), *What Should We Do with Our Brain?* New York: Fordham University Press.

Malpass, M. (2013), 'Between Wit and Reason: Defining Associative, Speculative and Critical Design in Practice', *Design and Culture*, 5:3, pp. 333–56.

Manovich, L. (2014), 'Software is the Message', *Journal of Visual Culture*, 13:1, pp. 79–81.

Marenko, B. (2016a), '*Filled With Wonder*: The Enchanting Android from Cams to Algorithms', in L. Atzmon and P. Boradkar (eds), *Encountering Things: Design and Thing Theory*, London: Bloomsbury.

Marenko, B. (2016b), 'The Un-designability of the Virtual: Design from Problem-Solving to Problem-Finding', in G. Sade, G. Coombs, A. McNamara (eds), *UnDesign*, London: Continuum.

Marenko, B. (2014), 'Neo-Animism and Design: A New Paradigm in Object Theory', *Design and Culture*, 6:2, pp. 219–42.

Marenko, B. (2010), 'Contagious Affectivity: The Management of Emotions in Late Capitalist Design', in *Negotiating Futures – Design Fiction*, Proceedings from the 6th Swiss Design Network Conference, Basel, pp. 134–49.

Marenko, B. (2009), 'Object-Relics and their Effects: For a Neo-Animist Paradigm', in B. Darras and S. Belkhamsa (eds), *Objets and Communication*, MEI *'Mediation and Information'*, Review nos. 30–1, Paris: Editions de l'Harmattan, pp. 239–53.

Matheron, A. (1998), 'Prefazione', in A. Negri (ed.), *Spinoza*, Rome: DeriveApprodi, pp. 13–19.

Monroe, D. (2014), 'Neuromorphic Computing Gets Ready for the (Really) Big Time', *Communications of the ACM*, 57:6, pp. 13–15.

Montag, Warren and T. Stolze (eds) (1997), *The New Spinoza*, Minneapolis: University of Minnesota Press.

Rajchman, John (2001), 'Introduction', in G. Deleuze, *Pure Immanence: Essays on A Life*, New York: Zone Books pp. 7–23.

Schmidgen, H. (2012), 'Inside the Black Box: Simondon's Politics of Technology', *SubStance*, 41:3, 129, pp. 16–31.

Simondon, Gilbert [1958] (1980), *On the Mode of Existence of Technical Objects*, trans. N. Mellamphy, London, Ontario: University of Western Ontario.

Simonite, T. (2014), 'IBM: Commercial Nanotube Transistors Are Coming Soon', *MIT Technology Review* (July); available at http://www.technologyreview.com/news/528601/ibm-commercial-nanotube-transistors-are-coming-soon (accessed 29 August 2014).

Simonite, T. (2013), 'Thinking in Silicon', *MIT Technology Review* (January–February), pp. 52–8.

Spuybroek, Lars (2011), *The Sympathy of Things: Ruskin and the Ecology of Design*, Rotterdam: V2_Publishing.

Spuybroek, Lars (2008), *The Architecture of Continuity: Essays and Conversations*, Rotterdam: V2_Publishing.

Talbot, D. (2013), 'Qualcomm to Build Neuro-Inspired Chips', *MIT Technology*

Review (October); available at http://www.technologyreview.com/news/520211/qualcomm-to-build-neuro-inspired-chips (accessed 29 August 2014).

Taylor, M. B. (2013), 'A Landscape of the New Dark Silicon Design Regime', *Micro IEEE Computer Society*, 33:5, pp. 8–19.

Thompson, D'Arcy (1961), *On Growth and Form*, Cambridge: Cambridge University Press.

Tingley, K. (2013), 'The Body Electric: A Scientist Takes Computing Power Under the Skin', *The New Yorker*, 25 November, pp. 78–86.

Winters, J. (2003), 'Remember the Adding Machine', *Mechanical Engineering* (September), pp. 50–2.

Chapter 6

Re-designing the Objectile

Derek Hales

Design and the Three Daughters of Chaos

> What would thinking be if it did not constantly confront chaos? . . . chaos has three daughters . . . the Chaoids – art, science, and philosophy . . . [Each] cut through the chaos in different ways. The brain is the junction – not the unity – of the three planes. (Deleuze and Guattari 1994: 208)

It is something of a cliché in design studies circles to say that design is a practice in which the two 'chaoids' (Deleuze and Guattari 1994) of science and art converge. Such sentiments are found, for example, in the design methods research of John Chris Jones, one of the founding figures of the field of design studies,[1] albeit that in his *Design Methods* this entails the separating out of mathematics, perhaps as the third philosophical chaoid? 'The view put forward [by Jones] is that designing should not be confused with art, with science or with mathematics. It is a hybrid activity which depends upon a proper blending of all three' (Jones 1992: 11). These sentiments are echoed in a supposed hybridity which comes to be by design, an hybridity requiring some systematisation, suggests Nicholas Negroponte, for whom design needs to be codified as the 'methods, principles and rules for regulating the science and art of design' (Negroponte 1975: 31). Sentiments echoed too by Pelle Ehn who makes similar claims for digital design in a thought that might have been born out of the Bauhaus: 'Designing computer artefacts is both art and science' (Ehn 1989).[2] To follow this view, however, would be to hold with design as the simple synthesis of art and science and to consign designing to a search for unity within a *hylomorphic* scheme – that is to say, as the imposition of an external idea or form onto an inert matter. It is, rather, that matter is a flow, a matter-flow, and that design, thought and the technological become formed in the production of structures and potentialities immanent to matter. This is the point from which Simondon critiques hylomorphism (1992, 2009)[3] and that also informs Deleuze and Guattari's position on the same subject (1987, 1994). This immanence of the production of matter and form is described in the chapter that follows as *speculative*. Design is a process of speculative artisanship with particular 'traits of expression' (Deleuze and Guattari 1987: 415). Designing considered this way becomes a process of speculative intuition in the following of matter-flow, matter in movement, as pure productivity. Speculative too in that design so described is a ceaseless swerve of deviances and alliances, as creative and in league with inhuman forces: design is out of chaos. So we can claim design – as Bernard Cache does for architecture (1995) – as a form of 'philosophy by other means', and by so doing the relationship between the chaoids sketched out by Deleuze and Guattari becomes complexified when design's ontogenetic production opportunities swerve into play.

There is therefore no need, no point even, in design studies laying out the planes of art or science simply as synthetic to processes of design and of the designed as correspondingly artificial. Instead a swerving path might be taken, bypassing – or at the very least short-circuiting – the tendencies within design studies to treat design as 'a science of the artificial', as Herbert Simon argued (1969). Instead follow a swerve that manoeuvres out of such conservative tendencies of design as a 'Royal science' of the artificial (Deleuze and Guattari 1987: 415). This chapter, then, proposes a swerved design as a 'minor' science of the machinic phylum. A swerving where natural or artificial, and both simultaneously, come into a dynamic, ceaseless being: a swerving designing in ontogenetic production.

To engage in the design of digital media *speculatively*, for example, is to be engaged in its aberrant forms – in eccentric forms of cybernetics rather than Norbert Weiner's normalising one:[4] the aberrant forms of a cybernetics of difference. This aberrance or eccentricity is also what it is to be sensitised to design's conjectural or prospective productivity. 'Conjectural' in the sense that design might be considered creative, incomplete and inconclusive; 'prospective' in so far as processes of design cease to be concerned with what Bruno Latour terms 'matters of fact' (Latour 2008), for example in ceasing to see functions as fixed or in ceasing to seek behaviours that are normalised or normalising; a design that instead speculatively reconfigures its norms as chaos, that gestures instead towards the open. In the place of 'matters of fact' Latour has suggested that design processes should deal with and therefore become 'matters of concern' (Latour 2008). Design, Latour suggests, has been

spreading continuously so that it increasingly *matters* to the very substance, to the matter and form of production. This speculative *mattering*
of substance, of the processing of technological objects as *concerns* is,
in a designing process, proximate with each of Deleuze and Guattari's
three chaoids of philosophy, science and art. Design so conceived would
be like the brain (Deleuze and Guattari 1994), a *junction* and not a
unity, not a synthesis but – like philosophy – a *thought synthesizer*:
'Philosophy is no longer synthetic judgement; it is like a thought synthesizer functioning to make thought travel, make it mobile, make it a force
of the Cosmos (in the same way as one makes sound travel)' (Deleuze
and Guattari 1987: 343). Here the synthesizer is expressive of the synthesis of sonic material, of simulacra[5] as the modification and movement of sonic force and the multisensory modulation of thought itself.
Such a non-homogenising synthesis is the conjunction and expression of
conditions and capacities of combination and recombination; capacities
teeming with the potencies of consciousness.

Any attempt to consider the speculative capacity for the design of
the technological object, once the notion of design as hylomorphic has
been circumvented, must also negotiate its way out of some of the other
tendencies within contemporary design that ally themselves with acts
of speculation. The most notable of these are *critical design*[6] and its
genealogies of the provocative and contestable, and *design fictions*[7] and
taxonomies of the futurological. While these tendencies of speculative
design should not be discounted out of hand, the discussion that follows
will evade the discourses of speculative design already coalescing as critical and fictional, and rather will suggest alternative ways of designing
speculatively as exceptions to these.

The interest of this chapter, then, is in a speculative approach to design
that revisits one of Deleuze's concepts: the *objectile* (Deleuze 1993). As
much as it relates to the computational and the cybernetic, the objectile,
as will be shown shortly, is also a cinematic concept for design. A cinematic concept where images are comprised of matter made up of signals:
'A signaletic material which includes all kinds of modulation, features,
sensory (visual and sound), kinetic, intensive, affective, rhythmic, tonal
and even verbal (oral and written)' (Deleuze 1989: 29–33). This revisit-
ing or redesigning of the objectile will provide for an encounter between
design, designing, technical media and philosophy, as an affirmation of
design and its manipulations of material conditions and processes of
consciousness. To accomplish this the chapter is concerned with design
in the following intermingling of ways: first, the practice of design as the
following of traits of expression in new 'signaletic material': design as an

expression of electrophysical material in speculative hardware; second, the ways in which design, as part of abstract culture,[8] modulates the industrially designed elements of electronic equipment, instruments, or digital devices and those designing interfaces characterised by generative processes.

For Deleuze, 'signaletic material' – 'a plastic Mass, an a-signifying and a-syntaxic material' (1989: 29–33) in the formation of movement-images – describes the situations and conditions of time. This chapter takes as a point of departure the position that design is implicated in these situations and conditions cybernetically. That is, in the sense of designing the signaletic as an abberant cybernetics where the intensely physical properties of electromagnetic waves, and the sensations, affects and percepts of audiovisual fields, form as the neuro-images of the electrophysical. The chapter examines these concepts as follows: first the section 'Hardware Design' considers technical media design and the design of speculative hardware. Then, 'Objectile Redux' introduces the concept of the objectile and then frees it from the stratum of architecture on which it has become lodged. In the section that follows, Lucretian atomism and 'pataphysics (Jarry 1996)[9] are introduced. This loosens the objectile yet further from its architectural stratum, and takes the form of its assimilation to the atomistic concept of the clinamen, first as suggested by Brian Massumi (2002), before swerving this trace into the pataphysics of a science of imaginary solutions (Jarry 1996; Deleuze 1998, 2004a, 2004b). The final section, 'Generative Design', examines the objectile as a concept arising in computational practice some twenty-five years ago, and recovers it for speculative practices and the signaletic material of contemporary generative design, as a concept productive of the new. The chapter concludes by assimilating design, as a 'minor' science (Deleuze and Guattari 1987) of the machinic phylum, to the pataphysics of a science of imaginary solutions. The chapter takes as its central trope, or design motif, the clinamen: the swerving principle, moving between design and hardware, between the design of synthesizers and designers as thought synthesizers.

Hardware Design

> Metallurgy is the consciousness or thought of the matter-flow, and metal the correlate of this consciousness . . . Artisans are those who follow the matter flow as pure productivity . . . Because metal is the pure productivity of matter, those who follow metal are producers of objects par excellence. (Deleuze and Guattari 1987: 411)

Deleuze provides little access to his thoughts on design, but in the extant material at the very least might be sensed an antipathy or even negativity towards design. Aside, that is, from praise for one Robert Gie, 'the very talented designer of paranoiac electrical machines' (Deleuze and Guattari 1984: 17). The paintings depicting the design of influencing machines by the schizophrenic Robert Gie, including his *Distribution d'effluves avec machine centrale* (1916), resemble bodies inextricably connected to energetic systems. Deleuze draws on Tausk's *On the Origin of the Influencing Machine in Schizophrenia* (1933), which portrays a world where everything is a machinic operation of flows and breaks, syntheses with and interruptions of other machines. Could Deleuze and Guattari be speaking of design with their interest in such paranoiac machines? And in the coupling of the latter with desiring machines as necessary for the production of the new, do they speak of designing and a pure productivity? When they say of such combinations of machines: 'The rule of continually producing production, of grafting production onto product, is a characteristic of desiring machines' (Deleuze and Guattari 1984: 7), is it not the same for contemporary software designers in their dependencies on hardware? This is just as it was for Marcel Duchamp:

> Always there has been a necessity for circles in my life, for . . . rotation. It is a kind of narcissism, this self-sufficiency, a kind of onanism. The machine goes around and by some miraculous process that I have always found fascinating, produces chocolate. (Marcel Duchamp, in Tomkins 1996: 125)

This, then, is where the trajectories of paranoiac electrical machines, 'chocolate grinders', the speculations of designers, and designing, intersect with a generalised and universalised software design; with the design, designing and designed of ready-made, standardised and industrialised components.

If there is an absence of any significant consideration for design or designing in Deleuze's published thought (alone and with Guattari), there is equally little that Deleuze has to say directly of the designed artefact. More specifically in the context of this chapter, there is little on the expression of electrophysical material in designed electronic instruments and digital media devices; and even less on the expressive capacities of their components or how these are assembled. Regarding the designed artefacts of electronic design and the technical media, together with the burgeoning of computers and digital networks, and the cybernetic cultures concurrent with his own creative output, Deleuze was strangely silent until the small essay 'Postscript on Control Societies' (1995). This silence has led media theorist Alex Galloway in *Computers and the Superfold* (2012) to describe Deleuze, with punning irony, as the 'analogue' philosopher par excellence, for the influence of Deleuze on a generation of digital media designers and theorists in the latter part of the twentieth century was in fact significant. Galloway also suggests that Deleuze's 'Postscript on Control Societies' entails a host of acceptances of conditions contingent to the control society. Within these conditions, amongst those suggested by Galloway,[10] should be appended design's allegiance to the production and consumption of numerical images.[11] We might also add to such conditions the sense that Deleuze's perception of the control society draws from William Burroughs's occult protocols of cybernetic control,[12] and the sense that it is within such conditions that vital and complex topologies of aggregation and disaggregation emerge. In this respect we should propose Deleuze and Guattari's own reference to the flows and counterflows of *Anti-Oedipus*. This recollection of *Anti-Oedipus* and its conjuring of new sensations affects and percepts, of a 'Burroughs experiment' (Deleuze and Guattari 1984: 370) with its a magickal, psychic and somatic effects, is a tendency that will be left aside for now but to which it will be necessary to make a swerving return to before concluding.

In *Cinema 1* (1986) and *Cinema 2* (1989) Deleuze makes occasional references to issues of technical design, referencing both descriptions of the apparatuses and informational concepts in designed devices and systems as well as occasionally employing technical terms from sceno-graphic design. For example, take the precision in Deleuze's thought in his choice of the term 'signaletic' (1989: 33) the precise effects of which 'remain to be determined' (1989: 265). This enigmatic, one might even say prophetic observation on the becoming of signaletic protocols of control suggests a familiarity on Deleuze's part with the cybernetic systems design term *signal*,[13] which, along with his own trans-semiotics of the Cinema books, provides an analytical and theoretical category of the technical media.

Deleuze and Guattari's expression of philosophy as a 'thought synthesizer' has already been encountered (1987: 343); this same passage allows us an insight into a precise expression of the design of a modular synthesizer: one expressive both of the synthesis of sound as well as the modulation of thought itself. Another design expression of this is the artist Martin Howse's 'blackdeath' noise synthesizer. This is the first open hardware[14] noise synthesizer containing the plague.

> Embedding epidemic and plague simulations amongst other data gen-
> eration algorithms for granular re-synthesis of incoming audio signals or

self-generated feedback, blackdeath represents a virulent yet highly control-lable noise/audio engine with built-in, switchable distortion. [The worm-code release . . .] offers a writhing, decidedly cut-up approach to contagion, sampling and feedback. (Howse 2013)

The 'blackdeath' synthesizer is the very model of a paranoiac electrical design: impossible to design without computers, manufactured from a file created with standardised software tools,[15] its performance embed-ded as a schematic layout and as parts lists capable of translation and inscription only by machines. It is a machine printed circuit board (PCB) in silk black silicon with mounted switches, inputs and outputs (also in black), simulating an abstraction of the black plague, the Black Death; it is a black-device, a black box[16] with which to process darkly, a dark interpreter of signals as noise.[17] It is designed by Howse as part of an ongoing series of actions investigating the immanence of code and mate-rial, which require a speculative hardware[18] to be designed. In this, and other of his hardware designs, Howse suggests a direct relation between software and substance, between hardware and the liberation of the forces of the earth or the Cosmos.[19] The design of hardware for Howse entails its continuity with a physical world. It demands the earth as an operating system: a world containing paranoiac-machines both under the influence of and influencing fields of electromagnetics, noise, sound and the body.

In Howse's practice, in what can be termed the 'Howse experiment', there is an affirmative, yet paranoiac, encounter with *design* and the technical media that allows us to exemplify the future affective possi-bilities of the signaletic. This takes the form of a speculative hardware, a hardware that can be defined as a technological object designed as a speculative relation with energetic flows. By designing such speculative hardware Howse joins forces with the schizophrenic flows of energy from which Gie was unable to free himself (Tausk 1992), and these allow Howse to connect to the paranoiac or miraculating machines of the earth. Speculative hardware thus expresses design's many allegiances to the combination and recombination of potent conditions and pro-cesses. It is in these conditions and processes that digital design becomes the expression of capacities in the modulation of materialities in the dataflow.

Objectile Redux

The new status of the object no longer refers its condition to a spatial mold – in other words, to a relation of form-matter – but to a temporary

> modulation that implies as much the beginnings of a continuous variation
> of matter as a continuous development of form. (Deleuze 1993: 19)

Deleuze's thought provides many concepts and variations on these as
alternatives to hylomorphism. That is, alternatives to the model of the
genesis of form as an imposition upon matter from the outside. One
concept in particular that is specifically geared to thinking the technological object for design ontogenically, that is to say as a becoming
or individuating difference, is that of the 'objectile': an object which
'no longer refers its condition to a spatial mold – in other words, to a
relation of form-matter – but to a temporary modulation', that is, to a
matter-flow. It is developed in parallel with Deleuze by the architect and
furniture designer Bernard Cache.[20] As a concept 'objectile' perhaps suffered from an initial over-use within architecture and its relatively privileged discourse on the computational, the numerical and the parametric
production of form.[21] This has led to the objectile becoming lodged on
the stratum of the architectural, and a once mobile concept is in stasis
to the extent that Cache has recently suggested (quoted in Frichot and
Loo 2013: 102) that what is now required is the pursuit of the objectile by philosophical rather than architectural means. Objectiles have
effectively been ossified as forms of disciplinary fabrication through
the simplistic application in architecture of techniques extracted from
Cache's texts, starting with *Earth Moves: The Furnishing of Territories*
(1995). Such stagnation has the unfortunate consequence of also rendering the objectile as determinate rather than being an expression
of the indeterminate. However, as an expression of design's capacity
for modulation – for this is the nature of its force – the objectile also
enables consideration of the workings of design in the ontogenesis of
technological objects.

The objectile enables design – and more specifically designing in the
form this appears in Cache's practice – to be thought and practised
ontogenically. That is, it is a concept for engaging with and driving the
becomings of digital design. This is to swerve around, but not to dimin-
ish, its importance as a concept for subject-object relations[22] and to
emphasise the objectile as a concept for design and the numerical image
and in the design of signaletic material. Neither should it be ignored in
our swerve that the concept of the objectile entails a changing status
of the subject as 'superject', as Deleuze suggests following Whitehead
(Deleuze 1993: 20).[23] Indeed, Cache subsequently notes of subject-
object relations that the difference between the concept 'objectile' and
the concept 'subjectile' is very subtle:

subjectile in French means the layer as basis for applying paint, so when one primes the wall before painting it means preparing the subjectile. It is a technical term, mostly used in industrial painting. However, the subjectile also refers to a redefinition of the subject. If one would consider the subject as a surface, then one precisely has the relationship between the specific technical meaning and the philosophical meaning . . . The terms subjectile and objectile are used to distinguish between open surfaces and closed surfaces. There is a strong difference between them since subjectile refers to surface and objectile to volume. (Cache quoted in Balkema and Slager 1999: 27)

However, for the purposes of this chapter objectiles will be considered simply as a way of conceiving 'technological objects'. As technological objects, plainly stated, objectiles relate to a set of things made up of software objects and hardware objects and entail the design of these soft- and hard-wares and their affects. The question Cache initially asked in *Earth Moves*, whilst creating continuities between media-based processes of designing and the fabrication of his furnishings for territories, was posed by asking quite simply: 'what is an object?' (1995: 89). Cache suggests that objects are already a 'set of things' and proposes that through its selection in frames any object has the status of simple image; that design with its 'different skills' works with such images as a 'cinema of things' (1995: 29). That is, an object is a set of things 'that industry conceives and fabricates and that we buy because they create use effects' (1995: 89).

Speculative practices – and Cache's practice as a software designer deserves this title – tend to run counter to normative and normalising design methods, those methods of standardising procedures that end up prototyping users and designers as much as their devices. In software design, if coupled with the speculative designing of paranoiac electrical machines, we find the kind of exceptions to normative laws governing use that Cache categorises under the heading 'consumption'. It is perhaps to such uses that Massumi refers when he describes the norm, somewhat pataphysically, as 'the proliferation of the inessential that comes when consumer choice interferes with design' (2009: 36–45). 'The purpose of the norm', Cache writes, 'is not to stabilize our movements; on the contrary, it is to amplify the fluctuations or aberrations in our behavior. Changes are the mode of the norm' (1995: 96). Cache's concept of consumption is that of Deleuze and Guattari – a desiring-production – a consumption which constitutes a field of forces where all production is recorded and across which all production is distributed by what appear to be 'miraculating machines':

> Conforming to the meaning of the word 'process', recording falls back on (*se rabat sur*) production, but the production of recording itself is produced by the production of production. Similarly, recording is followed by consumption, but the production of consumption is produced in and through the production of recording. (Deleuze and Guattari 1984: 18)

Cache enlists change as the condition of the norm for his reworking of this recording-production. He then offers a further five definitional headings for the objectile along with 'consumption'. These are production, representation, modelling, function and marketing (Cache 1995: 96–8). For marketing, which he links with forms of speculation as an uncertainty, he enlists the sense of an '*alea*' (1995: 98), or chance. Cache relates the predictable to this *alea*: from a non-human uncertainty to a choice between the *alea* of the open work of controlled chance (Pierre Boulez's work for example), an *aleatoric* indeterminacy (in the work of John Cage), or an aleatoricist randomness as the returned value of a variable number function. Nonetheless, even within these calculable limits an *alea* is apparently sufficient for Cache to enlist a 'state of fluctuation' giving rise to 'an ordinary object that may well entertain singular relations with the user' (1995: 98). Alternatively it is Deleuze's 'aleatory point', or the paradoxical element, to which Cache refers as this principle for design: 'the aleatory point which circulates throughout singularities' (Deleuze 2004a: 201). For Deleuze it is the aleatory point that draws chaos into a plane of consistency, a virtual that is no longer chaotic, and in which designing is the event of the actualisation itself; an aleatory point tracing an unfurling clinamen as a line of Aion, a pure becoming of 'proximate past and imminent future' (Deleuze 2004a: 74). Deleuze contrasts Chronos, the time of experience, with Aion, the paradoxical time of the combination of all pasts and futures. It is through such paradoxes as that of Aion, and that of nonsense and sense being co-present through Aion's precursory and premonitory anachronism in movements of pasts and futures, that Deleuze gives to philosophy pataphysical concepts. Take for example Alfred Jarry's neologism 'ethernity' (Jarry 1996: 100), which might, after Deleuze's incorporation of Jarry as conceptual personae,[24] become the seething, chaotic energy from which the cosmos emerges.

In his passage on the objectile in *The Fold*, Deleuze describes Cache's computational processes as a 'demonstration' of the objectile and thus: 'This new object we can call objectile. As Bernard Cache has demonstrated, this is a very modern conception of the technological object' (Deleuze 1993: 19). As but one demonstration it is clearly possible to provide of other versions. There is sufficient ambiguity in Deleuze's 'very modern' here to suggest that objectiles might be contemporary devices, current examples of the Baroque archetypes he enlists: a camera obscura, ceilings of painted skies, trompe-l'œil paintings, an infinite alignment of mirrors and their recursive pleatings and foldings. These are the Baroque devices preceding a generative aesthetic, devices in which a renewed interest in the corpuscular matter of Epicurean bodies, simulacral perception and philosophical objects came to figure in the regulation of boundaries between objects and subjects in the seventeenth and eighteenth centuries. These cunning designs of geometric curio-objects, perspective landscapes and architectural folds fluctuate, move and transform as perceptual screens. Similarly to such Baroque screens, Deleuze's 'modern' objects might refer to the paranoiac-, miraculat-ing-, influencing-machines of a twentieth-century thermodynamic and cybernetic modernity and the desiring machines of *Anti-Oedipus*. Here, in contrast to the Baroque world as theatre, in *Anti-Oedipus* everything in the world is instead a factory of machinic operation accelerating into the twenty-first century. Or equally, these very modern objectiles might refer to the cybernetic design of isolating black boxes – monads – of third generation machines that increasingly tend towards fabrication rather than fabulation, limiting rather than opening onto digital design's other speculative tendencies. Such speculative tendencies might be found in digital culture and generative design as tendencies towards the fantastic or the abstract. David Savat's (2009) essay on the objectile as a database form of modulatory control is helpful here at least in clarifying the objectiles's mediality. However, the nature of its modulatory power is not limited to the extent to which objects (and it follows subjects too) are 'no longer designed but calculated' using the numerical control functions of third generation machines (Cache 1995: 87), but instead, as we shall see, this modulatory power is that of a generation of machines with a rather more eccentric cybernetic genealogy. With this eccentricity in mind, Howse's designs for speculative hardware seem to fit the definition 'very modern' in the senses used here well enough. Furthermore, it would appear that the objectile is in urgent need of the modulations afforded by software running on just such a speculative hardware as that constructed by the Howse experiment. If the designing of the objects of a 'cinema of things' is to be productive of flows, breaks and interruptions, design will depend upon an operating system of exceptions. We might then re-pose Cache's question at this point, by asking once more, 'what is an object?', but asking it this time of the micro-temporal level of electrophysical media.

As Cache makes explicit, the objectile is an ontogenetic concept, one that he and Deleuze develop using concepts from Simondon and Bergson and one that does not distinguish images from things. Following Simondon, ontogenesis is a theory of the phases of being, the becoming of being in general. It replaces philosophical ontology as a preceding of ontology – what might be conceived as preceding or anticipatory of the ontological in ways not dissimilar, as we shall see shortly, to the ways in which pataphysics goes beyond physics and metaphysics, but nonlinearly and in reverse. For Deleuze, ontogenesis is an 'individuating difference' which must be conceived first within its field of individuation (Deleuze 1994: 252). Designing, then, is a becoming, an intensity forming out of its own field, out of differential intensities where problems without programmes only become visible through imaginary solutions requiring imaginary sciences. For Deleuze and Cache, designing technological objects proceeds according to Simondon and Bergson's account of ontogenesis as the actualisation of the virtual, in folding and unfolding procedures where access to problems and solutions can be achieved only discontinuously.

In returning to our questioning of the electrophysical object we can first recognise this object as ontogenetic modulation by accounting for it in Cache's sense of the object as a set or cinema of things. Such a cinema of things is in the unfolding of an object's dynamism. This unfolding unfurls across many sites and at a variety of scales including those beneath the threshold of human or cinematic perception, at the scale of the minerals as a sub-perceptual domain, at the infinitesimal dimension of matter. We can then give an answer to the question 'what is an electrophysical object?' – that it is the modulations of a cinematic set of things, it is in 'the modulation of the object itself' (Deleuze 1989: 27) designing across these sites and scales. The object so conceived constitutes those processes of individuation giving access to the teeming dimensions of the fold as electrophysical waves, in strata built up in micro-electronic aggregates of silica. An ontogenetic design *practice* in this context then is one that, as with the Deleuzian cinematic and the Baroque fold, entails different ways of involving movement and time in modulations of matter and in the artifice of following traits of expression. For Cache, this is in the framing of singular figures, what might be described as numerical screens or signaletic membranes. That is, as frames in the frequencies of movement-images, as topological surfaces and as volumes. If the subjectile is the extension of a surface topology, then at the micro-levels of electrophysical media, the objectile is a creative modulation of the volumetric stream of matter-flow.

In summary then, the significance of the objectile some twenty-five years after the event of its introduction is not a result of the production of architectural figures or of architectural fragments, building components, or of furniture design in the practice of post-Cacheian object creation. It lies rather in the expression of technical substances in processes of software design, hardware design and electronic design. With these preliminaries over, the objectile can now be further loosed from the stratum of architecture on which it has become lodged. By experimenting with the opportunities it offers, we might deterritorialise it further into/out-of code, accelerate its movement through both software and hardware. With this swaying and veering mobilisation of things and their infinitely varied dimensions in mind, the clinamen of this text now follows its own whim to swerve into other things that matter.

Clinamen

Anything that can serve as the basis for a relation is already of the same mode of being as the individual, whether it be an atom, an external and indivisible particle, *prima materia* or form. An atom can enter into relation with other atoms via the *clinamen*. It constitutes thereby an individual, viable or not, through the infinite void and the becoming without end. Matter can receive a form, and within this form-matter relation lies the ontogenesis. (Simondon 2009: 4)

In the Epicurean philosophy of Lucretius, the clinamen designates 'the smallest possible angle' (Motte 1986) by which an atom deviates from the laminar flow of the line of its fall through the void (Serres 2000). The deviance of the clinamen in the declination of its fall allows what would be the universal descent to death of all atoms to swerve into the teeming becoming of life. The clinamen marks the aberrant beginning of a world without cause.

Deleuze's conception of the clinamen, the simulacra and the perception of these and other aspects of Epicurean materialism in his work receives detailed and recent scholarly attention in Bennett (2013) and in Johnson (2014). Both of these authors provide a preliminary treatment of what Johnson terms the 'Deleuze-Lucretius encounter' (2014), however neither of them gives any attention to the supposed assimilation of the objectile to the atomistic concept of the clinamen suggested by Brian Massumi (2002), and it is primarily this that is taken up here.

The clinamen is a significant concept in mechanologist Gilbert Simondon's theories of ontogenetic individuation (Simondon 1992), and might be said to have swerved into Deleuze's thought as if a black atomic relation, as an inflection, as the becoming-modulation of the objectile. Bergson too engages the concept of the clinamen, and for him it is perhaps the refusal to reconcile materialism and mind. Bergson's *Philosophy of Poetry: The Genius of Lucretius*, a brief annotated essay on Lucretius' *On the Nature of Things*, provides his account of the Epicurean atomic theory of reality. With respect to the clinamen, Bergson suggests that:

> The human soul, like other bodies, is composed of atoms and subject to their laws. Its atoms also move naturally and inevitably by virtue of their weight as well as individually by virtue of their *clinamen*. When they move by virtue of their weight, the soul is passive and surrenders to their inexorable laws. But when they avail themselves of their faculty for deviating slightly by inclining to the right or to the left, the soul is active and takes advantage of its freedom. Finally, the soul will perish forever when death decomposes the body and frees its atoms. (Bergson 1959: 75)

Deleuze argues for a Bergsonism in which duration is in perpetual becoming. Bergson, duration and the clinamen intersect in his retrieval of the atomism of Lucretius, Gassendi and Leibniz. In Bergson's *Time and Free Will* (1910), *Matter and Memory* (1911) and *Creative Evolution* (1911) it is the background presence of eternally shifting cosmic matter, the irreducible swerve that folds time.

As has been observed briefly already there also exists the passing, yet insightful, comment by Massumi in a footnote to his *Parables of the Virtual* (Massumi 2002: 279–80, n.13) that the objectile might be assimilated to the clinamen. In this footnote Massumi provides what appears to be an extensive reference to the usage by Deleuze, both alone and with Guattari, of the clinamen. What is clear from Massumi's footnote and the brief survey of the concept undertaken in this chapter is that while Deleuze's introduction of the objectile comes in his work on Leibniz and the Baroque, the clinamen appears across Deleuze's project. This need to conduct a wider reading of Deleuze's work should not suggest a drive to form a homogenising unity of concepts, but rather to consider a fuller set of relations for any assimilation of the objectile to the clinamen.

In each of Massumi's references to the clinamen in Deleuze, the sense of Cache's account of the objectile is subtly reinforced, not as controlled chance but as the becoming of objects as a 'cinema of things' (Cache 1995: 29); that is, as a Simondonian and Bergsonian ontogenesis. Furthermore – to continue this brief review of Massumi's partial blind spot – the clinamen swerves into appearance as a proposition in Deleuze and Guattari's discussion of nomad science (Deleuze and Guattari 1987:

361), where they consider it a concept of an eccentric science. Other traces of the clinamen's fluctuating movement appear in the theses of the movement-Image (Deleuze 1986: 83), and it is of significance in the overturning of Platonism found in 'Simulacrum and Ancient Philosophy' (Deleuze 2004a: 291–320), where the clinamen is presented as a 'kind of *conatus* – a differential of matter' and 'by the same token, a differential of thought' (2004a: 306). In both *A Thousand Plateaus* and 'Simulacrum and Ancient Philosophy' the clinamen is defined as a becoming manifesting as 'neither contingency nor indetermination' (2004a: 306), as a unique movement in a 'unique direction in a minimum of continuous time' (2004a: 307).

It is certainly the case then, as Massumi intimates, that the clinamen has productive relations with the objectile in its conceptual development between the thought of Deleuze and the practice of Cache. Most intriguingly though, given Massumi's insistence that Deleuze 'adopts Bernard Cache's term "objectile"' (2002: n.13) in *The Fold*, missing from Massumi's survey is Cache's own explicit reference to the clinamen in his development of the objectile:

> Let us now return to the abstract functions of the frame. The frame selects a vector among a multiplicity of possibilities . . . vector to vector relations create action systems that are never simple. For action is in itself complex, as the vector is inseparable from a *clinamen*. (Cache 1995: 58 emphasis added)

Also missing from Massumi's footnote, almost certainly significant given Cache's preceding cinematic rendering of the objectile, is Deleuze's reference to the clinamen in *Cinema 1: The Movement-Image*:

> [the frame] does not 'terminate' the movement without also being the principle of its acceleration, its deceleration and its variation. It is the vibration, the elementary solicitation of which movement is made up at each instant, the *clinamen* of Epicurean materialism. (Deleuze 1986: 83; original emphasis)

In the temporal modulation of objectiles, in the continuous variation of matter of objectiles, matter is constantly exceeding its framing. If the clinamen can be defined by the framing of the fold that goes on to infinity, such a fold is the inflection that Deleuze says Cache names 'intrinsic singularity', Leibniz calls the 'ambiguous sign' and Deleuze himself 'the authentic atom, the elastic point' (Deleuze 1993: 15). The assimilation of the objectile to the clinamen then is that of the vectors of matter as excess overflowing: 'the vibration, the elementary solicitation of which movement is made up at each instant' (Deleuze 1986: 83).

The clinamen is a principle of ambiguity: it is the passing presence of a paradox, the ubiquitous creation of relation that repeats difference endlessly.

Whilst Motte, in chronicling the rehabilitation of the clinamen in twentieth-century continental thought, mentions neither Deleuze nor Simondon, he nevertheless declares Serres – one of Deleuze's known sources in *The Fold* – a 'Lucretian fundamentalist' (Motte 1986: 276). Motte's citation of Serres's account of the clinamen is worthy of reflection here, as it recollects Deleuze and Guattari's *eccentric* nomadic science:

> In the same way that the analysis of being produced atoms, the analysis of vectorial space produces the *clinamen*. Movement and rest are joined in turbulence, constancy and variation, life and death. There was perhaps nothing in all of Antiquity more accurately seen and stated. (Serres cited in Motte 1986: 276; original emphasis)

In *The Fold* Deleuze chides Serres for stressing not this 'turbulence of constancy and variation', but the importance of an 'architecture of vision' in the changing status of the Subject (Deleuze 1993: 21). In the passage in *The Fold* immediately following the introduction of the objectile, Deleuze credits Serres with suggesting a dynamism between the setting of a point of view for the centre-less subject in a 'world of infinity' and the status of the object as 'only existing through its metamorphosis' (Deleuze 1993: 21). In the metamorphoses of the clinamen described in *The Birth of Physics* (2000), Serres declares an isomorphism between the natural world and atomic physics of Lucretius' poem *De Rerum Natura* and a modernised negentropic nature inspired by thermodynamics and cybernetics. Massumi's assimilation of the objectile to the clinamen suggests in its isomorphism a topological continuity of Serres's view of nature, the clinamen operating as a complexifying temporal creativity, and the objectile as a designing modulation of a stream of variable matter. However, the earth, nature, is of course incomputable – as it must be for Cache and for all electrophysical signaletic design because it can never assemble its own elements into a whole[25] but instead coagulates into 'a pure multiplicity of ordered multiplicities and pure multiplicities' (Serres 1995: 111). Here Serres might as well be speaking pataphysically as well as literally of the clinamen, for what is required 'is the science of relations, of general links between atoms of different kinds . . . nature is formed by linkings; these relations, crisscrossing in a network' (Serres 1982: 114). From Lucretius' creation of *something by deviation* and the *deviation from a state of equilibrium* in the clinamen, Serres develops a kind of feedback system, a reflexive system capable of resisting 'disintegration, which is the whole of time, [and] operates by flux' (Serres 2000: 73). How could it be that the technological object might withstand such temporality? Are objectiles atemporal and universal, as Badiou suggests for the clinamen?

> The clinamen is outside time, it does not appear in the chain of effects . . . the clinamen has neither past (nothing binds it) nor future (there is no more trace of it) nor present (it has neither a place nor a moment). It takes place only in order to disappear, it is its very own disappearance. (Badiou 2009: 62)

But this is Badiou's error – the clinamen cannot be outside time. It is rather those forces of modulation within time, operating temporally as matter-flow, a negentropic and complexifying creative force. The objectile, as clinamen – as we have found previously in its sense of both ontogenesis in Simondon and Deleuze's Bergsonian becoming – is a becoming in processes of individuation and the teeming dimensions of the fold. It unfolds in the excesses of its unfurling frame. An ontogenetic design entails movement and time in modulations of matter, in traits of expression and in vortical waves. The clinamen is vortical – it is a vortex that operates 'in an open space throughout which things-flows are distributed' (Deleuze and Guattari 1987: 361). It would appear that the clinamen is that paradoxical negative entropy immanent to entropy. As such it is a temporal force: it is the growth of complexity and the production of novelty and innovation. The Lucretian world, the thermodynamic and the cybernetic world, might be 'globally entropic' but the world also contains certain negentropic 'swirling pockets' (Serres 2000: 124), variable streams in eternal flux, matter in temporary modulation, within which new sets of things form and create: objectiles. There are, however, other practices that might be implicated in the clinamen's swerve, and serve to further dislodge the objectile from its architectural strata and to recover it as a concept for design. These will now be drawn together in the entanglement of the clinamen and the technological objects of pataphysics: the science of solutions to imaginary problems.

Pataphysics

Pataphysics will examine the laws governing exceptions, and will explain the universe supplementary to this one; or, less ambitiously, will describe a universe which can be – and perhaps should be – envisaged in the place of the traditional one, since the laws that are supposed to have been discovered in the traditional universe are also correlations of exceptions, albeit more frequent ones. (Jarry 1996: 22)

The French Symbolist writer Alfred Jarry (1873–1907), or, more precisely, his fictional creation Ubu, King of Poland, founded the science of pataphysics in the late nineteenth century as the study of 'the universe supplementary to this one . . . a universe which can be . . . envisaged in the place of the traditional one' (Jarry 1996: 21). The science of pataphysics is described by Jarry in *Exploits and Opinions of Dr. Faustroll Pataphysician*, as investigating 'that which is superinduced upon metaphysics, whether within or beyond the latter's limitations, extending as far beyond metaphysics as the latter extends beyond physics' (1996: 21). In Jarry's plays, novels, poetry and speculative essays these proto-surrealist science fictions describe a variety of mechanical designs and contrivances. In *Clinamen Redux*, Motte suggests that it is via Jarry's literary output that the clinamen enters, or one might better say that it *veers* into, contemporary continental thought (1986: 263–81). Of particular interest for the remainder of this chapter will be the ways in which the careening movements of the clinamen intersect the designed artefact in the pataphysical machines invented by Jarry's fictional character Ubu. We shall return to one of these machines, *Clinamen*, the painting machine (Jarry 1996: 88), in due course. Indeed, across his philosophy Deleuze had recourse to a number of similar contrivances of the pataphysical, including for example the paranoiac electrical machines designed by the 'talented' Robert Gie. In their brief review of these in *Anti-Oedipus* Deleuze and Guattari cite the survey of fantastic machines conducted by Michel Carrouges (1954):

> Michel Carrouges has identified a certain number of fantastic machines – 'celibate machines' – that he has discovered in works of literature. The examples he points to are of many very different sorts, and at first glance do not seem to belong to a single category: Marcel Duchamp's painting *La mariée mise a nu par ses celibataires, meme* ('The Bride Stripped Bare by Her Bachelors, Even'), the machine in Kafka's *In the Penal Colony*, Raymond Roussel's machines, those of Jarry's *Surmale* (Supermale), certain of Edgar Allan Poe's machines, Villiers's *Eve future* (The Future Eve), etc. (Deleuze and Guattari 1984: 17)

Whilst these might be known better under a Duchampian sign as 'bachelor machines', what Deleuze and Guattari do not make explicit is that these machines – together it might be supposed with all of Deleuze's (and Deleuze and Guattari's) machines, indeed 'all machines' as Carrouges would have it – 'are first of all pataphysical' (Carrouges

1954: 44). These bachelor machines form alliances with other machines of desiring-production and the field of productivity. Similarly the pataphysical machines of designers, and those that modulate the designed artefacts of abstract culture, make fresh alliances between bachelor machines and the machinic phylum. The assimilation of the objectile to the clinamen suggested by Massumi is therefore tantamount to suggesting that, as technological objects or as cinematic sets of things, objectiles might first of all be pataphysical machines.

In its pataphysical treatment the clinamen is the principle of exception. As elaborated in Christian Bök's poetic work on the clinamen, it is a swerving principle: 'the atomic glitch of microcosmic incertitude' (Bök 2002: 43–5). The clinamen is ubiquitous, ambiguous and forms alliances or relations; as a principle of exception, a glitch rather than an inclination, the clinamen is deviance and difference.

For Bök, Serres and Deleuze, the Lucretian world is a swirling flux of things. This sense of a paradoxical entropy of clinamenic negentropy, rooted in the ideas of Epicurus and Lucretius, is the basis of theories of matter emerging in the nineteenth century. This theory of the diverse is claimed by Jarry, anachronistically, from the Lucretian materialism that undergirds Kelvin's theories in *Steps Towards a Kinetic Theory of Matter* (Thompson 2011). Jarry's anachronistic claim is made for pataphysics in his essays 'Concerning the Measuring Rod, the Watch and the Tuning Fork' and 'Concerning the Sun as a Cool Solid' (Jarry 1996: 100–6). Deleuze too proposes that the clinamen is the principle of the diverse, that it is a nonlinear and dynamic philosophy. For Deleuze, for Serres and perhaps for Bergson and Jarry then, the clinamen is matter and thought in constant motion and mutual generation. However, reality for Jarry's fictional character Dr. Faustroll is that which does not repeat but has an uncertain order. This might be expressed otherwise as the difference that is endlessly repeating.

Jarry's pataphysical machines are expressive of a nonlinear sense of the flow of time, as in the reversions of Aion present when 'the past created by the Machine when it returns to our Present and which is in effect the reversibility of the Future' (Jarry 1980: 114–21). Objectiles are similarly pataphysical time machines, their forms of design instances of the speculative, the becoming of laws of exception and the anomalous. And so design becomes a speculative branch of pataphysics, 'the science of imaginary solutions, which symbolically attributes the properties of objects, described by their virtuality, to their lineaments' (Jarry 1996: 22).

After Deleuze's brief essays 'An Unknown Precursor to Heidegger: Alfred Jarry' (1998: 91–8) and 'How Jarry's Pataphysics Opened the

Way for Phenomenology' (2004b: 74–6), Cache's question concerning the object and Heidegger's general question concerning technology swerve into clinamenic confluence. Deleuze it seems, in these two texts, is interested in asking pataphysical questions concerning technology through his creation of the schizoid personae Heidegger-Jarry and Heidegger-Ubu. Deleuze refers to pataphysics as 'the epiphenomena of a technological being' (1998: 92), to which we might add in a pataphysical pairing which might arise through such conceptual personae:[26] the milieu of the abyss-ethernity. Such a pairing would be a Heideggerian abyss of the cybernetic will to will, paired with Jarry's science-fictional neologism of ether/eternity as a cosmological doctrine of the technological world of pure becoming where whatever you will, you also will its eternal return. Within this abyss-ethernity, an abyss that exceeds metaphysics, Heidegger-Ubu would have that most kinetic of events, modern science, unfold in the technological. It is the technological that Deleuze has Ubu insisting upon as ubiquitous; 'anarchy is . . .', Deleuze (1998: 93) suggests, ventriloquizing Ubu, without the ellipsis but nonetheless inviting some addition; 'anarchy is . . .' in the ubiquity of the technological, in the clinamen of its becoming; the becoming of ambiguity and alliance. In such becomings Deleuze subsumes the thinking, the phenomenology, of the Heideggerian 'fat Being' of technology to pataphysics; he subsumes the thinking of the being of phenomena as the phantom of difference and its epiphenomena. It is epiphenomena that Jarry says the pataphysician studies: 'an epiphenomenon being often accidental, pataphysics will be, above all, the science of the particular . . .' (Jarry 1996: 22).

In turning towards the epiphenomenon, Deleuze suggests pataphysics as a means of overturning Platonism. It is 'the great Turning' he says, 'the overcoming of metaphysics' (Deleuze 1998: 91). In this he aligns his conceptual personae with Jarry's intention for pataphysics to exceed metaphysics in ways not dissimilar to the exceeding of physics by metaphysics. This does not so much *overturn*, however, as *accelerate* a suprametaphysical *deviance*. Nevertheless, viewed as an aberrant accelerant reversion, it is possible for Deleuze to 'consider Heidegger's work on technology as a development of pataphysics' (1998: 91). Indeed Deleuze suggests the adoption of the imaginary technology of pataphysics as the completion of metaphysics, or of its realisation in 'the outcome of metaphysics as planetary technology and a completely mechanized science, the science of machines in all its sinister frenzy'. Going further still Deleuze claims that 'Jarry's entire *oeuvre* ceaselessly invokes science and technology'; that Jarry's invocation of science and technology in the pataphysical is 'populated with machines and places itself under the sign of *Bicycle*. The bicycle is not a simple machine, but the simple model of a Machine appropriate to the times' (1998: 93).

Deleuze refers here to the frame of a bicycle for the connections it creates, a design for a frame that for Jarry is his simple model or design for a Time Machine.[27] In Jarry's 'How to Construct a Time Machine' (Jarry 1980: 114–21) it is the bicycle frame that is transformed into an altogether not so simple machine, a gyrostat; and it is the design of this as a frame, that of the gyrostat or gyroscope, which Jarry expresses as 'the transformation of a succession into a reversion' (Jarry 1980: 121).

Alongside such particularities as these, produced out of Deleuze's schizoid Heidegger-Jarry-Ubu, other encounters of a similarly multiple nature might be created. Following Deleuze's pataphysical genealogy for phenomenology to its logical conclusion, Alfred Jarry is henceforth to be recognised a precursor to the post-Heideggerian technical media theorist, Friedrich Kittler. Media theory (otherwise absent or occluded in Deleuze's writings) might then be folded into Deleuze's observations through other conceptual personae to the extent that it would be possible to employ – as well as the twofold thought of a Heidegger-Ubu – a schizoid Kittler-Ubu: the most Heideggerian of pataphysical media theorists.[28] For Kittler signaletic material is mineral and energetic, indeed, in 'There Is No Software' (1992) he declares that there is 'only hardware'. Kittler-Ubu's hardware is the design of a speculative probe-head: the becoming of a technological object, an objectile that can be assimilated to the clinamen; a speculative hardware, a creative relation between variables interrupting chaos, an eternal stream of vital materialities with the earth as its operating system. The clinamen might be taken here to be synonymous, for Kittler-Ubu, with an aberrant electronic difference Kittler himself would no doubt have discovered in his own engagement with electronic design through his construction of a modular synthesizer. Furthermore, in what might otherwise be considerably more oppositional, this is a concern he seems to share with Deleuze and Guattari:

> By assembling modules, source elements, and elements for treating sound (oscillators, generators and transformers), by arranging microintervals, the synthesizer makes audible the sound process itself, the production of that process, and puts us in contact with still other elements beyond sound matter. It unites disparate elements in the material, and transposes the parameters from one formula to another. The synthesizer, with its operation of consistency, has taken the place of the ground in *a priori* synthetic judgement: its synthesis is of the molecular and the cosmic, material and force, not form and matter, *Grund* and territory. Philosophy

is no longer synthetic judgement; it is like a thought synthesizer functioning to make thought travel, make it mobile, make it a force of the Cosmos (in the same way as one makes sound travel). (Deleuze and Guattari 1987: 343)

Such concern is for both the technics and the modulatory capacities of synthesizers: albeit that for Kittler the interest is with technical-media as material and for Deleuze and Guattari, in the above passage, it is with the synthesizer as paranoiac-, miraculating-, or influencing-machine and for its affective and intensive capacities.

In these constructive practices, and specifically in Kittler's physical construction of an analogue synthesizer in the 1970s – this tendency towards substance can be observed too in Simondon, in his construction of a television receiver in the early 1950s – we can sense concrete thought giving rise to the objectile as a concept. We might in fact now begin to refer to a Simondon experiment, a Tudor experiment, a Kittler experiment, as well as to a 'Burroughs experiment' (Deleuze and Guattari 1984: 370), as pragmatic design practices with electrophysical material. If this is an insistence in the mattering of media – that is, in designing modulations in the matter-flow, with the expressive traits of the structures and potentialities of matter as 'matters of concern' (Latour 2008) – then there arises an interest in how to design the softness, hardness and swervy-ness of the objectile. This interest is expressed well in Kittler-Ubu's double claim: first that 'there is no software' and secondly (and much more problematically) that 'design does not exist any more' (Kittler 1992). Each of these – software and design – has ceased to exist in the registers of the human-perceptible and appears now only in the modulations of hardware and in the temporal registers of electrophysical components.

Whilst there is no doubt much that might be set up in oppositional tendencies between Deleuze and Kittler, what needs stating explicitly here is that the modulation of hardware as objectile sets up topological continuities between biological life, memory and the modern technological object of technical media. The practice of designing speculative hardware – that is, the practice of the kind of pragmatic thought that designing is: a speculative production of the objectile – is to wrestle, to wrangle with code as a generative and asignifying material. This is a designing practised not as phenomenal inscription but as that from which hardware and signaletic material is constructed; speculative hardware designed as algorithmic-interface relations and connection-exception relations. Kittler claims that there is neither design nor software, but seems to suggest that we must go further still: for designing is the becoming material of the expression of technical substances; in continuities between technical and other images in signaletic material.

As much as he is a materialist, Kittler is also associated with certain tendencies within media theory towards an *imaginary* media that will need to be attended to: for what are pataphysical machines if not imaginary? Such imaginary machines as Gie's paranoiac machines, even Duchamp's bachelor machines or Howse's speculative hardware simulation of black putrefaction, must be conceived not at the level of identification but as part of a theory of consciousness. Such designs of speculative, imaginary and pataphysical machines are not distorted representations of real things but expressions of the exceptional and the anomalous. Pataphysical machines, bachelor machines and objectiles are sets of designed things that swerve through, career into, disrupt, cut and open-up new expressions of the real.

Following this it can now be said, without hesitation, that objectiles are first and foremost pataphysical machines. To say this is not only to confirm that one might approach the design of the technological object pataphysically, but also to suggest that in the ejaculate spasms of Jarry's pataphysical painting machine *Clinamen* (1996: 88), for example, one might find seeds of chaos. Such machinic pataphysical emissions plant the 'specific seeds' of Epicurean atomism (Deleuze 2004a: 307) in the various precursory registers of abstract culture. We will call this 'generative design'.[29]

Towards a Generative Design

> *Function*: a field of surfaces thus governs the object that has now become the set of possibilities of their intersection. But the surface of the object also becomes separated from its function when the latter is no longer mechanical but electronic . . . The shape of this new objectivity prolongs surfaces of resonance, whether screens or membranes, that restore the materiality of the numerical processes. (Cache 1995: 98; original emphasis)

Generative Design can be narrowly characterised as a software-based practice of digital design aware of the occultation of its own dependencies on the function of hardware; that is to say of the matter of abstract culture in its energetic flows and of the performance of its design in silicon and circuitry. Certain forms of generative design disassociate perception from our immediate needs and open it onto a universe of images and the flow of time.

In the chapter entitled 'Clinamen' in *Exploits and Opinions of Dr*

Faustroll Pataphysician, Jarry describes his machine, named simply *Clinamen*, as follows:

> Meanwhile, after there was no one left in the world, the Painting Machine, animated inside by a system of weightless springs, revolved in azimuth in the iron hall of the Palace of Machines, the only monument standing in a deserted and razed Paris; like a spinning top, it dashed itself against the pillars, swayed and veered in infinitely varied directions, and followed its own whim in blowing onto the walls' canvas the succession of primary colors ranged according to the tubes of its stomach, like a *pousse-l'amour* in a bar, the lighter colors nearest to the surface. In the sealed palace which alone ruffled this dead smoothness, this modern deluge of the universal Seine, the unforeseen beast *Clinamen* ejaculated onto the walls of its universe. (Jarry 1996: 88)

Jarry renders *Clinamen* as a painting machine which might be taken to be a symbolist apparatus for cinema's projection machines (Tortajada 2010: 97–114). Tortajada suggests that Jarry depicts a mechanical ecstasy in which *Clinamen* defamiliarises the then emerging physical means of projection. Clinamen deterritorialises *fin-de-siècle* engineering practices of the cinema as an imaginary symbolist painting machine, in the cinematic parallels between the fictional paintings Jarry attributes to his machine (1996: 97–114). In the 'deluge of the universal Seine' are painted Jarry's symbolist expressions of the matter-flow of 'blown' or projected cinematic images.

A pataphysical and generative design would actualise such a speculative hardware as Jarry's pataphysical machines. The modulation of exceptions, as pragmatic as the techniques of a Burroughs experiment, Tudor experiment, or Simondon experiment, would be its 'design methods'; the designing of images through functional equivalences; the arrival at solutions to imaginary problems in the unpredictability of the swerve or clinamen. This is not so different to the audiovisual practices of generative designers surveyed and collected in Hartmut Bohnacker et al.'s *Generative Design* (2012). This book contains numerous examples in which designing functions as a disruption of serial machines and as a modulation of the formless (chaos). For these designers the electrophysical is a ubiquitous difference that is endlessly repeated. This is expressed in both signaletic materialities and the temporalities enabled in the design of hardware.

Deleuze's Heidegger-Ubu might ask a question about technology at this point, researching by designing clinamenic probe-heads, problematising by drilling down to the metallurgical base of the silicon strata.[30]

This is what the developers of the generative design programming language and integrated development environment *processing* (Reas and Fry 2001) might suggest 'people doing strange things with software' do. But, as we have already seen, 'doing strange things with software' must already be a 'doing strange things' with hardware.[31] It is in such pataphysical *estrangements* of the technical media that generative design would be at its most speculative as it is mobilised from familiar to unimaginable forms. This speculation is expressed in the set of tendencies within digital design towards either fantasy or abstraction. For example, in the images by Field for SEA Design's *10,000 Digital Paintings* (2011), and Eno Henze's *Red Ambush* (2008) and *Subject Accelerator* (2008), there are surface-like, object-like, or form-like emergences[32] as well as tendencies towards naturalistic images of clouds and flows, of preturnaturalistic images of swarms or spectralities in ectoplasmic renderings of epiphenomena; the fictive materialities of the mercurial and the alchemical; of becoming-hybrid or -cybaroque and becoming-ecological or – to get down to the silicon – of becoming-metallurgical. These traits of exceptions are not software representations of things in the world, rather the signaletic material they contain are actualised folds designed into the hardware of the world.

The speculative hardware on which the designs of the generative studio runs, or executes, is found in a designer's set-up or 'rig'.[33] In these rigs, networks of components and modules, themselves the products of third generation machines, are put into relation with alphabets, choreographic notations, linguistic and scientific language-viruses, optico-acoustic intensities of the supergraphical and the hyperphysical. Such rigs can be configured by designers; can be modified to modulate the flows, cuts and stoppages of visual, sonic and physical syntheses. The conditions for these syntheses are modulated in designing modifications as framings. That is, in the framing or designing, assembly, dis- and reassembly of standardised modular – and therefore, highly refined and designed – technical objects. Through such a rig, design can approach the creation of certain kinds of exceptions that might be called breakthroughs: that which is termed the new. These exceptions arise in the 'continually producing production, of grafting production onto product' that is the design of paranoiac and desiring machines (Deleuze and Guattari 1984: 7). This is what Deleuze called the power of the new to remain forever new by 'beginning and beginning again' (Deleuze 1994: 136).

To conclude, the generative designer might follow the matter-flow of a clinamenic breakthrough in a practice sensitive to its traits of expression.

These include, but are not limited to, practices of patching, wiring, processing, sampling, hacking, bending and glitching.[34] For example, in the dataflow of *Pure Data* (Puckette 1996) the clinamen of an 'aesthetics of failure' (Cascone 2000) creates networks that molecularise and atomise, ionise optico-acoustic matter through sound, image and physical synthesis. *Pure Data*, *openFrameworks* (Lieberman 2005), *processing* (Reas and Fry 2001) and other programming environments favoured by generative designers reveal much in their naming. As thought synthesizers they are all approaches to the open. Another, named *Cinder* (Bell and Nguyen 2010), is the recent recipient of an award for innovation in advertising design.[35] *Cinder*: in whose dying embers time might form as 'crystal depositories sunk in ashes' (Serres 1982: 75).

In the design techniques of modular synthesis or dataflow programming, new worlds connecting software and electricity are made possible through the design of bespoke hardware controllers: hybrid analog digital interfaces attune connectivity between controllers; analogue effects units, oscillators, generators and transformers channel intensive frequencies. Generative design follows the expression of a creative production coaxed out of these intensive frequencies; out of the participation of the non-human in design, there is a production which arises as an exception. In designed software an exception is expressed at the seam of a failure or as a flaw in the way that something is assumed to function.[36] An exception then, a clinamen, is a certain kind of breakthrough of expression.[37] The breakthrough of the Burroughs experiment, for example, does not distinguish between the kinds of breakthrough of Raudive, tape recording or the paper cutup; the Howse experiment blurs instrumental and poetic distinctions in the breakthroughs of failure or leakage and in the detection of anomalies within processes of measurement and observation. These are, for the Burroughs experiment or the Howse experiment, clinamenic exceptions as expressive capacities across *spectral* contexts as well as the electromagnetic *spectrum*. In each of these experimental methods an exception emerges in recoded flows. This emergence is in the coding and decoding of flows in the organic and inorganic registers of memory and the transmission of these as new flows of energies.

Generative designers' rigs are configured (that is, they are tuned and designed) from technical, industrialised and machine-refined components. The potential for the handling of exceptions built into hardware enables generative designers to speculate within the exception itself to follow the expressive capacities of the anomalous. A generative designer operates within the singular and particular properties of the designed artefact for the multiplicity of exceptions that might be newly generated. The designer as pataphysician speculates on new laws governing such exceptions as these. As objectiles – for these are probe-heads of the pataphysician – these exceptions are volume-substrates creating isolated finite worlds, pataphysical machines of signaletic material designed to make cuts in the stream of variable matter. These cuts that the probe-heads of generative designers make, these processes of speculative artisanship within the traits of expression of the dataflow, are the viral pragmatism of the Burroughs experiment. In generatively designing with speculative hardware, clinamenic objectiles swerve and leak[38] through signaletic material and thus open the way for the breakthrough of the new. To suggest a Burroughs, Simondon, Kittler or Jarry experiment for design is to suggest a Deleuzian pragmatism in the designing of objectiles: a pragmatism for the design of technological objects. To design speculatively is to create pataphysical processes in the matter-flow, to make intuitive and generative cuts. This is the designing of an abstract culture in the foldings of the clinamen's negentropic deviances and its creative alliances.

Notes

1. Design Studies and Design Methods are recognisably distinct fields but are used interchangeably here. For example, see Horst Rittel's early work from the 1960s (Protzen and Harris 2010). For other notable proponents of 'synthetic' approaches see Jones 1970 and Simon 1969. Nigel Cross, current editor of the journal *Design Studies*, is notable in suggesting design methods research outside of straightforward science/art binaries.
2. It is of course to be acknowledged that teachers of the Bauhaus had wider syntheses than art and science in mind – take for example the preliminary course of Lazlo Moholy-Nagy who sought a synthesis of the senses: 'Man as construct is the synthesis of all his functional apparatus' (Moholy-Nagy 1922).
3. See also De Boever et al. 2012 and Combes 2012.
4. Norbert Weiner (1965, 1988) might be taken here as representative of a 'first-order' normalising cybernetics, where the 'second-order cyberneticians', for example British cybernetician Gordon Pask, might be taken as representative of an eccentric or aberrant cybernetics. For a broader discussion of the British cyberneticians, see Pickering 2010.
5. The use of the term 'simulacra' here is not to be confused with its use outside of Deleuze's thought – that is outside of Deleuze's dual use of the term found in the sections of 'The Simulacrum and Ancient Philosophy' (2004a: 291–320) subtitled 'Plato and the Simulacrum', and 'Lucretius and the Simulacrum'. The use in this chapter is with Deleuze's interest in the simulacrum as an Epicurean concept and where atoms are the limit of thinking matter and simulacra are the limit of thinking sensation.
6. See especially the work of Anthony Dunne 2008; Dunne and Fiona Raby 2001, 2013; and the critical overview by Malpass 2014.
7. See, for example, Bleecker 2009; Sterling 2009, 2013; Hales 2013.

8. Despite swerving around fictions the phrase 'abstract culture' can be taken to refer to the fictitious capital of design and material culture in its intersection with the imaginary science and remixology of sonic fictions and the many ways in which these fold and unfurl: 'in hip hop, science breaks it down in order to complexify not clarify' (Eshun 1998: 3), and in the 'double spooks of the world, the double of abstraction' is the construction of different matters into previously unimaginable relations. See Wark 2004.

9. Jarry suggests the inclusion of the apostrophe as part of the orthography of pataphysics 'to avoid a simple pun'. Following the College of Pataphysics the apostrophe is included here only once.

10. Those of the bioinformatics ecosystem: cybernetics, biological life, silicon.

11. 'If a modern reader thinks of a film projected in darkness, the film has nonetheless been projected. Then what about invoking numerical images issuing from a calculus without a model?' (Deleuze 1993: 27).

12. Deleuze never directly confronts cybernetics. In this he defers to Burroughs. The primary reference is likely to Burroughs 1971. *The Cybernetic Hypothesis* (produced by the Tiquun collective) refers to Burroughs 'mental manipulation' operations that were inspired by his 'cut-up' experiments, a combination of pronouncements based on the practice of interference, as 'Burroughs conceived it, and after him as hackers have' (Tiquun 2009 and no date).

13. See for example cyberneticist Norbert Wiener's 'spectrum of the signal' in Wiener 1942. Nam June Paik, for whom cybernetics is 'the science of pure relations, or relationship itself', cites Weiner: 'The signal, where the message is sent, plays [an] equally important role as the signal, where message is not sent' (Paik 1996: 433).

14. Open Source Hardware (OSHW) is defined as 'a term for tangible artifacts – machines, devices, or other physical things – whose design has been released to the public in such a way that anyone can make, modify, distribute, and use those things' (http://freedomdefined.org).

15. Kikad is an open source software suite for electronic design (the design of electronic machines, devices, or other physical things with electronic functionality). As well as kikad (the project management environment) the suite includes: eeschema, where schematic designs can be edited; cvpcb, where components specified to use in the circuit design can be selected; pcbnew, the PCB layout program for diagrammatic layouts; and the gerbview viewer.

16. A black box is a term given to a module that occludes its processing. Latour (1999) suggests that black-boxing is the 'way scientific and technical work is made invisible', that it is only 'inputs and outputs' that are visible in successful technologies and that internal complexities are paradoxically opaque and obscure.

17. That is, it simulates a scientific myth, as the material basis of the Black Death is an unknown. When played in Taipei, to accompany a presentation of a preliminary version of this chapter, whilst reading from *The Earth Moves*, accompanied by the sounds of the blackdeath synthesizer, the earth moved, affected by an earthquake of magnitude 6.2 Mw. Such are the frequencies through which the virtual is actualised. The next iteration of Howse's noise synthesizers is named the Dark Interpreter.

18. See the special issue of the *Digital Creativity* journal on Speculative Hardware (Hales 2015).

19. The components of computers are composed of the substance of the earth, silicon, copper and other minerals. This suggests that the cosmos could manifest its own computer.

20. Bernard Cache was a student of Deleuze.

21. See for example the parametricism of Patrik Schumacher, for whom the tendencies of continuous variation somehow also bear the traits of Platonism or at least the traces of a Neoplatonic mathematical interpretation of the ether: 'Parametricism differentiates fields', Schumacher (2008) claims, and 'fields are full, as if filled with a fluid medium', suggesting that this might be populated with furniture, presumably following Cache's 'furnishing of territories' with his own when he writes that 'we consider furniture not in terms of isolated objects but as pre-eminent space making substance'.

22. David Savat (2009) articulates this in relation to Deleuze's 'dividual'. See also for example Savat here: 'Technology is, as Deleuze stated, an expression of how we live. Technology expresses how we live our day-to-day existence and how we organize ourselves, in terms of both our relations to one another and the sorts of subjects we constitute ourselves as' (Savat 2012: 5).

23. Deleuze's brief comments regarding the subject-superject relate to Whitehead's *Process and Reality* (1978), but it is in his *Adventures of Ideas* that Whitehead directly confronts Lucretius' atomist cosmology: 'Atomic theory as adumbrated by Democritus, systematised by Epicurus, and finally explained in Epic shape by Lucretius. According to Lucretius the world is an interminable shower of atomic particles, streaming through space, swerving, intermingling, disentangling their parts, recombining them' (Whitehead 1961: 121–2). For a recent and thorough reading of Whitehead by a philosopher who is open to Deleuze and Guattari's thinking see Stengers 2011. See also Williams 2009; Shaviro 2009; and Massumi 2011.

24. Deleuze and Guattari write in *What is Philosophy* that 'conceptual personae carry out the movements that describe the author's plane of immanence' (1994: 63).

25. In the 'Simulacrum and Ancient Philosophy' Deleuze suggests the impossibility of bringing causes into a whole, but rather that effects refer to other effects in conjugations, affirming the independence of the plurality of causal series – the clinamen (Deleuze 2004a: 307).

26. Ubu is, for Deleuze, Heidegger's conceptual personae and, pataphysically, Jarry is Deleuze's.

27. For Jarry's obsession with cycling see Brotchie 2011, and Jarry 1999 for his narrative of the convergence of cyclist and machine.

28. There are of course others we might have considered here and certainly we might have worked with the Heideggerian Stiegler-Ubu for his concern with Simondon, technogenesis and mnemotechnics, or with a Zielinski-Ubu for an undeclared debt if not to Heidegger then certainly to Bergson's reflections on the depths of time.

29. The term 'generative' here in its computational sense is of course not new. See for example the 'programmed expressionism' of Manfred Mohr circa 1968, in which algorithms are designed to generate formal drawing machines thereby opening up conceptual spaces that would remain otherwise inaccessible.

30. 'As expressed in panmetallism, metal is coextensive to the whole of matter' (Deleuze and Guattari 1987: 411) and, regardless, silicon is metallic substance.

31. The debt here is to dorkbot – for all those people doing strange things with electricity. See also Goriunova 2012.

32. For a full description of such surface effects see Massumi's discussion of Gestalt psychologist W. Metzger's *Ganzfeld* experiments in Massumi 2002: 147–56.

33. The terms 'set-up' and 'rig' used here conjugate in the abstract culture of break-beat science as a modulation of matter – another lineage for generative design and the design of filters, valves and oscillators in traditions of dub that virally accelerate through electronic music: see Eshun 1998; Miller 2004; Goodman

2010. It is used here both to acknowledge the sonic origins of an *aesthetics of failure* (Cascone 2000) but also to recognise the increasing importance of customised 'desks' and controllers in contemporary audiovisual design practices and the viral contagion of these practices. Take, for example, the Monome controller and its relation with audiovisual software or in the hardware design contexts of postproduction; see for example the Davinci Resolve control desk by Blackmagick and its use in colour correction.

34. 'Patching' is the colloquial term, a skeuomorph of the physical patchcord networks of analog synthesizers, used in the visual programming dataflow environments MaxMSP, Pure Data and VVVV. 'Wiring' was the precursor to the Arduino hardware platform, the physical computing counterpart to the Processing software environment. The essential texts on 'hacking' culture are Sterling 2002 and Wark 2004. References to 'modding and bending' are to practices of circuit bending and hardware hacking; for its relation to the electronics of the Tudor Experiment see Collins 2014; see also High et al. 2014. The recent events 'Hacking the Barbican' (2013) and 'Disrupt NY hackathon' (2014) are illustrative of the virality of abstract culture infecting 'hackers, coders and designers' in exploratory software design and other contagious and 'discipline-bending' practices.

35. Innovation Grand Prix Cannes Lion award winner June 2013.

36. There are certain flaws, runtime errors, that standardised software design attempts to intervene in to prevent the perception of its use-effects: full system freezes and crashes.

37. The phrase 'a certain kind of breakthrough' used here can equally be taken to refer to the Breakthrough of Konstantin Raudive. See Raudive 1971.

38. The reference to leaking is to Burroughs: 'when you cut into the present the future leaks out' (2001).

References

Badiou, Alain (2009), *Theory of the Subject*, London and New York: Continuum.

Balkema, A. W. and H. Slager (1999), 'Bernard Cache: Inflection as Gaze', in A. Balkema and H. Slager (eds), *Territorial Investigations*, Amsterdam and Atlanta: Rodopi, pp. 23–40.

Bell, Andrew and H. Nguyen (2010), *Cinder*; available at http://libcinder.org/ (accessed January 2015).

Bennett, M. J. (2013), 'Deleuze and Epicurean Philosophy: Atomic Speed and Swerve Speed', *Journal of French and Francophone Philosophy*, 21:2, pp. 131–57.

Bergson, Henri (1959), *The Philosophy of Poetry: The Genius of Lucretius*, New York: Philosophical Library.

Bleecker, J. (2009), 'Design Fiction: A Short Essay'; available at: http://nearfuture-laboratory.com/2009/03/17/design-fiction-a-short-essay-on-design-science-fact-and-fiction (accessed 9 September 2014).

Bohnacker, Hartmut, B. Gross, J. Laub and C. Lazzeroni (2012), *Generative Design: Visualize, Program, and Create with Processing*, New York: Princeton Architectural Press.

Bök, Christian (2001), *'Pataphysics: The Poetics of an Imaginary Science*, Evanston, IL: Northwestern University Press.

Brotchie, Alastair (2011), *Alfred Jarry: A Pataphysical Life*, Cambridge, MA: The MIT Press.

Burroughs, William (2001), *Break Through in Grey Room*, Audio CD, USA: Sub Rosa.

Burroughs, William (1971), *Electronic Revolution*, St Louis, MO: Left Bank Books.

Cache, Bernard (1995), *Earth Moves: The Furnishing of Territories*, Cambridge, MA: The MIT Press.

Carrouges, Michel (1954), *Les machines célibataires*, Paris: Arcanes.

Cascone, K. (2000), 'The Aesthetics of Failure: "Post-digital" Tendencies in Contemporary Computer Music', *Computer Music Journal*, 24:4, pp. 12–18.

Collins, Nicholas (2014), *Handmade Electronic Music: The Art of Hardware Hacking*, London: Routledge.

Combes, Muriel [1999] (2012), *Gilbert Simondon and the Philosophy of the Transindividual*, trans. T. Lamarre, Cambridge, MA: The MIT Press.

De Boever, Arne, A. Murray, J. Roffe and A. Woodward (eds) (2012), *Gilbert Simondon: Being and Technology*, Edinburgh: Edinburgh University Press.

Deleuze, Gilles [1969] (2004a), *The Logic of Sense*, trans. M. Lester and C. Stivale, London: Continuum.

Deleuze, Gilles [2002] (2004b), *Desert Islands and Other Texts, 1953–1974*, trans. M. Taormina, ed. D. Lapujade, New York: Semiotext(e).

Deleuze, Gilles (1998), *Essays Critical and Clinical*, trans. D. W. Smith and M. A. Greco, London: Verso.

Deleuze, Gilles [1990] (1995), 'Postscript on Control Societies', in G. Deleuze, *Negotiations 1972–1990*, trans. M. Joughin, New York: Columbia University Press, pp. 177–82.

Deleuze, Gilles [1968] (1994), *Difference and Repetition*, trans. P. Patton, London: Bloomsbury Publishing.

Deleuze, Gilles [1988] (1993), *The Fold: Leibniz and the Baroque*, trans. T. Conley, Minneapolis: University of Minnesota Press.

Deleuze, Gilles (1989), *Cinema 2: The Time-Image*, trans. H. Tomlinson and R. Galeta, London: Athlone.

Deleuze, Gilles (1986), *Cinema 1: The Movement-Image*, trans. B. Habberjam and H. Tomlinson, London: Athlone.

Deleuze, Gilles and F. Guattari [1991] (1994), *What is Philosophy?* trans. G. Burchell and H. Tomlinson, New York: Columbia University Press.

Deleuze, Gilles and F. Guattari [1980] (1987), *A Thousand Plateaus. Capitalism and Schizophrenia 2*, trans. B. Massumi, London: Athlone.

Deleuze, Gilles and F. Guattari [1972] (1984), *Anti-Oedipus. Capitalism and Schizophrenia 1*, trans. R. Hurley, M. Seem and H. Lane, University of Minnesota.

Dunne, Anthony (2008), *Hertzian Tales: Electronic Products, Aesthetic Experience, and Critical Design*, Cambridge, MA: The MIT Press.

Dunne, Anthony and F. Raby (2013), *Speculative Everything: Design, Fiction, and Social Dreaming*, Cambridge, MA: The MIT Press.

Dunne, Anthony and F. Raby (2001), *Design Noir: The Secret Life of Electronic Objects*, Basel: August/Birkhauser.

Ehn, P. (1989), 'The Art and Science of Designing Computer Artifacts', *Scandinavian Journal of Information Systems*, 1, pp. 21–42.

Eshun, Kodwo (1998), *More Brilliant Than the Sun: Adventures in Sonic Fiction*, London: Quartet Books.

Frichot, Helene and S. Loo (eds) (2013), *Deleuze and Architecture*, Edinburgh: Edinburgh University Press.

Galloway, A. (2012), 'Computers and The Superfold', *Deleuze Studies*, 6:4, pp. 513–28.

Goodman, Steve (2010), *Sonic Warfare*, Cambridge, MA: The MIT Press.

Goriunova, Olga (2012), *Art Platforms and Cultural Production on the Internet*, London and New York: Routledge.

Hales, Derek (ed.) (2015), *Digital Creativity*, Special Issue: 'Speculative Hardware'.

Hales, D. (2013), '*Design Fictions*: An Introduction and Provisional Taxonomy', *Digital Creativity*, 24:1, pp. 1–10.

High, Kathy, S. M. Hocking and M. Jimenez (2014), *The Emergence of Video Processing Tools: Television Becoming Unglued*, Bristol and Wilmington, NC: Intellect Books.

Howse, Martin (2013) *Blackdeath Synthesizer*; documented at http://www.1010.co.uk/org/blackdeath.html (accessed January 2015).

Jarry, Alfred [1902] (1999), *The Supermale*, trans. B. Wright, Cambridge, MA: Exact Change.

Jarry, Alfred [1911] (1996), *Exploits and Opinions of Doctor Faustroll Pataphysician: A Neoscientific Novel*, Cambridge, MA: Exact Change.

Jarry, A. [1899] (1980), 'How to Construct A Time Machine', in R. Shattuck and S. Watson Taylor (eds), *Selected Works of Alfred Jarry*, New York: Grove Press.

Johnson, R. J. (2014), 'Another Use of the Concept of the Simulacrum: Deleuze, Lucretius and the Practical Critique of Demystification', *Deleuze Studies*, 8:1, pp. 70–93.

Jones, J. C. [1970] (1992), *Design Methods*, Hoboken, NJ: Wiley.

Kittler, F. (1992), 'There Is No Software', *Stanford Literature Review*, 9:1, pp. 81–90.

Latour, B. (2008), 'A Cautious Prometheus? A Few Steps Toward a Philosophy of Design (with special attention to Peter Sloterdijk)', in F. Hackney, J. Glynne and V. Minto (eds), *Proceedings of the 2008 Annual International Conference of the Design History Society*, Falmouth (3–6 September 2009), e-books, Universal Publishers, pp. 2–10.

Latour, Bruno (1999), *Pandora's Hope: An Essay on the Reality of Science Studies*, Cambridge, MA: Harvard University Press.

Lieberman, Zachary (2005), *openFrameworks*; available at http://openframeworks.cc (accessed January 2015)

Malpass, M. (2014), 'Between Wit and Reason: Defining Associative, Speculative, and Critical Design in Practice', *Design and Culture*, 5:3, pp. 333–56.

Massumi, Brian (2011), *Semblance and Event: Activist Philosophy and the Occurrent Arts*, Cambridge, MA: The MIT Press.

Massumi, B. (2009), 'Technical Mentality Revisited', *Parrhesia*, 7, pp. 36–45.

Massumi, Brian (2002), *Parables of the Virtual: Movement, Affect, Sensation*, Durham, NC: Duke University Press.

Miller, Paul D. (2004), *Rhythm Science*, Cambridge, MA: The MIT Press.

Moholy-Nagy, L. (1922), '*Produktion-Reproduktion*', *De Stijl*, 7, pp. 97–101.

Motte, Jr., W. F. (1986), 'Clinamen Redux', *Comparative Literature Studies*, 23:4 (Winter), pp. 263–81.

Negroponte, Nicholas (1975), *Reflections on Computer Aids to Design and Architecture*, New York: Petrocelli/Charter.

Paik, Nam June [1966] (1996), 'Cybernated Art', in *Theories and Documents of Contemporary Art: A Sourcebook of Artists' Writing*, Oakland, CA: University of California Press.

Pickering, Andrew (2010), *The Cybernetic Brain: Sketches of Another Future*, Chicago: University of Chicago Press.

Protzen, Jean-Pierre and D. J. Harris (2010), *The Universe of Design: Horst Rittel's Theories of Design and Planning*, Oxford and New York: Routledge.

Puckette, Miller (1996), *Pure Data*; available at http://puredata.info (accessed January 2015).

Raudive, Konstantin (1971), *Breakthrough: An Amazing Experiment in Electronic Communication with the Dead*, trans. N. Fowler, ed. J. Morton, Gerrards Cross: Colin Smythe Ltd.

Reas, Casey and B. Fry (2001), *Processing*; available at https://processing.org (accessed January 2015).

Savat, D. (2012), *Uncoding the Digital: Technology, Subjectivity and Action in the Control Society*, Palgrave Macmillan.

Savat, D. (2009), 'Deleuze's Objectile', in D. Savat and M. Poster, *Deleuze and New Technology*, Edinburgh: Edinburgh University Press, pp. 45–62.

Schumacher, Patrick (2008), 'Parametricist as Style – Parametricist Manifesto', presented at the Dark Side Club, 11th Architecture Biennale, Venice.

Serres, Michel [1977] (2000), *The Birth of Physics*, trans. J. Hawkes, Manchester: Clinamen Press.

Serres, Michel [1982] (1995), *Genesis*, trans. G. James and J. Nielson, Ann Arbor, MI: University of Michigan Press.

Serres, Michel (1982), *Hermes: Literature, Science, Philosophy*, ed. J. V. Harari and D. F. Bell, London and Baltimore: Johns Hopkins University Press.

Shattuck, Roger and S. W. Taylor (eds) (1965), *Selected Works of Alfred Jarry*, New York: Grove Press.

Shaviro, Steven (2009), *Without Criteria: Kant, Deleuze, Whitehead, Aesthetics*, Cambridge, MA: The MIT Press.

Simon, Herbert A. (1969), *The Sciences of the Artificial*, Cambridge, MA: The MIT Press.

Simondon, G. (2009), 'The Position of the Problem of Ontogenesis', *Parrhesia*, 7, pp. 4–16.

Simondon, G. (1992), 'The Genesis of the Individual', in J. Crary and S. Kwinter (eds), *Incorporations*, New York: Zone Books, pp. 296–319.

Stengers, Isabelle [2002] (2011), *Thinking With Whitehead: A Free and Wild Creation of Concepts*, trans. M. Chase, Cambridge, MA: Harvard University Press.

Sterling, Bruce (2013), 'Patently Untrue: Fleshy Defibrillators and Synchronised Baseball are Changing the Future', *Wired* (October); available at http://www.wired.co.uk/magazine/archive/2013/10/play/patently-untrue (accessed 28 November 2014).

Sterling, Bruce (2009), 'Design Fiction', *Interactions*, 16:3, pp. 20–4.

Sterling, Bruce [1992] (2002), *The Hacker Crackdown: Law and Disorder on the Electronic Frontier*, no place: IndyPublish.com.

Tausk, Victor [1933] (1992), 'On the Origin of the Influencing Machine in Schizophrenia', *Psychoanalytic Quarterly*, 2, pp. 519–56.

Tiquun (2009), *Tiquun 2*; available at https://archive.org/details/Tiqqun2 (accessed 9 September 2014).

Tiquun (no date), 'The Cybernetic Hypothesis'; available at http://cybernet.jottit.com (accessed 9 September 2014).

Tomkins, Calvin (1996), *Duchamp: A Biography*, The Museum of Modern Art New York: Holt.

Thomson, W. [1889] (2011), 'Steps Towards a Kinetic Theory of Matter', in W. Thomson, *Popular Lectures and Addresses Volume One: Constitution of Matter*, Cambridge: Cambridge University Press.

Tortajada, M. (2010), 'The Cinematograph Versus Photography, or Cyclists and Time in the Work of Alfred Jarry', in F. Albéra and M. Tortajada, *Cinema Beyond Film: Media Epistemology in the Modern Era*, Amsterdam: Amsterdam University Press, pp. 97–116.

Wark, McKenzie (2004), *A Hacker Manifesto*, Cambridge, MA: Harvard University Press.

Whitehead, Alfred N. (1978), *Process and Reality. Corrected Edition*, New York: The Free Press.

Whitehead, Alfred N. [1933] (1961), *Adventures of Ideas*, New York: The Free Press.

Wiener, Norbert [1954] (1988), *The Human Use of Human Beings: Cybernetics and Society*, Boston: Da Capo Press.

Wiener, Norbert (1965), *Cybernetics: Or, Control and Communication in the Animal and the Machine*, Cambridge, MA: The MIT Press.

Wiener, Norbert [1942] (1964), *Extrapolation, Interpolation and Smoothing of Stationary Time Series*, Cambridge, MA: The MIT Press.

Williams, J. (2009), 'A. N. Whitehead', in G. Jones, and J. Rolfe (eds), *Deleuze's Philosophical Lineage*, Edinburgh: Edinburgh University Press, pp. 282–300.

Chapter 7

Design, Assemblage and Functionality

Vincent Beaubois

By providing a concrete philosophy of artefacts as always being linked to the social, Gilles Deleuze and Félix Guattari's concept of 'assemblage' offers the opportunity of capturing the specificity of design: design does not consider the mere utility of objects but how they fit into a sociotechnical assemblage and participate in its maintenance. The aim of this chapter is to show that design is not simply interested in the mere interface between the object and the subject-user, but in the insertion of this item in a dwelling environment. In other words, in design, and according to Deleuze and Guattari, the object is always *in assemblage*. I will then show that the object, still inserted in a sociotechnical ensemble, is defined by the actual relationships it marks in its assemblage, thereby causing a redefinition of its functionality.

Design and Assemblage

Design should not be thought of as an aesthetic supplement to the technical object but rather as a shift in the way in which the artefact is viewed. To understand the specificity of design, one must not focus too closely on objects described as 'design' today (objects morphologically identifiable by a particular material and colourful sketch). Design cannot be defined by showing a chair by Eero Saarinen or Charles and Ray Eames; rather, the differences that animate it above and beyond craftsmanship and the simple technical production series of industrial premises should be taken into account. The classical history of industrial design, such as recounted by Nikolaus Pevsner, is not interested in identifying an absolute historical origin of design but in understanding what constitutes the emergence of this discipline: by identifying architecture and design, in *The Sources of Modern Architecture and Design*, Pevsner points to the fact that any artefact is related to the issue of dwelling (Pevsner 1968).

We do not only dwell amongst houses, but also amongst pens, tables, roads or clothes. As Reyner Banham and François Dallegret later stated: 'a home is not a house' (Banham and Dallegret 1965). Any artefact can materialise a home.

Design differs from other conventional technical production because it no longer perceives the object as the realisation of a simple utility or a simple beauty for individual use but is interested in the way objects create a dwelling technical and social environment. For example, William Morris, who spearheaded the Arts and Crafts movement in the late nineteenth century and was a key figure of British socialism, redefines a dwelling environment on the basis of an interrogation of its material conditions, with particular focus on the social organisation of technical production networks. Morris is interested in the status of the workers as they are embedded in their environment of production. Therefore, the objects produced by Morris and Co. are thought as polarising this environment. According to Morris, an artefact as mundane as a Sussex chair, produced by Morris and Co. between 1870 and 1890, is primarily the avatar of a production assembly (both craft and industrial). From this follows his theory of ornamentation: ornament is not primarily thought of as an aesthetic effect, but as a task endowed with dignity for the worker because it requires expertise. Ornamental forms are not justified solely by their decorative aspects, but especially by the recognition they bring to the labour of the operator: the pleasure of making rather than the pleasure of consuming (Morris 1901: 22).

This vision of emancipation of the labour of the worker, however, should not obscure the specificity of the approach: design does not focus primarily on objects but on a dwelling environment which then materialises in the form of objects. For Morris, producing a chair involves also producing the production system by which the chair is made possible. The Arts and Crafts movement, taking its inspiration from the guilds of the Middle Ages, placed the operation of design within the project of a community of labour, thereby defining its material conditions. Design does not *first* seek to produce beautiful or rational objects: it does not focus primarily on objects but on a dwelling environment which *then* materialises as objects.[1]

The purpose of design is not limited to a gross and passive materiality, closed on itself, but is rather characterisable, following Deleuze and Guattari, as an *object in* 'assemblage'. According to them, assemblage describes the space of an operation between different heterogeneous elements that define and transform each other (bodies, objects, languages, laws, and so on): 'An assemblage is precisely this increase in the dimensions of a multiplicity that necessarily changes in nature as it expands its connections' (Deleuze and Guattari 1987: 8). Assemblage focuses on the primacy of the relations prior to the formation of individuals. To think of objects as they perform in a dwelling environment is to think of the *assembling* effects of *assembled* objects. In order to incorporate this dual motion of the object into the environment and of the collection into the object one should consider the difference between a weapon and a tool as described by Leroi-Gourhan in his analysis of prehistoric percussion implements (Leroi-Gourhan 1971: 174–90), as well as Deleuze and Guattari's comments on this in *A Thousand Plateaus* (Deleuze and Guattari 1987: 395). Admittedly, they can distinguish a *weapon* from a *tool* in terms of use (destruction as opposed to production), but this category cannot fully account for 'a general convertibility between the two groups'. 'For ages on end agricultural implements and weapons of war must have remained identical' (Deleuze and Guattari 1987: 395). What is important in distinguishing between a weapon and a tool is the assemblage in which each operates, an assemblage determined by the formation of power of the social machine. We must understand the formation of power associated with a particular weapon or tool in order to designate it as such. However, in the absence of intrinsic distinctive properties, weapons and tools cannot easily be distinguished extrinsically: 'They have internal (and not intrinsic) characteristics relating to the respective assemblages with which they are associated' (Deleuze and Guattari 1987: 398), or, we may add, the assemblages with which they could be associated. Tools and weapons are both consequences and residues of formations of power in which they occur, and also support and consolidate the formations of power in which they operate. This is why they are said to be *assembled* and *assembling*: the context is no longer a fixed piece of data but continues to be transformed and consolidated by these very elements. The tool implies the organisation of work, while the weapon implies hunting or war, but, such organisation also implies these objects. The object is *assembled* because it differs (weapon or tool) depending on the assemblage (warlike or agricultural); but the object is also *assembling* because the weapon consolidates the warlike assemblage, in the same way that the tool consolidates the agricultural assemblage. The latter point reveals an object's capacity to transform the context, or rather to participate as part of a sociotechnical system in the co-creation of functional regimes that determine it, as well as the transformation of this sociotechnical field by these very practices. Therefore, technical reality cannot be said to differ depending on the 'context' in which it appears, but rather, given that it is always in assemblage, *technical reality is the context* (constantly changing). When considered from the point of view of their effects, technical machines cannot be dissociated from the social organisations that they enable and that condition them:

> That is why technical machines are not an economic category, and always refer back to a socius or a social machine that is quite distinct from these machines, and that conditions this reproduction. A technical machine is therefore not a cause but merely an index of a general form of social production: thus there are manual machines and primitive societies, hydraulic machines and 'Asiatic' forms of society, industrial machines and capitalism. (Deleuze and Guattari 1983: 32)

We never deal directly with a technical machine, but always with an assemblage involving a social machine. Furthermore, the interlacing between the two always involves a certain '*co-functioning*: it is a symbiosis, a "sympathy"' (Deleuze and Parnet 1987: 69).

Deleuze and Guattari will then extend the reflexions of Gilbert Simondon on technical objects (Simondon 1989) to the sociotechnical machine. Simondon defines a process of 'concretisation' of the technical object by its synergistic tendency towards greater internal consistency: 'The technical being evolves by convergence and by adaption to itself; it is unified from within according to a principle of internal resonance' (Simondon 1989: 20). According to Simondon, the various components of an 'abstract' technical object are treated independently and then juxtaposed with each other. They do not work in synergy. By solving its functional antagonism, the object becomes the site of an autocorrelation of its structure; it becomes concretised:

> The object causes and conditions itself in its operation and in the feedback effect of its operation upon utilization. The technical object, the issue of an abstract work of organization of sub-sets, is the theatre of a number of relationships of reciprocal causality. (Simondon 1989: 27)

According to Deleuze and Guattari, this concrete stage of an object that is physicochemically self-correlated to its milieu corresponds to the abstract stage of a sociotechnical apprehension of the object. Thus, in *Anti-Oedipus*, the Simondonian process of concretisation moves away from technical function towards the functioning of socius-related institutions. Deleuze and Guattari therefore describe the 'concretisation' of the State in its becoming-capitalist (with explicit reference to Simondon):

> As a machine it no longer determines a social system; it is itself determined by the social system into which it is incorporated in the exercise of its

functions. In brief, it does not cease being artificial, but it becomes concrete, it 'tends to concretization' while subordinating itself to the dominant forces. The existence of an analogous evolution has been demonstrated for the technical machine, when it ceases to be an abstract unity or intellectual system reigning over separate subaggregates to become a relation that is subordinated to a field of forces operating as a concrete physical system. (Deleuze and Guattari 1983: 221)

The State is concretised inasmuch as it is both a social and technical machine itself. Therefore, the right point of view for analysing technical efficiency lies in the relationships between the artefact and the collective.

The object still has traits not limited to its material properties but which bind it to a set in which it operates. The productivity of the object – in the literal sense of what it 'produces' – is not limited to its function of use, but resonates across the very assemblage. The object does not work just in a utilitarian way: functionality must be expanded so as to extend to all the effects it generates in and on a dwelling environment, thereby affecting the ways of inhabiting this environment. Thinking of artefacts in symbiosis with the socius, design redefines the notion of the functionality of the object and thus transforms the classical theories of the function of artefacts as they appeared in Larry Wright (1973) and Robert Cummins (1975) and in their contemporary commentators (Houkes and Vermaas 2010). These authors attempt to define an analytical concept of 'function' to explain functional statements particularly in the fields of technology. We will try to show how the opening of functionality in the field of design disrupts the very opportunity to forge such a unified concept.

Classical Theories of Function: Beyond a 'Hard Problem' of Functionality

The classic understanding of artefacts' functionality is maintained in a dualism. There are two incompatible ways to think functionality: either from the physicochemical functioning of the object, which defines its *technical function*; or from its *function of use* (Kroes and Meijers 2006: 1). The *technical function* corresponds to the causal role of an element of the artefact with regard to its overall functioning, and the *function of use* describes the purpose of the action that the object enables. For instance, the technical function of a refrigerator compressor is to increase the pressure of the refrigerant – the technical functions of the different elements define the technical functioning of the refrigerator (compression and expansion system of a refrigerant). This object's function of use, on the other hand, is to slow down the spoilage process, which reflects a strictly human concern. One function is physicochemical in nature, while the other is teleological.

Function theory differs depending on whether one focuses on the technical function or the function of use. Wright's (1973) and Cummins's (1975) theories represent the two poles of understanding of the functionality of the object. Wright formulated an etiological theory of function that refers to the theory of evolution by natural selection: the function of an artefact is the effect for which it has been selected. A refrigerator is socially reproduced because it keeps food fresh. Therefore, the etiological theory sheds light on the concept of the function of use of technical objects. It distinguishes between prescribed use and misuse based on an objective principle of selection.[2] Conversely, Cummins develops a systemic theory of the causal role of the function. This theory defines the function of an element by its causal role in an ensemble. Function is not understood in reference to a prior history, but develops its meaning in the current state of a system: if x is said to have a function F, this means that x plays a 'causal role' in the system that contains it and helps to create an effect in this set (Cummins 1975: 762). This theory perfectly characterises what we have referred to as the 'technical functions' of an artefact, namely the actions of the various technical elements of an object that update its overall functioning.

The current problem of these philosophers is the search for a ground of conciliation for these two definitions of the concept of function (causal and etiological). The problem of conciliating these two functional areas was recently the subject of a research programme entitled 'The Dual Nature of Technical Artefacts' conducted at the Delft University of Technology (Kroes and Meijers 2006: 1). Based on the opposition between etiological and systemic theories, the researchers in this programme placed this dual functional nature within the artefact itself. The description of a technical artefact may require two different conceptualisations at once because such an artefact is both a *physical object* (a wire is made of tungsten and has a length of 15mm) and *an object that is designed and produced for an end purpose* (a tungsten wire is produced for its electroluminescence). The object then becomes the site of a functional bias between an organised material and purposes at work in human gestures and intentions. Function appears in the object as a crystallised tension between two heterogeneous fields. If the overall aim of this research programme is to develop a coherent conceptual framework in the description of technical artefacts, it generates a dualism within the object. Houkes and Meijers even raise the hypothesis of a 'hard problem' in the philosophy of artefacts, much like the one encountered in the philosophy of mind (Houkes and Meijers 2006: 119).[3] This 'hard problem' formulated the idea that physical and teleological functions do not correspond without involving the idea of an arbitrary relationship between these levels (Houkes and Meijers 2006: 119). On the one hand, a same function of use can be achieved from different physical structures (underdetermination of the material basis as regards the uses that it enables); on the other, the same material basis offers several possible uses (underdetermination from the standpoint of the end purpose). Simondon, in *On the Mode of Existence of Technical Objects*, had already mentioned the non-correlation between what he calls the technical functioning and the use of the object:

> We can get the same result from very different functionings and structures: steam-engines, petrol-engines, turbines, and engines powered by springs or weights are all engines; yet, for all that, there is a more apt analogy between a spring-engine and a bow or cross-bow than between the former and a steam-engine . . . Usage brings together heterogeneous structures and functions in genres and species which get their meaning from the relationships between their particular functions and another function, that of the human being in action. (Simondon 1989: 19)

To understand this issue, we must return to its historical origins. This dualism between technical functioning and function of use is consolidated in the industrial organisation at the end of the nineteenth century by decentring the technical efficiency of the human body as operator. In a traditional craft society, the technical function is tied to the human being. A tool can only bring about true coherent functioning when coupled to the body of a human being, who in turn provides a flow of energy and information for conducting the technical operation. In this gesture, technical function and function of use are intimately linked by the body of the craftsman: the craftsman's own body proceeds technically while using. On the other hand, in the industrial era, the machine takes the place of the operator's body:

> Human being has played the role of technical individual to the extent that he looks on the machine-as-technical-individual as if it were a human being and occupying the position of a human being, whereas in actual fact it was the human being who provisionally took the place of the machine before real technical individuals could be made. (Simondon 1989: 81)

Industrial production decouples technical function – location of the machine – and function of use – location of the human body. The industrial machine no longer appears with its indissoluble link with the human body. The industrial object detaches itself from the corporeal halo, no longer appearing as an extension of the arm. Technical function and function of use appear in their heterogeneity.

However, the thought of Simondon does not seek to oppose these two types of functionality in a rigid dualism, but to understand their singularity and their modes of relationship. The problem of such a dualism and such functional fracture within the object is that it limits the life of the object to the simple interface with users, while the design is interested in all the functional resonances of the object in an assemblage, that is to say, in all its effects on the dwelling environment that it consolidates and affects. Design then accounts for a proliferation of functions. The term 'proliferation' comes from Deleuze and Guattari who use it to describe how an individual in a metastable situation with respect to its assemblage comes to be transformed by transforming the very assemblage:

> The development of the stratum into epistrata and parastrata occurs not through simple inductions but through *transductions* that account for the amplification of the resonance between the molecular and the molar, independently of order of magnitude; for the functional efficacy of the interior substances, independently of distance; and for the possibility of a proliferation. (Deleuze and Guattari 1987: 60)

This concept of proliferation is inspired by Simondonian thought. At the outset it is, in the words of Deleuze and Guattari referring to Simondon, a process of crystal individuation, a step-by-step formation around a germ in a rich solution of potential (Deleuze and Guattari 1987: 50). Proliferation reflects an operation of *transduction*, a process in which two or more incommensurable orders of reality resonate to become commensurate through the emergence of a dimension that connects them:

> Transduction occurs when there is activity, both structural and functional, which begins at a centre of the being and extends itself in various directions from this center, as if multiple dimensions of being were expanding around this centre. Transduction is the correlative appearance of dimensions and structures in a being of preindividual tension, that is to say in a being that is more than unity and more than identity, and that has not yet dephased itself into multiple dimensions. (Simondon 2005: 33)

The artefact, in relation to a sociotechnical assemblage, proliferates its functional meanings correlatively with respect to the relations that it establishes in this set. The concept of functional proliferation allows us to consider an effectiveness of the object that extends beyond its mere *utility*. It deploys a functional stratification of the object, acting on both the user and the various stakeholders of the object (manufacturers, dealers, repairmen, observers and so on), as well as all the elements with which it interacts (social organisations and relations, living beings, natural environment, identity, gender and so on). The term 'proliferation' is interesting also because it is the word used by Houkes and Vermaas, philosophers of 'The Dual Nature of Technical Artefacts', to describe the danger that hovers over any 'good' theory of function, where 'good' is synonymous with analytical categorical criteria (Houkes and Vermaas 2010: 388). According to them, a theory that allows an indefinite multiplication of functions would show a weakness due to the lack of a precise definition of its purpose. But this proliferation, of which design offers a glimpse, seems to be on the contrary constitutive of functionality and the way in which an object works and is worked in its insertion into an assemblage. Positioning oneself in this proliferation means no longer opposing the functional regimes seeking a principle of homogeneity, but making use of their heterogeneity (such as physical, social and economic effects) to understand how an assemblage takes on a consistency. To affirm the *functionality* of an object is to assert that it can always introduce new functions and produce new effects in sociotechnical systems.

Design and Functional Proliferation

To investigate the ways in which design makes an impact in this discussion, it is worth analysing the various regimes of functionality of a particular example, Raymond Loewy's Coldspot refrigerator from 1935.

In Loewy's design, the object is no longer the product of a technical function, nor the product of a use prescribed by this operation; it is understood as a generator of the dwelling environment. Its function is no longer confined to its material envelope, but expands within the sociotechnical assemblage in which it takes place. The Coldspot refrigerator was produced from an overall business strategy viewpoint, incorporating planned design refinements within an annual release cycle in a bid to encourage consumers to replace their current refrigerator at a time of economic recession (Lidwell and Manacsa 2009: 50–1). This attempt at enticement was achieved through the improvement of certain characteristics (ease of maintenance, user safety) as well as the development of an aesthetic and symbolic function of the object that redefined the role of its formal envelope. Loewy even admitted to having designed certain elements for facilitating the door opening action not only to increase the practicality of the artefact but also to provide a powerful advertising pitch, thereby creating a marketing and advertising function of the object:

> Another improvement was the 'feather touch' latch. This latch was designed so that a housewife with both hands full could still open the refrigerator by pressing slightly on a long bar with her elbow. In addition, it was connected by remote control to a small foot-operated pedal close to the floor. All these features combined made perfect advertising material for the copy boys and supplied the salesmen with great sales-talk features. (Loewy 1951: 128)

This attempt was duly rewarded by its commercial success: Coldspot sales increased from 60,000 in 1935 to 275,000 units in 1937 (Loewy 1951: 146–7).

The functionality of the object is not limited to use and technical efficiency, it includes all the effects the object generates: an advertising function through the show of the opening and closing of the refrigerator, but also an aesthetic function entrusted to seduce the consumer by its plastic forms. In this sense, Loewy identifies the objects he created with the movie stars created by Hollywood:

> Furthermore, it can be argued that Miss Grable's skin is really not a shield as such but a functional unit that serves the definite purpose of generating beauty, and therefore is desirable in itself. This shield, or housing, reminds me of a conversation I had, years ago, when streamlining was news. (Loewy 1951: 220)

The object works in different ways depending on the extent of the different affects it generates. The functionality of the object is no longer limited to the use phase but can incorporate other phases from the artefact life cycle as, in this example, phases of distribution and promotion. Moreover, the aesthetic function of such a streamlined object extends the purely visual effects of the object in a network of forms offering a unit style. Coldspot refrigerators weaved a network of formal referrals with various other streamlined artefacts – for example, Henry Dreyfuss's Model 150 vacuum cleaners (1935) or Robert Heller's Airflow fans (1937) – to define the aesthetic unity of a new mode of consumption. The generation of this design language consolidated a political and cultural function too, via the expression 'The American Way of Life' (which would become popularised during the Cold War). This amounted to a reversal of the use value by means of a symbolic value subject to fluctuations in fashion, reinforcing what is known as the 'planned obsolescence' of artefacts.[4]

The object is no longer just an item opposite the subject/user. The life and sense of an object is not confined to its use. Loewy's design is a powerful example, not for understanding the capitalist evolution of industrial design, but for apprehending the operation behind it. The object is no longer a mere object of use; its activity extends before and beyond the utilisation phase to encompass a multitude of stakeholders who become involved throughout its life cycle. The design of the Coldspot refrigerator includes a financial function for the Sears Roebuck Company, an advertising function for the seller, an aesthetic function for the ordinary beholder, and an economic function for the whole nation. Loewy places a lot of emphasis on the patriotic feature of industrial objects:

> And remember that for each man employed at the plant, there are three in the field: salesmen, advertising men, maintenance men, traffic and transportation fellows, warehousers and accountants, dispatchers and repair crews, electricians, statisticians, engineers, draftsmen, etc. That's another sixty thousand. If you add to that another two hundred and fifty thousand for dependents, you get a true picture. More than three hundred and twenty thousand people whose life is directly affected by the success or failure of what you put on paper. (Loewy 1951: 156)

Of course, before Loewy, all objects already possessed such effects, but the latter had yet to be designed as *functions* and were only technical production externalities. Design explicitly incorporates the systemic effects of the object within its specifications, acknowledging them as real functions. Thus, American Streamline design has established the difference between *products*, which are artefacts that are only perceived in a purely technical and functionalist approach, and *goods*, which are manufactured with the aim of being traded and sold before being used. The concepts of 'business strategy' and 'brand identity' were therefore unheard-of before the 1940s (Loewy 1951: 125). Thus the function of a consumer good involves both end users and company investors, with the latter developing widespread marketing, advertising and styling activities prior to the engineering phase.

For another example of functional proliferation we can look at eco-design since the 1970s, which has included the minimisation of environmental impact as a function of objects in their manufacture, use and recycling. By defining a heterogeneous multiplicity of functional regimes, design can therefore help us out of the 'hard problem' of the function. The concern is no longer to reconcile technical function and function of use within a unified theory, but instead to multiply the functional ruptures centred on the object. The aim is not to build a 'drawbridge' (Houkes and Vermaas 2006: 6) between different functional regimes but to assume a position in the rupture itself, to multiply breaks. The object is no longer the site of functional unity. It works in different ways in the dwelling environment that constitutes it and that it constitutes, as we have seen with the Coldspot example. This enterprise sets itself apart from the analytic philosophy of artefacts in that it does not focus as much on functional *allocation* (what *is* the function of this artefact?) as it does on the *creation* of new functions (designer's point of view: what *will be* the function of this artefact?). Deleuze and Guattari thus urge us to beware of dualisms by plotting a transversal path: 'The only way to get outside the dualisms is to be-between, to pass between, the intermezzo' (Deleuze and Guattari 1987: 277). What is meant by 'to pass between' when considering the functions of objects?

Functionality can not be expressed in the opposition of two functional regimes replaying both conventional poles of subject (use) and object (technical functioning). The *object in assemblage* must be understood as a potential functional creation, manifesting invention of new functional fields: technical, aesthetic, emotional, economic, mental, political, etc. To 'pass between' would then consist in demultiplying the functional regimes whose design is the operator. To position oneself 'between' does not mean unifying the differences but considering their coexistence. While contemporary theories of function (Houkes and Vermaas 2010) seek to bring into consonance the two functional regimes of the object, design displays a certain specificity: the object does not only function in a technical and utilitarian way, but also works aesthetically, symbolically, socially, politically, and so on. The aim is no longer to overcome ruptures but to multiply them.

The functionality of the object must be understood as a multiplicity of functional regimes working by rupture or synergy, changing as the socius changes. Houkes, Vermaas and Meijers do indeed begin to elucidate such a multiplicity, demonstrating that the object synthesises both a physical effect and an intended effect by supporting a purpose through use. Thus, these theories highlight two functional strata that should not be understood as being on opposing ends, but rather as plural and heterogeneous manifestations of the effects produced by the object itself. However, these two functional regimes are only the premises of a series that aims to apprehend the object as a functional stratification, functionality being the transversal path of such a heterogenesis. Positioning oneself within functional proliferation, for the philosopher, implies that one must stop thinking in dualistic terms by asking whether the functions are assigned to the object or by a human being, and position oneself in the middle instead, that is to say between the object and its environment, in its assemblage, in the relationship of recurrent causality linking, in the middle, subjects and objects.

A question arises over the specific position of the designer working from the very forces of the assemblage. Indeed, given that the proliferation of functional effects prevents a complete mastery of design by the designer, what is their role in such a process?

The Position of the Designer in this Functional Proliferation

The designer recognises new fields of action for the object and assigns a functional reality but cannot control the outcome of this operation. For example, while Streamline design makes the artefact into a fashion item with a planned obsolescence, the designer does not have control over the environmental effects correlating to the efficiency of the object with regard to failure or replacement (an ecological issue). If control of these externalities does not appear at first sight in the power of designers, it is from these externalities that they invest the new features of the object. Studying the object in assemblage, the designer focuses more on the multiplicities of functional opportunities than on the stabilised functions of the object. Design creates an object that cannot be reduced to its technical function because it includes, by functional proliferation, the capacity to transform the socius via this function. The relationships between the object and its assemblage are imperceptible at first, and then consolidate to form functions that are recognised as such by designers. To study an object with a view to grasping the meaning of its functionality is first and foremost to understand the object as being inseparable from its social organisation. The object cannot be studied in isolation but must always be viewed through the relationships it establishes with its physical environment, the individuals organised with and by it, and the social organisation that produces it and that underlies it (recurrent causality between the object and its assemblage).

To define design, Raymond Loewy, in *Never Leave Well Enough Alone*, considers a couple of Rube Goldberg's machines (Loewy 1951: 250). To Loewy, the famous cartoonist from New York was a 'poor industrial designer', and he took it upon himself to revisit two of Goldberg's machines, the 'Dishwasher' and the 'Self-Sharpening Razor Blade', to explain the operation of design. Here is how the 'Self-Sharpening Razor Blade' works: a gust of wind blows open a door and pulls a string attached to a hammer, which explodes a cap and wakes a sleeping cockroach that falls into a pail of water; the water splashes onto a washboard, causing a bar of soap to slide down, thereby releasing some goldfish; a hungry seagull swoops down on them, pulling on a string that starts the motor for sharpening the blade. One would expect Loewy to have revisited these bizarre and heterogeneous elements in a logical manner to create an opaque, smooth, streamlined and automated box, but in actual fact he did nothing of the sort. Admittedly, Loewy did integrate all the machinic elements into a synergistic whole, but his design did not do away with the cockroaches, washboard or seagull. Furthermore, it incorporated an additional patriotic dimension that was not found in the 1951 edition but shown later in the French 1963 edition, namely a tape recorder that automatically plays the national anthem when the blade is set in motion. The designer does not decide on the assemblage, but merely organises the overflowing functionality combining what Bruno Latour calls a network of humans and non-humans (Latour 2005: 72). It is no coincidence that Deleuze and Guattari included two of Goldberg's machines in the appendix to the French edition of *Anti-Oedipus* to complement their description of desiring machines (Deleuze and Guattari 1972: 464–5). The function is primarily a break-based function that generates effects on different planes. Although design is a process that seeks to grasp the *object in assemblage*, this does not mean that it is a design *of* the assemblage because assemblage consolidation starts off imperceptibly and is unanticipated. The designer does not know what will happen, but he/she knows that something will happen. He/she places the sociotechnical assemblage in this hesitation: between the desire for control and expectation.

Leaving the emerging sociotechnical process, the designer operates in this hesitation. He/she develops a specific viewpoint on the subject by extending technical efficiency to its social consequences, but the impossibility of anticipation due to the multiplicity of the forces involved defines their work as a social experiment. The designer, highlighting the different functional regimes of the object shows the artefact as producing unanticipatable effects. The figure of the designer differs from the image of the demiurge artisan, master of shaped material: their work is defined by the grasping of sociotechnical effects from ever new, unpredictable associations. If the activity of the designer is experimental, this experiment in the sociotechnical field would not own the designer him/herself, but the designed object transforming the dwelling environment and consolidating these transformations. It is not the designer who experiments, but the artefact which experiments with itself in connection with its assemblage.

This experimental dimension related to the life of the object in assemblage is attached to the possibility of a dysfunction always associated with the very functionality of the object. Dysfunction is the unexpected event that questions the stability of the functional regime. If dysfunction stops such a regime, it is not external to the functional itself. If Sears Roebuck uses Loewy to redesign their refrigerators, it is precisely because of the failure of the firm's economic function during economic recession following the 1929 crash. The aesthetic, symbolic and advertising regimes created by Loewy therefore arose from an economic dysfunction of the object, just as eco-design was born of environmental dysfunctions related to overconsumption and renewed obsolescence of objects integrated in fashion cycles. Dysfunction, far from being the negation of any functionality, is an explicit part of the sociotechnical sphere: it demonstrates the end of a functional regime and the emergence of a new functioning regime for the object. It is the index of new sociotechnical affects not yet perceptible as such.

Functionality appears to be *what we cannot escape*: while dysfunction may cause a function to cease, it does not necessarily mark the interruption of functionality. To dysfunction is to always redefine the relationship between different functional regimes; dysfunction calls for another way of functioning. The rupture of a functional regime does not leave the object in a powerless presence but suggests certain capacities and associated effects that were hitherto concealed. Functionality acts as a 'noise' surrounding the object, making way for new effects upon the cessation of an effect that is recognised as a function. An object cannot stop functioning or entering effective and affective relationships of transformation because it is always 'in assemblage'. In *Anti-Oedipus*, when Deleuze and Guattari initially assume that 'technical machines obviously work only if they are not out of order; they ordinarily stop working not because they break down but because they wear out' (1983: 31), it is only because they are imagining an abstract technical artefact that is separate from its assemblage and isolated in a physicochemical bubble. More precisely, dysfunction is not in the *crossing* – crossing from one regime to another still involves functioning, moving from one function to another – but in the permanent *superposition* of different regimes: the object is used while already operating as an aesthetic object that serves no purpose, or as recyclable raw material. The interaction between the various capacities of the object is the starting point for understanding what we call its functionality: functionality is always functioning and dysfunctioning at once, layering everything the object *can do* in an assemblage.

Conclusion

Deleuze and Guattari's concepts of 'assemblage' and 'proliferation' allow us to think the operation proper to design: to grasp an object always related to a dwelling environment that defines this object and is defined by it. The object appears as a functional node consolidating a sociotechnical assemblage. The object is not only designed as a simple passive material envelope for paths to intentions and human needs, but is thought of as being cross linked, organised in a dwelling environment thereby affecting forms of life inhabiting this environment. Thus, as being always in relationship with other objects and subjects in its assemblage, the designed object blurs the distinction between subject and object.

Although the classic examples like the Arts and Crafts' Sussex chair or Raymond Loewy's Coldspot may appear to be old and outdated compared to contemporary high-technology products, they do nonetheless reveal something fundamental about our time: design reflects a sociotechnical transformation of our ways of life. One major concern of this chapter was therefore not to relegate such old industrial design productions to a mere 'history of styles', but instead to draw on these examples to identify the underlying operations. The concept of assemblage enables functionality to traverse material and ideal sets, psychical and social sets. The functionality of an object is always multiple, following the different relationships of the object in its assemblage. A functional regime then appears as a 'refraining' (*ritournellisation*) (Guattari 1995: 16) of technical functionality, manifesting itself as an 'attractor' in the chaos of functionality. It is what maintains the unity of the object in its usage, compulsively repeating the same physicochemical effect or purpose of use. To assign a function is to assert the existence of a *stable* connection, whose stability cannot be explained physically but only historically. Functionality characterises the consolidation of this heterogenesis and design is directly concerned with this symbiosis, for better or for worse.

Notes

1. This utopian understanding of design is still valid when design becomes an integrated instrument of capitalism because its interest in social sculpture clearly resonates with a capitalist organisation seeking to rationalise social relations and their compatibility with the requirements of the market. The capitalist integration of the design object is precisely due to the interest in the social insertion of this item (Baudrillard 1981: 186).
2. Wright's theory is clarified and defended by Millikan (1984) and Neander (1991).

While Millikan and Neander only briefly mention a possible application of the etiological theory to artefacts, Beth Preston (1998) rigorously defines the function of use of artefacts by modifying the etiological theories to apply them in biology as well as technology.

3. According to the expression introduced by David Chalmers, the 'hard problem' of consciousness, in philosophy of mind, characterises the impossibility of establishing a strict correlation between the activity of neuronal processes and the subjective and phenomenal experience of consciousness.

4. The term 'planned obsolescence' comes from a chapter published by Bernard London in 1932 during the New Deal, entitled 'Ending the Depression Through Planned Obsolescence', from his book *The New Prosperity*. He made the observation that, as a result of the economic crisis, Americans were no longer in the habit of getting rid of their possessions before they were completely worn out, and that they were determined to keep their goods for much longer periods than predicted by statisticians, thus going against the 'law of obsolescence'.

References

Banham, R. and F. Dallegret (1965), 'A Home Is Not a House', *Art in America*, 2, pp. 70–9.

Baudrillard, Jean (1981), *For a Critique of the Political Economy of the Sign*, trans. C. Levin, St Louis: Telos Press.

Cummins, R. (1975), 'Functional Analysis', *Journal of Philosophy*, 72:20, pp. 741–65.

Deleuze, Gilles (1994), *Difference and Repetition*, trans. P. Patton, London: Athlone.

Deleuze, Gilles (1990), *The Logic of Sense*, trans. M. Lester and C. Stivale, New York: Columbia University Press.

Deleuze, Gilles and F. Guattari (1994), *What is Philosophy?* trans. Hugh Tomlinson and Graham Burchell, New York: Columbia University Press.

Deleuze, Gilles and F. Guattari (1987), *A Thousand Plateaus. Capitalism and Schizophrenia* 2, trans. B. Massumi, Minneapolis: University of Minnesota Press.

Deleuze, Gilles and F. Guattari (1983), *Anti-Oedipus. Capitalism and Schizophrenia* 1, trans. R. Hurley, M. Seem and H. Lane, Minneapolis: University of Minnesota Press.

Deleuze, Gilles and F. Guattari (1972), *L'Anti-Œdipe, Capitalisme et schizophrénie* 1, Paris: Éditions de Minuit.

Deleuze, Gilles and C. Parnet [1977] (1987), *Dialogues*, trans. H. Tomlinson and B. Habberjam, London: Athlone.

Guattari, Félix (1995), *Chaosmosis: An Ethico-Aesthetic Paradigm*, trans. P. Baines and J. Pefanis, Indianapolis: Indiana University Press.

Houkes, W. and A. Meijers (2006), 'The Ontology of Artefacts: The Hard Problem', *Studies in History and Philosophy of Science*, 37:1, pp. 118–31.

Houkes, W. and P. Vermaas (2010), 'Théorie des fonctions techniques: combinaisons sophistiquées de trois archétypes', in J. Gayon, and A. de Ricqlès (eds), *Les fonctions: des organismes aux artefacts*, Paris: PUF, pp. 381–404.

Houkes, W. and P. Vermaas (2006), 'Technical Functions: A Drawbridge Between the Intentional and Structural Natures of Technical Artefacts', *Studies in History and Philosophy of Science*, 37:1, pp. 5–18.

Kroes, P. and A. Meijers (2006), 'The Dual Nature of Technical Artefacts', *Studies in History and Philosophy of Science*, 37:1, pp. 1–4.

Krohs, Ulrich and P. Kroes (eds) (2009), *Functions in Biological and Artificial*

Worlds: Comparative Philosophical Perspectives, Cambridge, MA: The MIT Press.

Latour, B. (2005), *Reassembling the Social: An Introduction to Actor-Network-Theory*, New York: Oxford University Press.

Leroi-Gourhan, André [1964–5] (1993), *Gesture and Speech*, trans. A. Bostock Berger, Cambridge, MA: The MIT Press.

Leroi-Gourhan, André (1973), *Milieu et techniques*, Paris: Albin Michel.

Leroi-Gourhan, André (1971), *L'homme et la matière*, Paris: Albin Michel.

Lidwell, William and Manacsa, G. (2009), *Deconstructing Product Design: Exploring the Form, Function, Usability, Sustainability, and Commercial Success of 100 Amazing Products*, Beverly, MA: Rockport Publishers.

Loewy, Raymond (1990), *La laideur se vend mal*, Paris: TEL Gallimard.

Loewy, Raymond (1951), *Never Leave Well Enough Alone*, New York: Simon and Schuster.

Millikan, Ruth G. (1984), *Language, Thought, and Other Biological Categories*, Cambridge, MA: The MIT Press.

Morris, William (1901), *Art and its Producers, and the Arts and Crafts of Today: Two Addresses Delivered Before the National Association for the Advancement of Art*, London: Longman.

Neander, K. (1991), 'Functions as Selected Effects: The Conceptual Analyst's Defense', *Philosophy of Science*, 58:2, pp. 168–84.

Pevsner, Nikolaus (1968), *The Sources of Modern Architecture and Design*, London: Thames and Hudson.

Preston, B. (1998), 'Why is a Wing Like a Spoon? A Pluralist Theory of Function', *The Journal of Philosophy*, 95:5, pp. 215–54.

Simondon, Gilbert (2005), *L'individuation à la lumière des notions de formes et d'information*, Grenoble: Jérôme Millon.

Simondon, Gilbert [1958] (1989), *Du mode d'existence des objets techniques*, Paris: Aubier.

Simondon, G. (1961), 'Psychosociologie de la technicité', *Bulletin de l'École pratique de psychologie et de pédagogie de Lyon*, 3, pp. 197–238.

Wright, L. (1973), 'Functions', *Philosophical Review*, 82:2, pp. 139–68.

Chapter 8

Milieu and the Creation of the Illustrator: Chris Ware and Saul Steinberg

John O'Reilly

Don't forget to go out of the house every once in a while or you'll lose your source of pollination. (Clare Louise Ware (1905–90), from opening dedications to Chris Ware's *Building Stories*)

The first thing we see in the introduction to *A Thousand Plateaus* (Deleuze and Guattari 1987) is an image by Sylvano Bussoti. What might we think if we called it an 'illustration'? We could think that it is an example, a visual example of a concept, a second-order representation of an idea. We can think of illustration as an applied art that is generally commissioned and briefed, unlike the supposedly freely motivated product of the fine artist. There are deeply territorialised visual languages of illustration – from the highly confected surfaces of airbrushing, to the 'naivety' of unpolished drawing, to the 'folk' vernacular of woodcuts, to the figurative brushstroked watercolours of greetings cards – where technique is coded as message and on the plane of commerce consumption is coded as style. It is arguable that illustration exists/emerges at the point where the conceptual flows of Fine Art are contained and moated in recognisable craft form.

Yet illustration's forms of image making are not solely defined by being commissioned or briefed, and they are not really made to be seen on canvas, or framed in art galleries.[1] Illustration is created for: newspapers and magazines; children's books; billboards; textiles; packaging; wallpaper; wine labels; skateboards; CD sleeves; arms, legs and torsos as tattoos; moving as animation and computer games; emojis. Generally, illustration is figurative, representational and narrative.

Sometimes using the word *illustration* can be a little awkward when bringing it into conjunction with Deleuze's work. For these actions – figuration, representation and narration – are ones that Deleuze might be expected to interrogate as static or linear forms. The opening section of *A Thousand Plateaus* for example explores the notion of the rhizome as a map not a tracing. Furthermore, illustration is most highly visible as the visual form of memorialisation, of anchoring time through birthday cards, seasonal cards, as the surface of gifts such as chocolate boxes, as the visual language of the static – the image where the notion of 'experience', of birthdays and weddings, is when becoming is most heavily codified by illustration. At the same time, illustration has generated a whole sub-genre of greetings cards that mocks the traditional format through the expression of different voices.[2] Illustration is both an official 'vernacular' visual language, a minor visual language that evolved official functions, and the unravelling of that language through humour. Yet the word 'illustration', like its traditional role, serves a functional purpose, and this may take us away from these general conceptions of illustration. So at the back of *A Thousand Plateaus*, Deleuze and Guattari (or perhaps the editor) provides a 'List of Illustrations' within the book. In an interview in *Negotiations* Deleuze, describing the editorial furniture of *A Thousand Plateaus*, says that each plateau, 'has a date – an imaginary date – and an illustration, an image too. It is an illustrated book. What we're interested in, you see, are modes of individuation beyond those of things, persons, or subjects: the individuation, say, of a time of day, of a region, a climate, a river or a wind, of an event' (1995: 26). Illustrations accentuate the exploded nature of the book through individuations that connect each plateau to different milieus; and the seemingly simple figurations, representations and narrativisations of illustration's functional acts are themselves complexified by the milieus that they help create. Deleuze's account of illustration begins to make it more interesting, connecting philosophy to the creatively rich and odd things that illustrators create and engage with, and vice versa.

While illustration includes the world of greetings cards and chocolate boxes, it is also the world of Dr Seuss, of Heath Robinson, the animation of *Ren and Stimpy*, where the eccentric becomes central, nonsense a black hole that threatens to absorb all worldly order. While Theodor Geisel uses only 236 words for *The Cat in the Hat* (1957), and fifty words for *Green Eggs and Ham* (1960), the impact of such books comes through the relationship of word and text, in the rhyming, the *ritornello*, the experience of image, thought, word and sound together. Inna Semetsky argues in a paper on Deleuze and Education, that knowledge, growth and adaptation emerge from affective experience. She writes:

> For Deleuze, knowledge is irreducible to a static body of facts but constitutes a dynamic process of inquiry as an experimental and practical art

embedded in experience. Thus experience is not confined to a personal Cogito of a Cartesian subject but represents an experiment with the environing world: we can, and should, learn from experience. Experience is that quasi-objective *milieu* which provides us with the capacity to affect and to be affected; it is a-subjective and pre-personal. (Semetsky 2009: 443)

Semetsky highlights the individuation of experience given and provided for by the construction of a milieu; it is as affective as it is instructive, experimental as it is informative. The visual languages of illustration are so familiar, that when they are exposed by the illustrator, for example in *Ren and Stimpy* or Dr Seuss when sense and nonsense merges, it delivers an affective experience exposing the temporariness, the contingency of order.

In this way illustration gives social licence for chaos and disorder, and this licence allows illustration to play this out across all its everyday platforms of expression. Deleuze and Guattari give themselves a similar licence in *A Thousand Plateaus*, to play with the edges of the book, to frame the book in a way unfamiliar to the history of philosophy, but as readers we can have a tendency to seek out the content and screen out the signals at the edges: the 'illustrations', or even the dates and chapter titles which could belong to a science fiction novel or a comic. The titles of *A Thousand Plateaus* position the reader differently as they seek out a different sensibility to conventional academic work. Deleuze explains in an interview collected in *Negotiations*:

> The fact that each plateau's dated, given an imaginary date, is no more important than the fact that it's illustrated or includes proper names.
> But the telegraphic style of the titles has a force that goes against mere abruptness. Consider a sentence like 'Jules to come 5 P.M.' Nobody would want to write like that. But it's interesting how the words actually convey a sense of imminence, of something about to happen or something that's just happened behind our back. Proper names belong primarily to forces, events, motions and sources of movement, winds, typhoons, diseases, places and moments, rather than people. Infinitives express becomings or events that transcend mood and tense. The dates don't refer to some single uniform calendar; each refers to a different space-time . . . Together, these elements produce arrangements of utterance: 'Werewolves swarming 1730' . . . and so on. (1995: 34)

This imminence, something about to happen, is the book as 'event', the book as an affective experience. So while the often-cited notion of 'the end of the book', or 'the end of print' may convey little more than cultural drama, the fact is that the medium of print and the format of the book is surrounded by constantly evolving audio and visual technology. Deleuze recognises this, writing in 1968 in the preface to *Difference and Repetition*: 'The time is coming when it will hardly be possible to write a book of philosophy as it has been done for so long' (1994: xxi), prefiguring the affective experimentation of *A Thousand Plateaus*. Deleuze's description of this new kind of book ('Werewolves swarming 1730') is not traditional academic discourse, and is much closer perhaps to pulp cinema, horror, or – with the dates that do not belong to a 'uniform calendar but a different space-time' – sci-fi. Just as he describes the Nietzschean aphorism as a kind of 'intensity' (Deleuze 2004: 257)[3] it might be possible to call these titles 'intensities': they are not meant to be translated, or directly represent content, these titles take us elsewhere, they are a connector with an outside of philosophy, they are vectors heading beyond familiar philosophical territory.

So when Deleuze gestures towards an idea of what it might be like to do philosophy differently he is creating a milieu, an environment where a new image of thought, a new style of thinking, will live, adapt, connect with other living thinking. In social rather than philosophical terms this thinking will find/connect with an audience. It is partly that he conceives philosophy as invention, creating new conceptual forms and moments (or moments in/as forms), and it is also simply that traditional philosophical presentation appears to be no longer interesting.[4] In 'On Nietzsche and The Image of Thought', a 1968 conversation with Jean-Noel Vaurnet collected in *Desert Islands*, Deleuze muses:

> The search for modes of expression (both a new image of thought and new techniques) must be essential for philosophy. Beckett's complaint: 'Ah, the old style!' takes on its full significance here. We get the feeling that we can't go on writing philosophy books in the old style much longer; they no longer interest the students, they don't even interest their authors. So, I think everyone is on the lookout for something new. (2004: 141)

These new modes of expression using both new images of thought and 'new techniques' we have seen already at work in *A Thousand Plateaus*, and I will explore them further in terms of milieu and style in the work of Chris Ware and Saul Steinberg, two illustrators who have produced work that extends the idea of what it might be like to produce illustration.

Part of illustration's popular, easy, appeal is that, unlike Fine Art, it is always 'like' something. Its vernacular language is always recognisable, sometimes rendering that which was not previously recognisable familiar, either in political cartoons on editorial pages, or through the narratives of children's books, or sometimes though borrowings from Fine Art. Originality is a complicated issue for illustration, at least in the terms of Fine Art.

On the food chain of professional image makers, illustration has historically been caught in the middle between the commercial management of Graphic Designers who commission illustrators, and the cultural capital of Fine Artists who, even when responding to a commission, don't lose their status as Fine Artist – the aura of 'freedom' both in a creative and especially moral sense isn't erased by being commissioned. For the commercial purposes of such projects the client as well as buying the work is also buying for their brand (private or public) an association with the transcendent values of Fine Art. Beyond the content of the work, whether the client is a private company or a public body, they are purchasing the semiotic value of Art as 'Art'.

So for professional illustrators the issue of the future of illustration is felt keenly, not only in terms of the creative anxiety that this in-betweenness promotes, but also as a deep economic fear as they are on the front line of print publications determined to cut budgets. It appears that the innovation illustration offers the work of philosophy can be returned as the work of philosophy provides lines of flight for illustration to reconfigure its modes of thinking and doing.

In this chapter, therefore, I will examine Deleuze's notion of milieu in terms of the work of the illustrators Saul Steinberg and Chris Ware. Both Steinberg and Ware have made successful careers in traditional areas of illustration – cartoons and the graphic novel respectively. During his career *The New Yorker* regularly commissioned Steinberg for covers and individual cartoons, and Ware is frequently commissioned for covers and single pages within the magazine. But crucially, while professional illustrators deliver work using familiar codes of illustration, their illustration also interrogates a notion of milieu that challenges conventional illustrative forms of narrative. This notion of milieu is an incredibly useful tool for advancing an expanded notion of illustrator and illustration, of thinking illustration not just as representation, but as mapping played out in popular form that not only configures new lines and directions between image, book and world but helps illustrators understand the mobile and elastic characteristics of these entities – to think of illustration and illustrator as a practice of the contingent rather than the execution of visual formulae. Illustration as a discipline and a profession (not as a practice) is both extraordinarily conservative and anarchic, sometimes separately, sometimes at the same time. It can be fashionably empty, charmingly empty, culturally mobilised by its own circulation through being shared in blogs, pushed out by creative media newsletters and showcased in viral videos commissioned by brands – where illustration suddenly becomes content in videos of illustrators painting on the walls of galleries, shops and buildings. And of course illustration is a significant vehicle by which we are socialised in children's books, the latter being arguably the reason why illustration can still lay such emotional claims on us as adults. It is also so wedded to representational forms, as the accompaniment to text, that its function as visual support can become simply visual imitation of text. Jean-Jacques Lecercle makes a similar observation about nonsense (a key driver of illustration's anarchic sensibility from comics to cartoons to greetings cards) in writing on Deleuze and Lewis Carroll:

> I am struck by the fact that nonsense is on the whole a conservative-revolutionary genre. It is conservative because deeply respectful of authority in all its forms: rules of grammar, maxims of conversation and of politeness, the authority of the canonical author of the parodied text. (Lecercle 1994: 2)

One could extrapolate from Lecercle's observation the idea that illustration is the schizo-art par excellence, delivering imagery that's deeply respectful of the codes of the format where it is published, and often scandalously disrespectful of authorities in its satire, storytelling in children's books, cartoons, magazine and book covers, and the kind of viral advertising whose popularity is fuelled by an affective image, a visually affective concept. Yet there is something remarkably Cartesian about illustrators, and those who commission illustrators in the belief that visual thinking is goal-directed towards some 'clear and distinct' idea (the brief) rather than being process-driven, immanent and inclusive of the geography of contingency called 'milieu'. What makes the works of Ware and Steinberg significant images of thought for an illustrator is their openness to the adaptive contingency of a milieu, to its internal and external forces; their work becomes creative as it maps the ecology of space.

The Ecology of Milieu

One of the sources of Deleuze's conception of milieu is the philosopher of science Georges Canguilhem's essay 'The Living and Its Milieu', where he traces the evolution of this concept. Deleuze had taken a course under Canguilhem, and 'The Living and Its Milieu' was originally given as a lecture at the *Collège Philosophique* in Paris in 1946–47; it was then published in *La Connaissance de la vie* in 1952 (Canguilhem 2001: 29;

translator's note). It is not difficult to see why Canguilhem had such an impact. The opening sentence of this essay reads: 'The notion of milieu is in the process of becoming a universal and obligatory means of registering the experience and existence of living things and one could almost speak of its constitution as a basic category of contemporary thought' (Canguilhem 2001: 7). There were many intellectual currents running through French philosophy at the time, from the influence of Alexander Kojève's lectures on Hegel at the Sorbonne in the 1930s, to Sartre's *Being and Nothingness* published in 1942, to the necessity of taking up a philosophical position regarding the French Communist Party and the Soviet Union, to Sartre's criticism of Surrealism in *Les Temps Modernes* in 1947 and George Bataille's subsequent open letter to Merleau-Ponty in the pages of *Combat* magazine, edited at the time by Albert Camus. Yet, amidst the questions that animated French intellectual life, George Canguilhem wrote a paper that parked Hegelian dialectics and History as the generative motor of humanity, focusing instead on geography and ecology. Canguilhem tracks milieu from being an idea in mechanics and biology, to an idea that serves a function in the nascent discipline of sociology, to the moment where biology and geography and relationships between the organic and the environment become the product of each other. After his examination of these intellectual and practical currents from the eighteenth century to his present, Canguilhem brings the reader to Jakob von Uexküll's studies of animal behaviour. Von Uexküll's appeal is in highlighting milieu *as a relationship*, the relationship that guides the development of an organism and that complicates the boundaries of organism and environment. Canguilhem writes:

> The individuality of the living does not come to an end at its ectodermal boundaries, no more than it begins at the level of the cell. The biological relationship between the being and its milieu is a functional one, and as a result it changes as the variables successively change roles. (Canguilhem 2001: 19)

In this way Canguilhem maps out the evolution of a rich notion of milieu that has a source in the science of biology, but at the same time extends and transforms the biological. Milieu operates at an 'intra-cellular level' and, scaled-up, at the level of the organism – and it is the relation in-between. Canguilhem cites Jakob von Uexküll's theory of *umwelt*, the behavioural milieu of an organism, giving the example of the *umwelt* of the tick. The tick grows by extracting the warm blood from a mammal, and completes its reproductive function by climbing onto a tree and waiting for a mammal. The tick, sensing the smell of 'rancid butter' coming from the cutaneous glands of an animal, as well as its blood temperature, will fall and attach itself to the animal on a hairless area of skin (Canguilhem 2001: 20). Deleuze (1994) highlights the seemingly limited number of stimuli in the production of the tick's milieu: the attraction of the light in the sky that leads to it climbing the tree, and the smell of the animal that affects its drop. The animal and the human live as part of a milieu they create and by which they are created, and the relationship between the organic and the environment in a milieu is, according to Deleuze and Guattari, an immanent function of both art and nature. A song's refrain of goes to work in many different regimes of signs, from the love song to the religious, but it always synchronises with a land or a territory (1987: 312). The territory, argue Deleuze and Guattari, is the act that 'affects milieus and rhythms, that territorialises them' (1987: 312, 314). What appeals to Deleuze and Guattari (and Canguilhem) is von Uexküll's multi-layered vision of development that isn't teleological or purposive. This melodic perspective of the organism is a kind of biosemiotics (Buchanan 2009: 8). In *What is Philosophy?* Deleuze and Guattari write,

> every territory encompasses or cuts across the territories of other species, or intercepts the trajectories of animals without territories, forming interspecies junction points. It is in this sense that, to start with, Uexküll develops a melodic, polyphonic, and contrapuntal conception of Nature . . . The tick is organically constructed in such a way that it finds its counterpoint in any mammal whatever that passes below its branch, as oak leaves arranged in the form of tiles find their counterpart in the raindrops that stream over them. This is not a teleological conception but a melodic one in which we no longer know what is art and what nature ('natural technique'). (1994: 185)

A milieu is what sustains an organism, and is remade by that organism; each of the different elements of the milieu rearranges its relation with the others. The milieu locates a dynamic geography of the living: it is rhizomatic. In that felicity of language that does not communicate immediately in English, milieu is at once environment and middle, the middle without beginning or end. Milieu is the generator of multiple connections, and these connections form and reform the milieu. It is not a fixed context, the final origin of causality, or the 'ether' of causality. It's not a set of coordinates or the meeting point of a timeline. Milieu is climates, terrains, proximities and distances, organisms, and the forces and relations produced from the mobile geography of circumstance. Milieu is Deleuze and Guattari's conception of 'circumstance' (where circumstance in dictionary terms is seen as giving form to an activity or a thing), that is temporary, provisional and contingent. 'Geography', write Deleuze and Guattari,

> is not confined to providing historical form with a substance and variable places. It is not merely physical and human but mental like the landscape. Geography wrests history from the cult of necessity in order to stress the irreducibility of contingency. It wrests it from the cult of origins in order to affirm the power of a 'milieu'. (1994: 96)

It is mental just like the landscape created by the songbird. When a component of the milieu is extracted and deployed as expression against the chaos of forces, a milieu is territorialised, given a specific landscape, and subjectivity emerges. Deleuze and Guattari tell the story of the child in the dark singing a refrain, the song as an audio sketch of a 'happy place', marking a territory. Or the way the sound of television or music marks out a domestic space, a marking that is also semiotic, the house-wife/husband doing the ironing while singing or listening to music as they 'marshal the antichaos forces' of their work (Deleuze and Guattari 1987: 311). Territory and subjectivity are created simultaneously. Deleuze and Guattari argue that 'From chaos, *Milieus* and *Rhythms* are born' (1987: 311), and rhythm is the emergence of form. Rhythm is not the repetition of the same, or simply the attribute of a thing, but the relationship of difference between milieus. In this way we can think of space as composed not of static homogeneous elements but of blocs of heterogeneous space-time. Deleuze and Guattari suggest that when emergence is territorialised as expression, this is what we call Art.

> The artist: the first person to set out a boundary stone, or to make a mark. Property, collective or individual, is derived from that, even when it is in the service of war and oppression. Property is fundamentally artistic because art is fundamentally poster, placard. As Lorenz says, coral fish are posters. (Deleuze and Guattari 1987: 316)

Property, expression and art, as we will see, are the components of the milieu of illustrator Chris Ware's *Building Stories*. While I do not want to focus too much on Deleuze and Guattari's concept of the rhizome, one of the ways they highlight its operation is via milieu. It is important in relation to the notion of the book, the reader and, in the case of *Building Stories*, the notion of the image-maker. The rhizomatic aspect of milieu, and the milieu of the rhizome, is a more conceptually dynamic and material notion than, say, Derrida's intertextuality. While Derrida rejected the criticism that intertextuality was simply an operation of language, the word itself is anchored, rooted, in the notion of text. The way rhizome and milieu work together is to deterritorialise invested intellectual landmarks such as the notion of 'book' itself, with its roles of authors and readers. So when Deleuze and Guattari write that the rhizome 'has neither a beginning nor an end, but always a middle (*milieu*) from which it grows and which it overspills' (1987: 21), it transforms how we might think of the relationality of the book. It is not a question of an essential quality of the book, how 'open' it is for example, it is rather an issue of what the book activates and is activated by. Thinking of the book as a rhizome, as a middle and medium, at once both removes from the 'book' the sentimentality it has as a cultural artefact, and makes us consider the milieu in which it roams, connects and animates. This is why Deleuze and Guattari can say of the book (and especially *A Thousand Plateaus*) that the book is not an image or a representation of the world. The book creates a rhizome with the world, 'there is an aparallel evolution of the book and the world' (1987: 11). In the relationship between book and world the convention among readers and critics is to build resemblances between each other, to build on what's gone before. But the relationship is not a bridge between two static entities. Each is changed by the other. Deleuze and Guattari tease out this relationship of book and world, a relationship that is not simply imitative, with the example of a classic children's cartoon featuring an animal that illustrates the world.

> Mimicry is a very bad concept, since it relies on binary logic to describe phenomena of an entirely different nature. The crocodile does not reproduce a tree trunk, any more than the chameleon reproduces the colors of its surroundings. The Pink Panther imitates nothing, it reproduces nothing, it paints the world its color, pink on pink; this is its becoming-world, carried out in such a way that it becomes imperceptible itself, asignifying, makes its rupture its own line of flight, follows its 'aparallel evolution' through to the end. (1987: 11)

Book and world are never simply inside-and-outside to each other. When the Pink Panther paints the world don't ask what it means – it is asignifying – follow the line of flight, see where it goes and what it does. The child watching *The Pink Panther* waits with expectation for the swooning affect of the world becoming pink, when the screen itself is absorbed by and painted pink, when the chaos of the 'Pink Hole' liquifies the order of the conventional narrative, turning everything pink. The semiotic provides the structure of memory, memory territorialised on previous forms of anchored identity, whereas as the rhizome creates milieu, is anti-genealogical. This is one reason why Chris Ware's *Building Stories* is such a compelling book, driven by the territorialisation and deterritorialisation of memory.

Building Stories

Chris Ware is a US illustrator, born in 1967, whose talent was initially recognised by Art Spiegelman (creator of *Maus*), who commissioned Ware while he was still a student, for Spiegelman's highly influential RAW magazine. During the 1990s he began producing a series of experimental comics called the *Acme Novelty Library* and since 1999 has contributed regularly to *The New Yorker* magazine – *The New Yorker* remains the most prominent magazine to exclusively feature illustration on its cover, and extensively inside. The title *Acme Novelty Library* nods to the folklore of comics and cartoon culture – *Acme* is the generic name of a commercial corporation (mid-twentieth-century American capitalism?) featured by animator Chuck Jones in Warner Brother's Looney Tunes cartoons such as *Road Runner*. In *Road Runner,* the singularly bespoke products of the ACME corporation – the 'ACME Instant Icicle Maker – freeze your friends, loads of laughs', the 'ACME Earthquake Pills' or the fake holes – are bought by Wile E. Coyote to codify the rhizomatic Road Runner, who creates and erases 'road' as pure running, often as a cloud of dust.

In 2001, Ware's *Jimmy Corrigan: The Smartest Kid on Earth* won the Guardian First Book award, the first time a comic novel had won a literary prize in the UK. *Building Stories*, his most ambitious work to date, was published as a box-set of reading materials in 2012, elements having appeared weekly in *The New York Times Magazine* from September 2005 to April 2006, and nominated in the UK's Designs of the Year in 2014. It is this piece of work which explores storytelling as a *milieu* in the sense that is being developed here: an ecology of mutable elements whose shifting arrangements shift the notion of story as a sequence of moments in time to the idea of story as a geography of spatial bodies and arrangements, as blocs of space-time. *Building Stories* makes contingency the driver of narrative and story. Ware's epic experiment in the printed book, in thinking narrative as geography and ecology, as milieu, echoes our twenty-first-century digital milieu of storytelling. A milieu in which we pick up and aggregate information across different platforms, in different spaces: at our desks on our computers; on our laptops on the train; on our smartphones in a café; on our tablets while watching TV. In the introduction on the *Building Stories* box (posing the question of where a book begins) Ware writes: 'With the increasing electronic incorporeality of existence it is reassuring – perhaps even necessary – to have something to hold onto.' Ware's book is an analogue vision that disrupts but also connects to our experiences of digital, networked existence. There's a dark humour in Ware's work and one can only assume a note of humour in the description of a 'reassuring' corporeal object, for his book changes every moment it is selected, every moment it is set in motion in relation to each different booklet the book contains (I shall return to the 'contents' below).[5]

The notion of building a story nods to the idea that stories by necessity are always territorialised, are the territorialising of fluid circumstance, like the refrain sung by the child in the dark referred to by Deleuze and Guattari (1987: 311). Ware's *Building Stories* is about the fluidity of memory and memorialising, of past, present and future, and how these made and unmade as geography.

Each book in *Building Stories* creates a slightly different geography and map of reading – in this way it rethinks the book as narrative, re-imagining it as milieu. The books contained within *Building Stories* are heterogeneous elements, like a milieu with its mobile internal and external forces. While each book can stand alone, Ware's narrative blending of past and future and his reconfiguration of comic narrative construction – page spreads flow over double-pages, and simultaneously stand as single pages – serve to keep us guessing about the relations between wholes and parts. The surface of each page and each panel – with vector arrows often pointing diagonally to non-contiguous panels/images – is fluid. Like *A Thousand Plateaus*, *Building Stories* 'is made of variously formed matters, and very different dates and speeds' (Deleuze and Guattari 1987: 3). Again, like *A Thousand Plateaus*, *Building Stories* is a travel book designed with the various protocols of a more familiar genre – in the case of Deleuze and Guattari, philosophy, in the case of Chris Ware, the comic book.

One of two extended projects Ware worked on since 2000 (the other is his irregular series, *Rusty Brown*), *Building Stories* tells the story of an apartment block in Chicago as a milieu that makes us think about what happens as we build stories – how we add together different 'times' and 'directions'. 'Direction' is a useful geographical word that frees up the conjugation of elements we conventionally call narrative (though here we might call them 'points') and helps us get a sense of what storytelling consists of in *Building Stories*.

The front surface of the box is a collage of different styles and sizes of lettering that is worth describing in some detail. One might call it a cover, and it is, but it also problematises the notion of a cover as the exterior representation of the 'real' content that begins 'inside'. There are many different approaches to book cover design, and it depends very much on genre, but despite the design coding (or perhaps because of it) the book cover is intended to feel 'transparent', a window on to the interior of the book, onto its soul. In the case of *Building Stories* the cover is a map, not just of a space, but of the way to think about this space, or an introduction to how this space will both make you think and inhabit you. The image on the box is divided horizontally in half by a line of white space, and by an arrangement of shapes and angles giving the illusion (which is also real) of a divide vertically down the middle. There is a mixture of lettering and icon-style images framed in regular squares and oblongs: an eye; sky; a face; a baby; a wall; a map; a bee; a snowflake; an engagement ring; a finger on a buzzer; a woman lying asleep over the bedclothes; a book; a globe; a 25-cent coin; the corner of a room where wall, ceiling and door-frame meet. In the corresponding

Fig. 8.1 *Building Stories* Box Lid. *Building Stories* was first published by Pantheon © Chris Ware 2012. Reprinted by permission of Chris Ware and Aragi Inc.

four quadrants of the surface (whose image of the four quadrants is only as stable as the reader's perceptual focus) can be made out the words, 'B-u-IL-ding S-TO-R-I-e-S' (Fig. 8.1). This map introduces us to the world of the combinatory, of text and image – the letters 'ding' for example are white serif letters on a blue background with a little blue electric flash connecting to a finger on a bell underneath. A world where the conventions of language are there to be broken down, where we can hear the sounds of language breaking, and listen to what this breaking might say in its becoming broken.

The basic visual language of illustration is traditionally the addition of an image to the text that has already been created by a writer; in this way the image is a visual 'example' or extension of the text. Ware turns the words into image, breaking down the words then adding them together to see what it might sound like as an image: B-u-IL-ding S-TO-R-I-e-S. For Deleuze this is 'creative stammering' (1995: 44): the semiotic regime broken up and become multiple, a series of visual additions and non-textual relations, the central meaning-delivering authority of a title become eccentric, fluttering in and out of nonsense:

> AND isn't even a specific conjunction or relation, it brings in all relations, there are as many relations as ANDS, AND doesn't just upset all relations, it upsets being, the verb . . . and soon. AND, 'and . . . and . . . and . . .' is precisely a creative stammering, a foreign use of language, as opposed to a conformist and dominant use based on the verb 'to be'. (Deleuze 1995: 44)

This brief, titular eccentricity could be termed 'transcoding'. The name of the work becomes multiple and different, like the 'and . . . and . . . and . . .' of the boards, books and comics inside the box. The surface of the box is an interface, a map, training the reader in the visual, material and spatial languages of the milieu inside: the unconventional relationships between word and image, the improvised and discontinuous connections between narratives, and the nonlinear approach to reading that these require. Through the creation of milieu as book and book as milieu, Ware reimagines the possibilities of illustration, as well as of writing and the moments of their interaction. This is what a new kind of book might sound and look like: B-u-IL-ding S-TO-R-I-e-S. The challenge of *Building Stories* as a rhizomatic book, one that deforms and reforms on each occasion of reading, is its encounter with the notion of memory. On the one hand this is a book about someone recalling her life through the medium of an apartment building. On the other hand conceiving the book as milieu in Deleuzian terms means that on each occasion of reading, previous narrative relationships are always being configured in a different way. 'There is no difference between what a book talks about and how it is made. Therefore a book also has no object', write Deleuze and Guattari (1987: 4): the point is not to ask what a book means, but what it does, what and how it connects with other objects. The central character (a former art student) appears on the cover of one of the books, writing the story that is *Building Stories*. As Ware explained to *Publisher's Weekly*:

> the main character is doing these stories for a creative writing class and those stories are part of the stories she's written for the class. She's used the building as a character itself and its sort of this self-conscious way for her to get inside of it. I left it very vague. I didn't make it super explicit, which is probably a mistake. It's not necessary to the understanding of the story. But I think anybody who's read *Pale Fire* by Nabokov eventually ends up wanting to make a book where the book is the reason for its own existence. (Reid 2012)

This sense of the book as experiment and generator of experience rather than meaning is the driving impulse of *Building Stories*. The book as the entity that is writing itself, that is building its own story. The book is not simply a book-as-object, a book constructed from different objects; the story of the book itself is a diagram, a plan, of the book as object. Such a book has to rethink the 'contents' page as a map – or at least the concept of a map – to help the reader navigate the creative opportunities it contains, to reconsider the chronology of the contents page, to rethink the predictive power of the 'contents' page, to rethink chronology. *Building Stories* helps us re-imagine the book as an affective machine that channels materials into sensation.

So the back of the *Building Stories* box features advice and a diagram of how the reader might put together contents: 'A pictographic listing of all 14 items (260 pages total) appears below, with suggestions made as to appropriate places to set down, forget or completely lose any number of its contents within the walls of an average well-appointed home' (Fig. 8.2). Each of the differently sized print formats that make up the contents of the book is pictured in the diagram, with dotted lines linking to a wireframe architectural drawing of a house. Via the dotted lines each print object is connected to a particular room, to an imaginary milieu where the reader can experience reading the story of a building that is built (and destroyed) differently each time the print formats are read in a different relation. A book might offer us different kinds of experiences of its contents and we might want to find different places to access these

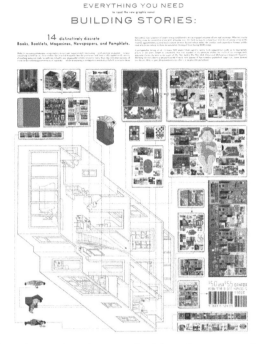

Fig 8.2 *Building Stories* Box Bottom. *Building Stories* was first published by Pantheon © Chris Ware 2012. Reprinted by permission of Chris Ware and Aragi Inc.

contents. Or as an experiment in what it is to experience this book we might want to forget it, lose it, to discover an untimely book. The map of an experimental book may then become a map of forgetfulness, in the way Deleuze and Guattari value the power of forgetting as espoused by Nietzsche. 'Nietzsche opposes history not to the eternal but to the subhistorical or superhistorical', they write: 'the Untimely, which is another name for haecceity, becoming, the innocence of becoming (in other words, forgetting as opposed to memory, geography as opposed to history, the map as opposed to the tracing, the rhizome as opposed to arborescence)' (1987: 296). This map does not define the contents of a book as a sequence of/in time, or as anterior to the experience of the book standing as some transcendent system of organisation, but distributes the contents as virtual possibilities that can be made differently through each reading.

Deleuze and Guattari write: 'the diagrammatic or abstract machine does not function to represent, even something real, but rather constructs a real that is yet to come, a new type of reality. Thus when it constitutes points of creation or potentiality it does not stand outside history but is instead always "prior to" history' (1987: 142). With countless possibilities to form and reform content, the map of the barely contained explosion of a book that is B-u-IL-ding S-TO-R-I-e-S opens itself up to the possibilities of its own re-creation, by developing the mutually creative relationship between the milieus and contents it generates. It is untimely and diagrammatic, oscillating between its aesthetic expression and its figuring, between the possibilities that occur now, and those yet to come. Ware's use of the diagrammatic, which appears throughout the different books, functions both as content that directs and organises information and as a graphic that undermines realism and narrative continuity, a visual eruption halting any attempt at chronological momentum of the narrative. Reading the book each time means holding in suspense, or partially forgetting, the previous arrangement of the story. In this way *Building Stories* is a diagrammatic process of production and destruction, of time and milieu.

In her 2011 essay, 'A Line with Variable Direction, which Traces No Contour, and Delimits No Form',[6] Susanne Leeb highlights two kinds of diagrams, the retrospective and the projective. The retrospective diagram visually systematises a particular thought process and establishes a sequence of relations, causalities and hierarchies. The projective diagram 'is rather the structural possibility of putting relationships in the foreground, so conceiving of the diagrammatic as something which describes the alignment of words, shapes, objects and persons' (Leeb 2011: 31). Referring to Kenneth Knoespel's (2001) essay 'Diagrams as Piloting Devices in the Philosophy of Gilles Deleuze', Leeb highlights his unpacking of the Greek etymology of *diagramma* via Deleuze's work on Leibniz and the Baroque (1993). Quoting Knoepsel she defines *diagramma* as that 'which is marked out by lines, a figure, form, or plan, but also carries a secondary connotation of marking or crossing out'. Correspondingly, diagrams would not only take care of 'order and stability' but would also be a means to 'destabilisation and discovery' (Leeb 2011: 31).[7] Both of these dynamics are at work in Ware's diagram on the box: diagrams as systematising a set of reading relations providing stability, and the diagram as a plane providing different connective possibilities. Most importantly it is the geography that is 'prior to' history – in Deleuze and Guattari's own words the diagrammatic plays a piloting role. The diagrammatic or abstract machine does not function to represent, even something real, but rather constructs a real that is yet to come, a new type of reality. Thus when it constitutes points of creation or potentiality it does not stand outside history but is instead always 'prior to' history (Deleuze and Guattari 1987: 142).

Ware presents the book not as a chronology of chapters, a sequence of reading, but as an interaction, that poses the issue of relationality: the book as a changing relationship between a set of physical elements. In Ware's diagram, a 'factual', instructional image visualises places one might read the book, leave different parts of it around and where one might move on within a house to continue reading it. He offers spaces to contextualise reading, opportunities for 'order and stability' that might otherwise be difficult to attain given such an exploded construct. We will see, too, that Ware uses the diagrammatic structure as layout to visualise fluid temporality.[8] Just as Ware uses the nomenclature of comics' culture to extend the milieu of his work,[9] so the diagram becomes the figuration that functions as content and conceptual map maker. In *Building Stories* the diagrammatic form functions as a semiotic figure and as expressive surface, echoing Deleuze and Guattari's conception of the diagrammatic operation: 'The diagram knows only traits and cutting edges that are still elements of content in so far as they are material and of expression in so far as they are functional, but which draw one another along, form relays, and meld in a shared deterritorialization: particles-signs' (1987: 142).

Entries and Exits

Boiled down to a tale, *Building Stories* documents the intersecting lives of people within a ninety-eight-year-old Chicago building. The central protagonist is a female, former art school student, now a florist, and with a prosthetic leg. Although depending on which book you choose to open first, you might be reading the story from the perspective of the bee or the building itself. Lifting the top off the box, on one the side of the container there is a circular panel, with an image of the main character stirring a pot on the stove and explaining to a former boyfriend that 'I don't think you can make yourself into an artist . . . you just have to be born that way, like being gay, or something . . . that was my problem, I think, I was always just art-curious.' Other characters include the landlady of the building who has lived there all her life (another former art school student), a couple living a miserable relationship, a bee and, most of all, the building itself.

Opening the box reveals materials of varying shapes, sizes and papers, including: a square-shaped hard-back book; a set of A4 comic-size magazines; a 3 x 7 inch strip that unfolds to 27 inches; some A3-size papers that open like broadsheet newspapers. There is also a 16 x 10 inch piece of hardboard that, as it opens out, reveals four large panels on one side, each panel containing single image pictures and an almost wordless narrative of the building in a seasonal cycle. On the reverse of each panel there are architectural diagrams of different floors. Any single act of removing these items from the box leaves them gathered in different arrangements, moving towards and away from each other, folding over one another, suggesting different possibilities of connection or repulsion, depending on the set of affects between the contents and container, the reader(s) and the milieu within which the whole event is taking place. The book organises itself spatially, with points of entry and exit changing according to the contingencies of any reading-event.

Deleuze and Guattari make a similar point that the minor literature of Kafka deterritorialises a major language and its familiar codes. They write that Kafka's work:

> is a rhizome, a burrow ... We will enter then by any point whatsoever: none matters more than another and no entrance is more privileged even if it seems an impasse, a tight passage, a siphon. We will be trying only to discover what other points our entrance connects to, what crossroads and galleries one passes through to link two points, what the map of the rhizome is and how the map is modified if one enters another point. Only the principle of multiple entrances prevents the introduction of the enemy, the Signifier and those attempts to interpret a work that is actually only open to experimentation. (Deleuze and Guattari 1986: 3)

Ware's experimental book is a challenge to the reader as it challenges the idea of reading that demands an over-arching narrative; the fluid *connection* between the sequence of books that you read becomes the experience and experiment. While design conventions of conventional books are designed to produce a static/stable memory of the connection between sections/chapters/essays, Ware's is a variable and rhizomatic map of memory, a map that maps its disappearance. As Deleuze and Guattari write:

> Neurologists and psychophysiologists distinguish between long-term memory and short-term memory (on the order of a minute). The difference between them is not simply quantitative: short-term memory is of the rhizome or diagram type, and long-term memory is arborescent and centralised (imprint, engram, tracing, or photograph). (Deleuze and Guattari 1987: 15–16)

Rhizomatic mapping, as opposed to the arborescent linear narrative, has long been a part of comics and cartoon tradition where the immanent becomes the map, most famously in the Warner Brothers 1951 animation *Duck Amuck* where Daffy Duck's form and shape is constantly redrawn by the animator. The content of animation often feeds off the given to explore the conditions of possibility of the given.

In the most obvious sense, *Building Stories* deterritorialises Literature and Art's official languages of cultural expression. But Ware's work also has a minor relationship to the dominant semiotic regimes and visual forms of comic book literature: the iconography, symbols and furniture of comic books. *Building Stories* challenges the traditional boundaries of panels and their sequencing, directions of reading, and in the diagrammatic conventions it vectors in from other image-making platforms (manuals and architecture, for example). It maps its experimental possibilities through its centripetal condensing of comic book panels and its centrifugal use of white space: announced, as already mentioned, on the outside of the box, B-u-IL-ding S-TO-R-I-e-S.

Most of all though, it is the invitation to experimentation over interpretation that provides the book with its minor opportunities: in the way the work is constructed as rhizomatic, without boundaries; in the way it spills into the space of the reader; the way it modifies the experiential milieu, extending it beyond the printed page to create a domestic geography of reading.[10] Bernard Cache writes in *Earth Moves: The Furnishing of Territories*, that geography

> is not the surroundings of the building, but rather the impossibility of its closure. But it is not a context either, for architectural punctuation is never final. We will therefore not speak of geography as a superior scale to the built frame, but rather as a principle of rupture of scale. And in this way, there will be no object, no matter how small, that does not have its geographical component. (1985: 70)

The book as an affective, eventful and experimental thing is a function of multiple geographies: material, narrative and the different life forms that traverse these. So as much as *Building Stories* is about a character writing the stories of *Building Stories*, it is also folded into and over by the story of the building itself, which comments and reflects on the inhabitants, the text occasionally becoming part of the image of the building. The building observes and talks and feels.

All this is also cut across by an entomological story, itself with multiple layers and points of entry and exit. The booklet *Branford The Best Bee In The World* features a bee who also appears in a four-page A3 newspaper *The Daily Bee* and in an A5 comic book tracking the life of a bee who lives, feeds off and pollinates the space, before concluding and starting the cycle again as *Branford The Benevolent Bacterium*. Branford the Bee emerges too in another story, one that a mother tells to her daughter.

In this way, if we consider *Building Stories* as furniture, architecture and diagram of a book, we must also consider it as geography, as a terrain that is mapped each time it is read, and a milieu that is created each time it is mapped. 'We think too much in terms of history, whether personal or universal', Deleuze explains in *Dialogues*, 'Becomings belong to geography, they are orientations, directions, entries and exits' (Deleuze and Parnet 1987: 2). And these becomings of milieu are non-human too. *Building Stories* is the book's journey of orientation: how one might rethink the space of the book, its inside and outside, its maker and reader. We will see next how experimentation impacting milieu, illustrator, audience and everything in between can burgeon also from just one line.

The Line and Milieu

Born in Romania in 1914, Saul Steinberg studied philosophy and then architecture in the 1930s, graduating in 1940 from the *Politecnico di Milano* before emigrating to America when anti-Jewish laws were brought in by the Fascist government. His work was first published in *The New Yorker* in 1941 and he became a regular contributor, providing nearly ninety covers and numerous drawings inside the magazine by the time of his death in 1999.

His most well-known image is a geography: the 1976 *New Yorker* cover, *The View of the World from 9th Avenue*, where the rest of the US and the world recedes into tiny distant shapes. Steinberg's work is about milieu in many different ways: sometimes with the illustrator in the middle of the piece, sometimes capturing the illustrator creating work. Or else it is the milieu of the visual language of representation within which illustrators find themselves that provides material for Steinberg's experimentations. His self-portraits are self-generating: *Untitled* (1948) pictures a line flowing in a loop, slowing, drawing an outline of a man walking. Here the illustrator is not so much the creator of spatial self-differentiation as if from an authoritative, transcendent position, but is rather the function of a spatial self-differentiation whose individuality requires the line to remain open. Unless the line and the space of the image are kept in focus, and their difference reinforced by the act of looking, the body disappears. The boundary between the internal and external in this image of the illustrator is fluid, the drawing creating itself as it draws, and both illustrator, audience and image oscillating between moments of 'order and stability' and those of 'destabilisation and discovery' (Leeb 2011: 31). It is the illustrator thinking themselves immanently. In '1837: Of the Refrain', Deleuze and Guattari remark of the power of the circle that 'to improvise is to join with the World, or meld with it' (1987: 311). Steinberg's drawing is an improvised subjectivity, experience and experiment, a line in search of a form. It reterritorialises as a recognisable representation, but is always on the edge of deterritorialising as the line opens into white space, its movement breaking free of a simple resolution.

There are many of these kinds of images throughout Steinberg's work; self-portraits as different experiments of self that are always in the process of being built, playing with readability and ontogenesis. Steinberg experimented with the familiar forms of representation, particularly the signifying regimes of art, in order to amplify the possibilities of visual communication itself. So another 'self-portrait' from *The New Yorker* in 1954 has the illustrator begin drawing with an ink pen in his right hand, the line tracing the shape of a body until it flows from the illustrator's left-shoulder into a calligraphic, multiple 'S', forming swirls that allude to his name ('SS'). While there is continuity through the image, the line wanders away from the body creating its own experience of form that is not pre-meditated. There is a sense here that we have looked in at this line in the middle of its journey and that its existence stretches infinitely in all directions.

The great advantage that Steinberg had in being a professional illustrator rather than an artist was the requirement to communicate to an audience of readers; or at least to give the appearance of communication. As an immigrant in America he could also be a foreigner in the visual language of his profession, cartooning. Steinberg stammered this language, the language of the figurative cartoon. He energised familiar figurative forms such as question marks, speech and thought bubbles, freeing them to become life forms animated by their own ink. Harold Rosenberg writes of Steinberg's speech balloons in *Saul Steinberg*, published as a companion to a 1979 exhibition at the Whitney Museum, New York:

> Having risen to the status of three-dimensional entities, the speech balloons take to meeting secretly in hotel bedrooms . . . Perhaps as a result, the balloons develop images within themselves that in turn produce their own speech balloons, indicating that talk and its imagery result in thoughts that have thoughts of their own. (Rosenberg 1979: 27)

The signifier becomes sensation; the body becomes producer of new emergent forms. Neither the figurative form nor the square of the cartoon limit thinking within Steinberg's work: it stammers, exceeding form and frame with a line that creates and unravels. His lines reterritorialise onto familiar semiotic regimes while simultaneously deterritorialising given forms. When E. H. Gombrich writes of Steinberg in *Art and Illusion*: 'There is perhaps no artist alive who knows more about the philosophy of representation' (2002: 202), he simultaneously misses the point and hits it. It is Steinberg's 'knowledge' of representation that allows him to experiment with ways of actively forgetting it in favour of something more affective and creative. But, as we can see, it is Steinberg's milieu creation that affords him opportunities for unpacking the strictures of many different systems of control and power. Steinberg's drawing, then, is always in transit: between art and the comic, between draughtsmanship and cartooning, between an image-maker steeped in a history of representational form and one who highlights the material surface of the white page; and, as we will see below, the wall. This has the effect of sucking into its milieu the familiar visual furniture of a magazine page – the columns, the gutters, the framing of the image – and foregrounding the geographical and cognitive habits that have positioned us as reading subjects in our relation to type, journeying from left to right, top to bottom, trained as we are in navigation around white space and lettering. Steinberg's drawing defines and dissolves boundaries through his material line of becoming: 'What I draw is drawing, that drawing derives from drawing. My line wants to remind constantly it's made of ink . . . The reader by following my line with his eyes becomes a draftsman' (Steinberg 1965: 59). If the line activates as draughtsman, the draughtsman is activated as becoming-a-reader-of-maps, as the drawing takes hold of space.

In August 1954, at Milan's Design and Architecture fair, Steinberg presented another image of the illustrator as the creation of his creative milieu. His drawing *The Line* was enlarged for a mural on a children's labyrinth designed by the architectural firm BBPR (Banfi, Belgiojoso, Peressutt and Rogers). Steinberg made drawings, which were then enlarged and applied to the wall by local craftsmen using a technique called *sgraffito*. The labyrinth was in the shape of a three-leaf clover and at the heart of the mural was a line that unfurled for thirty-three feet.

Beginning with an image of the nib of Steinberg's pen, *The Line* unfolds as a picture of an illustrator thinking heterogeneous spaces and being thought by heterogeneous spaces; the becoming of the line is the expression of a variation that generates a milieu and is itself generated by that milieu. The line becomes the surface of a canal with a gondola and Venetian buildings in the background; then it is a laundry line with a sock and tea-towel; then a railway line on a bridge framing mountains in the distance. Now the line positions me at the top of a Parisian apartment building looking down to the line where building and pavement meet; and then in an Egyptian desert landscape with pyramids. It becomes a Spanish tabletop, a bridge, the dividing line in a mathematics sum. The line is in continuous variation, shaping new spaces and being shaped by them in an immanent unfolding of itself, differing itself, unfurling as the multiple becomings of the illustrator.

Paul Klee famously defined a drawing as a line going for a walk.[11] Steinberg's *The Line* is much more energetic than this, going for a swim, a train journey, a dance, a road trip. Letting the line create a milieu allows it to act vectorially rather than teleologically: it launches from points rather than to them. In doing this it creates a different space where one creates differently, and where one is created differently. This is the milieu affect, where it emerges from that which it creates, which in turn allows for different drifting possibilities on what and how the milieu becomes. *The Line*, as with any line, is immanent thinking: 'The plane of immanence is not a concept that is or can be thought but rather the image of thought, the image thought gives itself of what it means to think, to make use of thought, to find one's bearings in thought' (Deleuze and Guattari 1994: 37). Illustrator and image are created in their mutual co-creation of the milieu that creates them. All of this is thinking too. The illustrator is taken for a walk, swim, road trip and so on by the line drawn, and is no longer the passive individual waiting for commissions, to be hired, with a fixed place determined by others. *The Line*, a line, is an image of thought of the illustrator as a migrant, as a foreigner, as someone in the process of creating their own milieu and being created by it.

Conclusion

Illustrators are weighed-down by the memory of illustration as a function in the chain of commercial production, how illustrators memorialise their subjectivity as technicians. Both Steinberg and Ware draw lines of flight from this memory through the production of new space, through becoming foreigners in the language of illustration, stammering and stuttering, breaking down and creating. Their work creating experimental milieus is both organised and chaotic. Ware says in an interview in *Publisher's Weekly* that while most books move from a beginning to an end, and a character changes along linear lines, he was aiming for something that expressed

> What it's like to be inside a body experiencing the world with all the myriad multi-layers of thoughts and memories that happen at the same time. And then the way that those things contradict each other and then the way that we think of ourselves as people, somehow all layered together. Of course if you try to imitate that exactly then it's just going to be a mess. So as you're saying, to me trying to have a sort of clear chaos about the thing, may not be a good approach necessarily but it's kind of what I try for. (Reid 2012)

Ware here highlights not only the way his work engages with chaotic, nonlinear life, but also that such life should not be simply represented. There needs to be order and stability, disorder and instability. That is why the diagrammatic is a core element of *Building Stories* as visual territorialisation, but it also plays out as an affective image. Illustrators need to become the mapmakers, architects and geographers of a different future, creating images and books from the visual language of illustration that no longer repeat the fixed memory of illustration, that – like the works of Ware and Steinberg – are untimely.

Deleuze and Guattari ask: 'How can the book find an adequate outside with which to assemble in heterogeneity, rather than a world to reproduce?' (1987: 24). We can ask the same question of the illustrator: how can the book find an adequate outside maker with which to assemble in heterogeneity, rather than reproducing the role of illustrator as supplier of representations? Former Artistic Director of the literary magazine *Granta*, Michael Salu, made a similar point in *Varoom* illustration magazine, asking whether as a medium illustration 'might need to do more than vocationalise aesthetics' (Salu 2012: 23).

Deleuze and Guattari's concept of milieu is a tool to enable illustrators to think of the role and subjectivity of the illustrator as part of a fluid and dynamic space, and therefore to rethink and more importantly remake the activity of illustration itself for clients, commissioners and most of all themselves. Illustrators and the people who brief them extract the concept of a work, the thing that makes it engaging, funny, sad – in short affective – as surplus value and circulate it as a charming fiction. Chris Ware quotes Picasso on the inside of the box of *Building Stories*: 'Everything you can imagine is real.' Milieu, the contingency of making and thinking, making as thinking, enables the illustrator to encounter the affective as what produces work and what creates the illustrator as illustrator, what creates the illustrator as the untimely.

Notes

1. The House of Illustration opened in London in 2014. The project to establish a site for illustration was led over a number of years by the noted children's illustrator Quentin Blake. The title of the space suggests a marking of territory that is different from 'Gallery' and 'Museum'. The house is of course a key narrative space of children's books.

2. One sub-genre of greetings card addresses both the buyer and the semiotics of the traditional card, which through text and image is entirely directed to the considered construction of 'sentiment'. Part of the function of the traditional greetings card is a process where the card produces through text and image the space for a consensual emotion, visualising the feeling of the buyer for a named relation (rather than a particular individual). The *Edward Monkton* range of cards (by artist Giles Andreae) has proved itself commercially successful by drawing attention to the emotional demand at the heart of birthday cards. For example a recent birthday card addressed to 'My Brother', features a framed portrait of a young man, a flower poking out of a hole in his head, his tongue sticking out with the 'handwritten' thought: 'DARE TO BE DIFFERENT . . . but not so different that you become a Menace to Society and they have to take you off to the HEAD HOSPITAL and conduct experiments on your BRAIN. That would just be too DIFFERENT, OK?' Or, playing with a different tradition of 'Hate Mail', the illustrator Mr. Bingo who will, for a £40 fee, send a vintage postcard with a drawing and an offensive message.

3. 'The aphorism is not only relationality with the outside. Its second characteristic is relation with the intensive. And they're the same thing' (Deleuze 2004: 257). The thinking of the aphorism as we say it generates and sparks different connections – the aphorism as technique is intended to be 'said'. An aphorism is the riposte of thinking to the representation of thinking. The aphorism thinks – it is in the 'middle', au milieu, it is active, living material. As a linguistic style, the aphorism is both immersive as a way of capturing thought in movement, and its characteristic of openness enables it to attach and connect and reshape the arrangement of thoughts adjacent to it.

4. Both of these – philosophy as the creation of concepts, and philosophy as interesting (rather than true) – drive much of what Deleuze and Guattari write in *What is Philosophy?*

5. *Building Stories* is not the first book to create unpredictable readings through an assemblage of parts. English author B. S. Johnson's *The Unfortunates* (1969) delivers twenty-seven unbound sections, and only the first and last chapters are prescribed a place. Ware has said that the prominence of BS on the cover of Building Stories was a reference to the initials of Johnson. Originally published in French in 1961, Marc Saporta's *Composition No. 1*, was recently published by Visual Editions in London, with an iPad edition designed by studio Universal Everything. The novel consists of 150 unbound single-sided pages that can be reshuffled each time.

6. The title is a quotation from Deleuze and Guattari (1987: 499). It is an image of the line.

7. Knoespel does not, however, want this insight to rest purely on etymology, with its echoes of Heidegger, but refers to the practice and technology of writing on a wax tablet, where one would write on a surface with words already erased and disfigured. This has a different echo in Derrida's analysis of Freud's discussion of the apparatus of the mystic writing pad in 'Freud and the Scene of Writing' (Derrida 1978).

8. The inside cover of Chris Ware's *Jimmy Corrigan: The Smartest Kid on Earth*

features a two-page 'instruction guide', an exam and a narrative strip visualised in the form of a diagram.

9. Not only is *Acme Novelty Library* a reference to cartoon folklore but Ware's comic *Quimby the Mouse* (2003) features a mouse which some suggest bears a resemblance to Ignatz Mouse in George Herriman's *Krazy Kat*. And of course Fred Quimby was the producer of the *Tom and Jerry* cartoons.

10. The sheer weight and size of the book means that it seeks out different objects: my daughter has found one of the smaller booklets by a set of adaptor plugs on the floor 'charging up'.

11. Deleuze and Guattari use a similar image early in *Anti-Oedipus*: 'A schizophrenic out for a walk is a better model than a neurotic lying on an analyst's couch' (1984: 2).

References

Buchanan, Brett (2009), *Onto-Ethologies: The Animal Environments of Uexküll, Heidegger, Merleau-Ponty, and Deleuze*, New York: SUNY Press.

Cache, Bernard (1985), *Earth Moves: The Furnishing of Territories*, Cambridge, MA: The MIT Press.

Canguilhem, G. [1952] (2001), 'The Living and Its Milieu', trans. J. Savage, *Grey Room*, 3, pp. 6–31.

Deleuze, Gilles [2002] (2004), *Desert Islands and Other Texts, 1953–1974*, ed. D. Lapoujade, trans. M. Taomina, New York: Semiotext(e).

Deleuze, Gilles [1990] (1995), *Negotiations 1972–1990*, trans. M. Joughin, New York: Columbia University Press.

Deleuze, Gilles [1968] (1994), *Difference and Repetition*, trans. P. Patton, London: Athlone.

Deleuze, Gilles [1988] (1993), *The Fold: Leibniz and the Baroque*, trans. T. Conley, London: Athlone.

Deleuze, Gilles and F. Guattari [1991] (1994), *What is Philosophy?* trans. G. Burchell and H. Tomlinson, London: Verso.

Deleuze, Gilles and F. Guattari [1982] (1987), *A Thousand Plateaus. Capitalism and Schizophrenia 2*, trans. B. Massumi, London: Athlone.

Deleuze, Gilles and F. Guattari [1975] (1986), *Kafka: Towards a Minor Literature*, trans. D. Polan, Minneapolis: University of Minnesota Press.

Deleuze, Gilles and F. Guattari [1972] (1984), *Anti-Oedipus. Capitalism and Schizophrenia 1*, trans. R. Hurley, M. Seem, and H. Lane, London: Athlone.

Deleuze, Gilles and C. Parnet [1977] (1987), *Dialogues*, trans. H. Tomlinson and B. Habberjam, New York: Columbia University Press.

Derrida, Jacques [1978] (1981), 'Freud and The Scene of Writing', in J. Derrida, *Writing and Difference*, trans. A. Bass, London: Routledge and Kegan Paul, pp. 196–231.

Gombrich, Ernst H. (2002), *Art and Illusion: A Study in the Psychology of Pictorial Representation*, 6th edition, London: Phaidon Press.

Knoepsel, K. (2001), 'Diagrams as Plotting Device in the Work of Gilles Deleuze', *Littérature, Théorie, Enseignement*, 19, pp. 145–65.

Lecercle, Jean-Jacques (1994), *Philosophy of Nonsense: The Intuitions of Victorian Nonsense Literature*, London and New York: Routledge.

Leeb, S. (2011), 'A Line with Variable Direction, which Traces No Contour, and Delimits No Form', in *Drawing a Hypothesis: Figures of Thought*, Vienna: Springer-Verlag, pp. 29–42.

Mullarkey, John (2006), *Post-Continental Philosophy: An Outline*, New York and London: Continuum Press.

Reid, C. (2012), 'A Life in A Box: Invention, Clarity and Meaning in Chris Ware's "Building Stories"', *Publisher's Weekly*; available at http://www.publishersweekly.com/pw/by-topic/booknews/comics/article/54154-a-life-in-a-box-invention-clarity-and-meaning-in-chris-ware-s-building-stories.html (accessed 30 August 2014).

Rosenberg, Harold (1979), *Saul Steinberg*, London: André Deutsch.

Salu, M. (2012), 'Art Directing Taste', in J. O'Reilly (ed.), *Varoom*, 19, Special issue on Taste, pp. 20–3

Steinberg, Saul (2011), *The Line*, Zurich: Nieves Books.

Steinberg, Saul (1965), 'Straight from the Hand and Mouth of Steinberg', *Life magazine*, 10 December, pp. 59–70.

Topliss, Iain (2005), *The Comic Worlds of Peter Arno, William Steig, Charles Addams and Saul Steinberg*, Baltimore: The Johns Hopkins University Press.

Ware, Chris (2012), *Building Stories*, London: Jonathan Cape.

Ware, Chris (2003a), *Quimby the Mouse*, Seattle, WA: Fantagraphics

Ware, Chris (2003b), *Jimmy Corrigan: The Smartest Kid on Earth*, London: Jonathan Cape.

Chapter 9

Sustainable Design Activism: Affirmative Politics and Fruitful Futures

Petra Hroch

If, for Deleuze and Guattari, art makes percepts and affects, science deals in prospects or functions, and philosophy creates concepts (1994: 24), how then are we to think of an interdisciplinary activity like design – a creative endeavour at the interstices of artistic, scientific and conceptual thinking? Design draws upon and contributes to all three of Deleuze and Guattari's 'domains of thought': it shares with art its concern with percepts and affects, with science its interest in prospects and functions, and designers often think of themselves as creating 'design concepts'. We might assume, then, that design is exactly the kind of experimental exercise, the sort of hybrid multiplicity, the type of creative, critical and conceptual assemblage that Deleuze and Guattari would have found promising. And yet, while they refer extensively to art, literature, music, theatre, opera and film in their work, they pay remarkably little attention to design. Moreover, while they find promise in creativity expressed through these various artistic modes, they are overtly hostile when they do – albeit briefly – turn their attention to design. They write: 'Finally, the most shameful moment came when computer science, marketing, design and advertising, all the disciplines of communication, seized hold of the word "concept" itself and said: "This is our concern, we are the creative ones, we are the ideas men!"' (1994: 10).

This chapter focuses on design as a discipline in relation to Deleuze and Guattari's three domains of thought. I argue, first, that the *problem of design* – that is, Deleuze and Guattari's critique of the discipline and its complicity with capitalism as 'the great Major' (1994: 149) – is critical to understanding the context and driving force for Deleuze and Guattari's thought and, as such, should not be overlooked by designers wishing to engage with their work. However, I also argue that the *problem posed by design* as a discipline – particularly by what I call 'minor' (Deleuze and Guattari 1986: 16) modes of design such as emerging forms of 'design activism' (Fuad-Luke 2009; White and Tonkinwise 2012; Julier 2013a, 2013b; Markussen 2013) that provide alternatives to mainstream neoliberal capitalist logics – challenges Deleuze and Guattari's overly narrow and negative conceptualisation of design as a discipline. In fact, emerging directions in design that challenge taken-for-granted assumptions, structures, systems and distributions of power resonate with concepts in Deleuze and Guattari's oeuvre by sharing a common interest in challenging *doxa*, experimenting with intensities, and creating heterogeneous connections in the interest of promoting more equitable forms of future flourishing.[1] Indeed, as Marcelo Svirsky observes in the *Deleuze Studies* supplement on 'Deleuze and Political Activism', 'Deleuze and Guattari's political philosophies have created some of the conceptual tools which may be put to use in activism that seeks to break with repressive traditions' (Svirsky 2010a: 4). Although a comprehensive analysis of Deleuzo-Guattarian politics is beyond the scope of this chapter, as is an extensive overview of the many definitions of design activism emerging in debates today, my interest here is simple and specific: to focus on how Deleuze and Guattari's work in *What is Philosophy?* can be mobilised as part of this conceptual toolbox for emerging design activisms, particularly in light of their critique of design and its complicity with the repressive regimes of neoliberal capitalism in this, their last, text. A focus on this issue – it is my hope – will contribute to emerging debates on art, design and politics in Deleuze and Guattari (Massumi 2013), as well as design, activism and neoliberalism (Julier 2013a).

To propel this twofold line of argument (or what I call, respectively, the *problem of design* and the *problem posed by design*), I propose an intensive method of reading *What is Philosophy?* that first seeks to deterritorialise the three domains of thought by seeking to understand the domains not in static terms of what they are, but rather along the more Spinozist lines of flight that ask what they can do (Deleuze and Guattari 1983: 108). Extending this methodological approach, I suggest design be re-thought as an 'intra-domain' mode of thought and re-conceptualised *intensively* through a re-consideration of how design works and what it can do. This approach reminds us to remain critical of examples of design that territorialise creativity onto reductive, difference-diminishing, monopoly-oriented outcomes. As I argue in the second part of the chapter, this approach also opens up fields of design that may not be conventionally recognised *as* design in order to demonstrate the potential of design to have effects other than what Deleuze and Guattari characterise as 'shameful moments' (1994: 10). In sum, this chapter invites us to read Deleuze and Guattari's domains of thought *intensively* and also to consider the potential capacities of design activism to effect *intensive resistances* to the present (Hroch 2013b: 22). I invite us to ask what kind of design expresses both critiques and creative alternatives to problems such as ecological destruction and waste, economic disparity and collapse, and social inequality. In other words, I consider *what design can do* as a set of practices intent on engaging with and re-making the material world in more ecologically, economically and socially sustainable ways.

To this end, I am particularly interested in design activism focused on environmental sustainability that uses the social realm as its medium. I focus especially on a close analysis of one example, Toronto's *Not Far From the Tree*, to highlight some of the ways their activities operate as an expression of design activism that, by re-conceptualising, re-organising and deterritorialising material flows of fruit, people, private property and profit, reconfigures a system of deeply enmeshed social, environmental, as well as economic 'problems' into a rich web of opportunities for the flourishing of different, more equitable, and perhaps surprising or unforeseen connections.

Deleuze and Guattari's Critique of Design (The Problem of Design)

In this section I start by delineating Deleuze and Guattari's three domains of thought in relation to what I call the *problem of design* in their work. I underscore Deleuze and Guattari's critique of the discipline and its complicity with contemporary capitalism as 'the great Major' (1994: 149) and argue that it is critical to understanding the context out of which Deleuze and Guattari's thought arises and the impetus that drives it. To begin, Deleuze and Guattari's overt criticism of the 'disciplines of communication' including computer science, marketing, design and advertising (1994: 10) is rooted in the wide-ranging critique of capitalism that grounds their collective work in *Anti-Oedipus* (1983) and *A Thousand Plateaus* (1987). Indeed, the subtitle that connects these two tomes, *Capitalism and Schizophrenia*, offers what we might think of as their summary assessment of the state of things and identifies the problem with which the two volumes take issue.

In their last book, *What is Philosophy?* Deleuze and Guattari argue that the disciplines of communication including design are troublesome because no matter how 'creative' they purport to be the so-called 'creativity' of these disciplines produces little if anything 'new'. By 'new', these thinkers who had a passion for inventing tools for thinking that work against the capture of life's forces and flows by capital refer to concepts, percepts and affects that do just this. That is, they argue against concepts, percepts and affects that create – or themselves become – the 'new' as in new commodities. The 'new' for Deleuze and Guattari is not the 'new' in neoliberal capitalism, but rather, its intensive resistance – or resistance through the ongoing creation of difference. Indeed, for designers drawn to Deleuze and Guattari's vocabulary of concepts, to ignore their indictment of advanced capitalism is to risk reproducing the very same problematic they critique: using design as simply another capital-creating enterprise and reducing concepts such as the 'rhizome', 'assemblage', 'deterritorialisation', 'concept', and, indeed, the term 'new' to mere slogans. As Deleuze scholar Adrian Parr argues in her recent work on Deleuze and Guattari and architectural design, if concepts such as 'the fold, force and becoming are not connected to the larger political impulse driving Deleuze and his collaborations with Guattari', then 'the concepts are no longer tools in the way that Deleuze insisted they need to be treated' and in their political disengagement become 'profoundly un-Deleuzian' (Parr 2013: 204).

Deleuze and Guattari's collective work takes aim at the way in which capitalism eliminates – rather than creates – difference and 'newness' (that is, the production of ongoing differentiation). They warn, for instance, that capitalism today has appropriated, instrumentalised and commodified the concept of the 'concept' for the purposes of sloganeering, seduction and sales. Deleuze and Guattari not only critique the way in which the 'concept' is used by the disciplines of communication such as design, but also foreshadow the rise of contemporary neoliberal capitalism's championing of concepts such as the 'knowledge economy', the 'creative class', the 'enterprising individual', and 'design thinking' when they write:

> Information and creativity, concept and enterprise: there is already an abundant bibliography. Marketing has preserved the idea of a certain relationship between the concept and the event. But here the concept has become the set of product displays (historical, scientific, artistic, sexual, pragmatic), and the event has become the exhibition that set up various displays and the 'exchange of ideas' it is supposed to promote. The only events are exhibitions, and the only concepts are products that can be sold . . . The simulacrum, the simulation of a packet of noodles, has become the true concept and the one who packages the product, commodity, or work of art has become the philosopher, conceptual persona, or artist. (Deleuze and Guattari 1994: 10)

In an era in which ubiquitous capitalism is the new normal within which images of thought reside, Deleuze and Guattari have this to say about the role of philosophy in creating concepts:

> Certainly, it is painful to learn that Concept indicates a society of informa-tion services and engineering. But the more philosophy comes up against shameless and inane rivals and encounters them at its very core, the more it feels driven to fulfill the task of creating concepts that are aerolites rather than commercial products. It gets the giggles, which wipe away its tears. So, the question of philosophy is the singular point where concept and creation are related to each other. (Deleuze and Guattari 1994: 11)

In the face of the concept's appropriation by the capitalist machine Deleuze and Guattari seek to defend the concept of the concept from the way it is used to commodify ideas – what they call an 'absolute disaster for thought' (1994: 12).[2] At the same time, the distinction they draw between the concept in philosophy and its instrumentalisation by 'rivals' is also an attempt to defend philosophy as a discipline from conservative forces within the discipline of philosophy itself. In other words, their defensive argument against 'rivals' is a twofold attempt to deflect forces that reduce what philosophy can do from within as well as from without. Like their critique of majoritarian modes of design, Deleuze and Guattari's critique of the conservative forces at work in philosophy champions experimen-tal, presentational (not representational or recognition-based), and 'new' (as difference-producing) modes of concept-creation. Indeed, as Svirsky observes, although Deleuze and Guattari 'do not provide ready-made blueprints for revolution' they do certainly promote a 'minor' art of thinking/doing as a way to challenge oppressive structures including rep-resentational forms of thought (Svirsky 2010a: 5).

In order to argue that the problem posed by 'minor' modes of design (Deleuze and Guattari 1986: 16) such as emerging forms of 'design activism' challenge Deleuze and Guattari's reductive conceptualisation of design as a discipline, I begin by proposing in the next section an intensive method of reading *What is Philosophy?* that deterritorialises the three domains of thought by understanding them in terms not of what they are, but rather of what they can do (Deleuze and Guattari 1983: 108).

Deterritorialising the Three Domains of Thought

Throughout their collaborative work, beginning with *Anti-Oedipus*, Deleuze and Guattari are not as interested in setting up *extensive* categories as they are in exploring, expressing and experimenting with *intensive* processes (DeLanda 2002; Hroch 2013a). These thinkers' emphases on processes of desiring-production reveals their interest not in what things are called, what they mean, or what they call 'extensities' (extensive measures of things), so much as in 'intensities' and intensive capacities – what things are capable of, what becomings they engender, what effects they can have, what they produce, *and what they can do.* As they underscore, 'the question posed by desire is not "What does it mean?" but rather *"How does it work?"'* (Deleuze and Guattari 1983: 108; original emphasis). It strikes a reader as strange, then, given Deleuze and Guattari's insistence on intensities and intensive processes rather than extensities (such as categories and classifications) that in *What is Philosophy?* they shift from a style of thinking and writing focused on breaking down categories and building connections that they put to work in *Anti-Oedipus* and *A Thousand Plateaus* to one that attempts rather rigidly to delineate disciplinary territories and erect conceptual boundaries around the 'three domains of thought': 'art', 'science' and 'philosophy' (Deleuze and Guattari 1994: 24). Isabelle Stengers notes that, for her, as it was for many readers, Deleuze's last book, co-authored with Félix Guattari,[3] came as 'a surprise', even 'a disappointment' (Stengers 2005: 151). In her essay on *What is Philosophy?* entitled 'Deleuze and Guattari's Last Enigmatic Message', she observes that we suddenly 'face a strong differentiation between the creations which are proper to philosophy, to science, and to art' which has 'caused many to wonder or even to feel betrayed' (2005: 151). After all, these were the thinkers associated with 'the affirmation of productive [connections], the creation of deterritorialising processes escaping fixed identities, transgressing boundaries and static classifications, destroying the power of exclusive disjunction, that is the either/or alternatives' (2005: 151). Deleuze and Guattari's last work together thus left many readers – especially those who appreciated their previous critique of categories such as 'Royal science' (Deleuze and Guattari 1987: 361) wondering why, as Stengers asks, they chose to create a trifecta – 'a seemingly "classical picture"' (2005: 151).

So, why this approach in *What is Philosophy?* Why this tripartite territorialisation? I suggest – and here I agree with Stengers's insightful reading of Deleuze and Guattari's writing on philosophy in relation to science[4] – that the shift in style and the concerted effort to clarify and simplify (and perhaps in a sense even *over-simplify*) concepts (such as their effort to clarify the role of philosophy suggested by the title itself) can be seen as a purposeful attempt at once to defend each domain from the reductive tendencies encroaching upon them, as well as to launch an offensive strategy to remind readers of the potential of each domain to continue to be creative, to resist the present, and to refuse not only to be treated reductively in terms of disciplinary definitions, but also to resist being instrumentalised in the service of capital.

I support Stengers's argument that *despite* the 'classical' delineation of tripartite categories, the text may be the most 'political' of Deleuze's books in so far as the crucial problematic it tackles is their observation that 'we lack resistance to the present' (Deleuze and Guattari 1994: 108). Stengers adds that by 'resisting the present', Deleuze and Guattari do not simply mean criticising or denouncing but rather creating and constructing (2005: 152). It is in this spirit that I invite us to revisit these categories of 'art', 'science' and 'philosophy', and suggest that rather than simplistically denouncing or uncritically fetishising them, we should heed Deleuze and Guattari's own advice to 'resist the present', to create and to construct – and not simply to repeat what they said, but rather, to 'do what they did'. I follow in Stengers's steps in my approach to this text – an approach that, in the following passage, she describes as an engagement that seeks to 'actualise' or 'effectuate' ideas. I will not stay within Deleuze and Guattari's text but rather follow Deleuze's own advice, as noted by Stengers: 'we should be interested in tools for thinking, not in an exegesis of ideas. An idea is always engaged in what he called a matter, always a specific one . . . in order [to ask] how and why [the idea] matters, the kind of difference it makes' (2005: 151).

The style of reading Stengers suggests is in keeping with Deleuze and Guattari's own style of engagement with other authors' ideas. Following Deleuze and Guattari's advice, we should read their own concepts by asking *what they do* (Deleuze and Guattari 1994: 28) and continuing, as they did, to create concepts 'adequate' for and 'worthy' of the ever-changing present (Braidotti 2006: 272; 2013: 184). I thus suggest that we regard Deleuze and Guattari's seemingly territorialising gesture in *What is Philosophy?* as one that attempts to concentrate on the intensities – and indeed *to concentrate the intensities* – of each 'domain' in the face of what they may have regarded as their potential 'collapse' (Deleuze and Guattari 1987: 161). As they point out, stratification, or staying 'organised, signified, subjected' as a strategy is 'not the worst that can happen', but experimenting with strata is the approach they champion (1987: 161). My intention, then, is not simply to repeat these categories by tracing the contours that delineate their territories, but rather, to ask *what these categories do*. In deterritorialising these domains, we can draw connections that actualise and effectuate the intensities – the forces that resist the present – that inhere in them.

Following Deleuze and Guattari's advice to problematise existing concepts and postulate concepts – in other words, to do the work of philosophy – I suggest that not only their categories of 'art', 'science' and 'philosophy' but also their critique of 'design' require reconsideration. Moreover, I suggest that thinking about these categories in relation to the work of design and *vice versa* enable us to do this work – that is, to reconsider their own previous work in the ways they advised. This kind of re-reading is important not only as Deleuze and Guattari's work – and in particular their attention to the three domains of thought – is continually taken up by designers and architects, but also as the fields of design and architecture shift towards projects and activities that Deleuze and Guattari may not have identified as 'design', projects and activities that stand in a different – sometimes problematic and sometimes also *problematising* – relation to capitalism or what they call 'the great Major' (1994: 149).

From Extensive Models to Intensive Modes: Understanding the Three Domains of Thought as Images of Thought

In order to extend this deterritorialising movement as a methodological approach, in the following section I suggest that the three domains of thought be understood as images of thought; that is, I posit that we move from understanding Deleuze and Guattari's categories as extensive models to understanding them as intensive modes. Following this line of argument, I propose that design be re-thought as an 'intra-domain' mode of thought and be re-conceptualised *intensively* through a reconsideration of how design works and what it can do (Deleuze and Guattari 1983: 108). This approach enables us to consider 'minor' modes of design as examples of design that Deleuze and Guattari overlooked in their analysis, at the same time that it reminds us to remain critical of examples of design that territorialise creativity onto reductive, difference-diminishing, monopoly-oriented outcomes.

In *What is Philosophy?* art, science and philosophy do not function as 'extensities'. Rather, given the overtly political thrust of their previous work, and in keeping with Stengers's observation that *What is Philosophy?* is implicitly political, these categories or 'domains of thought' attempt to re-intensify each domain, to wrest each free of its impotent state, and to re-focus, re-charge, re-new each domain of thought so that they might work together again with their full critical and creative force. At the end of his life, Deleuze turned his focus from 'doing philosophy' to the question of 'what philosophy *is*' in order to ask 'what philosophy *does*'. That is, the question posed in terms of the 'identity' of philosophy here is a final attempt, approached perhaps with more clarity and certainly more urgency, to underscore philosophy's strengths and to emphasise its potencies and potentials. Deleuze and Guattari's parallel focus on the other domains of thought does not separate them from philosophy once and for all. Rather, it invites us to be critical of increasingly common, habitual and reductive approaches to each and to encourage us to find each domain's creative force and, in turn, to afford us each domain's full capacity to 'resist the present'. In this way, Deleuze and Guattari's seemingly conservative manoeuvre can be read, paradoxically, as a radical gesture.

In this section, then, I attend to the concept of the 'concept' in Deleuze and Guattari's oeuvre by suggesting that to understand the 'three domains of thought' in their work – art, science and philosophy – requires that we understand these 'domains' as *modes* through which thought-events happen rather than as *disciplines* to which a particular image of thought belongs. I propose that deterritorialising the territories that define these 'domains of thought' affords us the ability to engage more productively with Deleuze and Guattari's oeuvre and with interdisciplinary disciplines such as design – those 'perpetually interbreeding' (Deleuze and Guattari 1994: 24) disciplines that are uniquely prepared to tackle some of today's most pressing conceptual, perceptive, affective and prospective problems, namely problems of sustainability or, more precisely, problems of what I elsewhere term 'sustaining intensities' (Hroch 2014). Indeed, I suggest that this deterritorialisation of the domains is an always-present and yet often-underemphasised dimension of *What is Philosophy?* and perhaps reveals less about the authors of the text and more about us as readers and what 'lines' of reading we have been prepared to 'effectuate' (Stengers 2005: 151). Indeed, Deleuze and Guattari recognise their own over-simplification and outline their methodology as follows:

> At present we are relying only on a very general hypothesis: from sentences or their equivalent, philosophy extracts concepts (which must not be confused with general or abstract ideas), whereas science extracts prospects (propositions that must not be confused with judgments), and art extracts percepts and affects (which must not be confused with perceptions or feelings). In each case language is tested and used in incomparable ways – but in ways that do not define the differences between disciplines without also constituting their perpetual interbreeding. (Deleuze and Guattari 1994: 24)

Deleuze and Guattari begin their delineation of the 'three domains of thought' by pointing out that the 'sciences, arts, and philosophies are all equally creative' (1994: 5). Although all three are creative,[5] what distinguishes philosophy from science and from art is that it is 'the art of forming, inventing, and fabricating' or '*creating*' concepts (1994: 2, 5). Deleuze and Guattari address the work of science and art in order to distinguish it from the work of philosophy, and to defend a creative mode of philosophy from being encroached upon by reductive scientific and artistic paradigms.[6] At the same time, from their first definition of philosophy, despite distinguishing it from science and art, Deleuze and Guattari already forge connections between philosophy and art, by conceiving of philosophy as one kind of creative process the object of which, by definition, is to create 'new' concepts (1994: 5). This definition already compels us to ask: if philosophy creates concepts, *is it not the case that wherever there is the creation of concepts there is philosophy?* This may sound like an analytical gesture but I think it addresses the issue at the heart of how to read this text by placing the emphasis on what things *do* as opposed to what things are and are *called*. Philosophy creates concepts and so even when something isn't necessarily called 'philosophy', if a concept is being created, philosophy is being done, or one is working in a philosophical *mode*. Deleuze and Guattari concur when they write: 'So as long as there is a time and a place for creating concepts, the operation that undertakes this will always be called philosophy, or will be indistinguishable from philosophy even if it is called something else' (1994: 9).

It follows, then, that if we read Deleuze and Guattari's definition of philosophy not as a disciplinary model but rather as an image of thought, then we can say that aspects of artistic, scientific and even *design practice* can be philosophical if they create concepts in the philosophical *mode* and, concomitantly, engage in the posing of problems (1994: 27). For Deleuze and Guattari, when doing philosophy – or thinking philosophically – problems must be posed 'just as concepts must be created' and 'new concepts must relate to our problems, to our history, and, above all, to our becomings' (1994: 27). Deleuze poses philosophy as a problem-solving endeavour that involves the positing of questions, the putting forth of propositions, and the creation of always-provisional concepts that respond to an ever-shifting context. By posing problems and creating concepts that relate to our current and ever-changing context, we remain immanently rooted in – while using philosophy as a way to resist intensively– the present.

As the second part of this chapter unfolds, I turn to focus on activist design as a set of philosophies that are critical of capitalist waste and accumulation and as a set of practices intent on making and re-making the material world in more ecologically, economically and socially sustainable ways. I am interested particularly in activist design practices that, rather than create objects, artefacts, or 'products' (or, 'services', which, David Noble argues in *Trading the Future*, commodify relations), re-conceptualise existing 'problems' and re-organise existing territories in order to contribute to the design of more equitable and yet difference-sustaining connections among humans and their more-than-human environments (Deleuze and Guattari 1994: 81). What is at stake in this section is this: deterritorialising the domains of thought allows us to expand the concept of the concept from applying only to the work of philosophy proper to include activist aspects of 'design thinking' which, in turn, can open up ways of not only conceptualising but also of materialising more sustainable modes of collective becoming.

Lodging the Self on a Stratum: Design as Thinking/Doing Differently

At the same time as Deleuze and Guattari's work compels us to critically interrogate design's complicity with capitalism, their concepts – not to mention modes of 'minor' design themselves – also enable us to see the complexity of capitalism in its contemporary neoliberal modulations (Harvey 2005; Hroch 2013b). Design practices are products of, co-produce, and at times intensively resist in a myriad of complex ways, the ways capitalism is both conceptualised and materialised (Julier 2013a, 2013b; Svirsky 2010a, 2010b). Design, by engaging the material world through a practice that includes conceptualisation, also exceeds it by doing the work of conceptualisation through more-than-abstract media thereby complexifying what concepts are and what they can do. Design methods and 'ways of knowing' (Cross 2001) experiment with a variety of modes of thinking, doing, thinking and/as doing, and doing and/as thinking. By engaging the material world, and re-making it differently (through concept, practice, concept-as-practice, and practice-as-concept) design understands an ideological/material practice such as capitalism less abstractly than critical theoretical conceptualisations of capitalism alone. Design enables a less reductive understanding of capitalism – not only as a totalising abstraction, but as itself a design: a series of practices, habits, ideas, patterns, materialities, fabulations and fabrications (Deleuze and Guattari 1994: 2) that are made, and thus, can also be un-made and re-made (Julier 2013b: 224).[7]

Design practices might be said, then, to enable what Deleuze and Guattari invited us to do: 'lodge [oneself] on a stratum, experiment with the opportunities it offers, find an advantageous place on it, potential lines of deterritorialisation, possible lines of flight, experience them, produce flow conjunctions here and there' (Deleuze and Guattari 1987: 161). We might even say that engaging with 'minor' design practices is an experiment in 'lodging oneself' on the great Major stratum of capitalism in particular. As I discuss in the following section, 'minor' modes of design such as the social design activist practices I explore, produce two related flow conjunctions: 1) they conceptualise the world differently in order to re-make or re-materialise it in different ways; and 2) they materialise the world differently in order to re-make or re-conceptualise it in different ways. Through the design process, conceptualisation happens through materialisation, materialisation happens through conceptualisation, and both modes of engagement – the conceptual and/as the material, and the material and/as the conceptual – engage, lodge on, find an advantageous place in the made world in order to experiment, find potential lines of deterritorialisation, possible lines of flight, and re-make the world differently, producing different connections and different conjunctive flows.

Let us address, prior to proceeding further, what I mean by 1) design, 2) activism, and 3) the term design activism. Following the work of Deleuze and Guattari in *What Is Philosophy?* I am interested in positing intensive definitions of design, activism, and design activism – definitions that focus on how things work and what they do (rather than what Deleuze and Guattari call an 'extensive' one – namely, what things are called or what they mean) (Deleuze and Guattari 1983: 108). Alastair Fuad-Luke provides an intensive working definition of design as 'the act of deliberately moving from an existing situation to a preferred one by professional designers or others applying design knowingly or unknowingly' (Fuad-Luke 2009: 5). Interestingly, Fuad-Luke's definition of activism is remarkably similar – and similarly intensive – to his definition of design. He defines activism as 'taking action to catalyse, encourage, or bring about change, in order to elicit social, cultural and/ or political transformation' (2009: 6).

Of course, in spite of the similarities between design and activism as modes of change, transformation, movement and differentiation, not all design is activism, and not all activism is design. Likewise, not all those doing design (often called 'designers') are doing (or claim to be doing) activism, and not all those doing activism (often called 'activists') are doing (or claim to be doing) design. Still, it is interesting to note that design and activism have much in common in their focus on imagining possible futures and working towards their actualisation. Indeed, design and activism as modes of engagement with the world share a number of similar characteristics that makes their intra-action particularly synergistic: both design and activism fit very much within a Deleuzo-Guattarian strategy of producing different connections, experimenting with intensities, actualising latent potential and engaging in processes of transformation of the status quo.

So what, then, is 'design activism'? In *Design Activism*, Fuad-Luke provides a combined definition of 'design activism' as 'design thinking, imagination and practice applied knowingly or unknowingly to create a counter-narrative aimed at generating and balancing possibilities of social, institutional, environmental and/or economic change' (2009: 27). I suggest this definition is 'intensive' because, like the definitions of design and activism above, it too focuses on what design activism does rather than by whom it is done, or what it is called (that is, whether the doing is explicitly defined as design, activism, or activist design). Indeed, as Fuad-Luke adds, speaking of 'design activism' is to imply 'that it already exists and has an established philosophy, pedagogy, and ontology' (2009: 1), although this is not necessarily the case. Rather, to speak of design activism is to gesture towards the existence of what Fuad-Luke describes as 'an emergent' phenomenon with the 'potential to help us deal with important contemporary societal issues' (2009: 1). Guy Julier's definition of design activism adds to this broad definition the idea that design activist practices, like Deleuze's 'minor' modes of art, are 'collective and constructive struggles' concerned with the 'public sphere rather than the individual' (Julier 2013a: 146). For Julier, design activism 'reallocates resources, reconfigures systems, and reprioritises interests' and is thus 'necessarily broad in its scope and aims' (2013a: 145), intersecting with other practices such as 'social design, co-creation, sustainable design, and critical design' (2013a: 146) as well as 'community design' and 'participatory design' (2013b: 226). In order to elaborate upon and ground these ideas about design activism I will focus predominantly on one example that fits within these broader trends, as well as an emerging trend that Ezio Manzini has called 'design for social innovation': Toronto's *Not Far From the Tree* urban fruit-picking project. *Not Far From the Tree* is an example of the kind of activity that 'analyzes and critiques systems of provision, looking for or proposing non-mainstream models to create alternative constellations of people and artifacts and rearrange channels between them' (Julier 2013a: 146), and, as such, can be seen as a form of 'minor' design that intensively resists neoliberal systems of power that deregulate, individualise, privatise and 'free' up to market machinations what was once shared, collective or 'common' (Hardt and Negri 2009).

Design Activism: Difference as Intensive Resistance

In this second part of the chapter, I turn to fields of 'minor' design in order to demonstrate the potential of design to have effects other than what Deleuze and Guattari characterise as 'shameful moments' (1994: 10). In other words, I invite us to ask *what can design do* as a set of practices intent on engaging with the made world and re-making the world in less ecologically resource-intensive and less polluting, less economically unequal and monopolistic, and more socially just and equitable ways. I refer to Toronto's *Not Far From the Tree* to highlight some of the ways their activities operate as a model of design activism that, by re-conceptualising, re-organising and deterritorialising flows of fruit, people, private property and profit, experiment with the reconfiguration of a system of deeply enmeshed social, environmental as well as economic 'problems' into a rich web of opportunities for the flourishing of different, more equitable, and perhaps even surprisingly fun, connections.

Many designers today recognise that in a world in which non-renewable resources are quickly becoming depleted and where waste – whether landfill, water pollution, or greenhouse gas emissions – is exceeding critical limits, we cannot 'design' our way out of these issues merely by innovating technologically or by producing more 'stuff' within a design context that ignores ecological limits.[8] Manzini, echoing the work of designers such as Victor J. Papanek in *Design for the Real World* (1971) and *The Green Imperative* (1995), as well as the many critiques of environmentalists, sociologists, political theorists and critical economists, points to the tension between the results of our current consumptive patterns and the impossibility of the promise of unending capitalist growth and expansion when he underscores that today '20 percent of the world's population . . . consumes 80 percent of the available physical resources' (Manzini 2008b: 11). If this trend continues, the other '80 percent of the worlds' population, to whom we are trying to sell the same dream, will have to make do with the remaining 20 percent of these resources' (2008b: 11). He points to this inconsistency in order to drive home the point that the promise of ongoing consumption of 'stuff' is a promise 'we now recognise is impossible to keep' (2008b: 11). This very predicament – the tension between the economy's growth imperative and the environmental, social and political limits with which this 'growth' and 'expansion' conflicts – leads the designer Nathan Shedroff to argue provocatively that 'design is the problem' and to go so far as to suggest that even 'sustainable' design too often results in the production of more stuff (2009: xxiii). Ann Thorpe reinforces this observation when, in *Architecture and Design versus Consumerism*, she remarks that although 'sustainability' is taught in design school:

> outside of the studio or class that investigates 'sustainability', students are often immersed in the business context for design. Students are groomed for conventional market expansion rules through standard portfolio development, final year shows and 'design management' modules. Individual practitioners and researchers may meet at conferences to examine inspiring activist case studies and assemble systemic and necessary transdisciplinary approaches, only to return to institutions . . . that reward siloed expertise, profitability and disciplinary purity. (Thorpe 2012: viii)

A potential issue with these critiques is that, in not being specific enough about *what kind of* 'sustainable design' and *which kinds* of sustainable design schools and institutions, they risk generalising and dismissing what is in fact a varied landscape of sustainable design pedagogies and practices. Although there is room for more specificity, what I think is valuable in their critique is similar to what I think is valuable in Deleuze and Guattari's, namely, that they pointedly address the missed opportunities of modes of design that simply perpetuate the individualist, consumerist, expansion-oriented, monopolistic, neoliberal capitalist status quo. Although these designers' critiques may be excessively broad – and indeed, this chapter is interested in adding nuance to Deleuze and Guattari's own generalisations on design – they are motivated by an interest in promoting sustainable design solutions that challenge dominant capitalist paradigms. In so doing, they echo Deleuze and Guattari's critical questions about activities that follow, reinforce and reproduce contemporary capitalist logics, assumptions and mechanisms, all the while promising 'the new'. Deleuze and Guattari ask, rhetorically, whether these promises of 'the new' or 'the innovative' do not often lead us right back 'to the simple opinion of the average capitalism, the great Major?' (Deleuze and Guattari 1994: 149). Of course, many designers are themselves asking critical questions about what is specific, unique and, indeed, 'innovative' or *different* about what designers can bring to the world. Some designers, such as those participating in recent colloquia on design activism,[9] are interested in activities that, rather than creating new commodities or services, focus on the creation of systems or the re-creation of existing systems that prioritise more equitable social, economic and ecological relations.

One example of an organisation that takes this approach is Toronto's *Not Far From the Tree*. *Not Far From the Tree* is a grassroots project that engages creatively with a series of existing, entrenched, 'wicked' problems. As Fuad-Luke notes, sustainability is one such 'wicked problem', first described by Horst Rittel in the 1960s, whose definition Fuad-Luke quotes as follows: 'a class of social system problems which are ill-formulated, where the information is confusing, where there are many clients and decision-makers with conflicting values, and where the ramifications of the whole system are thoroughly confusing' (Fuad-Luke 2009: 142). In the case of *Not Far From the Tree*, the complex or 'wicked' problem involves issues related to social cohesion among neighbours, food going to waste by people who don't have time to harvest it, and lack of access to produce by lower-income individuals and families. *Not Far From the Tree* confronts these problems not merely by 'problem solving', but by identifying a series of complex needs that may go unseen in the first place, by seeing these from a different perspective, and by re-conceptualising, re-configuring and creatively re-inventing a set of existing relations into potentially different, surprising and more equitable – and even more joyous – connections among trees, fruit, cargo bikes, neighbourhoods and people.

Although *Not Far From the Tree* does not define itself as a design project or as an activist project – indeed, the organisation prefers to focus on what they do rather than what they are called – I am describing it as an example of design activism following a definition of design activism that focuses not on what is called design or activism, but rather on what a given activity or design does. I am inspired here by not only Deleuze and Guattari but also Tony Fry, whose definition of design is a process-oriented one. He suggests that design need not be practised by a designer, nor does a person need to recognise that s/he is doing design for it to be design. For Fry, design is defined by what it does: 'design designs' (Fry 1999: 176; see also Fry 2009, 2011). Similarly, we can say that activism need not be done by activists, nor pre-defined as activism, for it to activate people and effectuate social, environmental or economic change. We might say, similarly, taking inspiration from the work of Rosi Braidotti, that activism activates affirmative affects and latent potentials in people, places and things (Braidotti 2010: 45). Although *Not Far From the Tree* may not self-define as a design, activist, or design activist project, organisations like *Not Far From the Tree* not only demonstrate a keen attention to matters of system design but are also becoming increasingly interesting to designers, whose own discipline – where 'minor' design modes such as activist activities are concerned – continue to take inspiration from a range of community activities and actions that do not necessarily consider themselves 'design'. To name just one further example of this trend, the recent emergence of 'participatory design' similarly borrows from the kind of community organisation and action that has a long history in grassroots local political activity (such as neighbourhood associations) and practices of direct democracy (such as those perhaps most prominently on public display during the Occupy Movement). Thus, what I suggest here, following Manzini, Julier and others, is that design activism today is intermingling with, inspired by, and also inspiring – especially, as I go on to explain, where 'design for social innovation' is concerned – other kinds of interventions that may not consider themselves design or activist per se. In the section that follows I point to other emerging examples of such practices, while focusing on *Not Far From the Tree* in order to flesh out in greater detail its connections to what I have called 'minor' modes of design.

Not Far From the Tree: Intensive and Affirmative Modes of Design Activism

Inspired by Los Angeles's *Fallen Fruit* project and itself inspiring other fruit-sharing projects in numerous cities, Toronto's *Not Far From the Tree* is a not-for-profit organisation that mobilises volunteers to harvest produce that would otherwise go to waste from fruit-bearing trees in private yards across the city. Founded by Laura Reinsborough in 2008, this experiment in social, economic and environmental sustainability has grown into an organisation that since 2008 has mobilised 1,600 volunteers to pick 71,159 pounds of fruit from 1,500 downtown trees in fourteen neighbourhoods (notfarfromthetree.org). *Not Far From the Tree*'s harvest – as diverse as cherries, apricots, plums, grapes, elderberries, pears, apples, mulberries, service berries, gingko and walnuts – is picked by volunteers, distributed by cargo bikes and shared in equal thirds among fruit-pickers, fruit tree owners, and local food banks. Reinsborough describes the project as a 'logistics' operation that 'moves all the pieces' and 'mobilises' people, property lines and produce using a modular design (Reinsborough 2013). The organisation does not itself pick the fruit – rather, it works to facilitate a series of new connections and flows. Fruit tree owners who can't keep up with the amount of fruit their tree is bearing, don't have time to harvest the fruit, or can't make use of all of the produce, register their trees with *Not Far From the Tree*. Volunteers who have the time and have registered their interest in picking fruit, sign up for the fruit-pick neighbourhood by neighbourhood. The fruit that is picked by volunteers is divided in thirds among fruit tree owners, tree-picking volunteers, and food banks and shelters for those who need food but may not be in a position to volunteer. The fruit-picking tools and ladders, as well as the produce that is picked, is distributed by cargo bicycles stored in central, accessible, and also volunteered, storage locations in each of the participating Toronto neighbourhoods. The organisation's simple mandate, to 'pick fruit and share it' responds to a series of complex needs – for environmental sustainability, social justice, food security and economic equity, and offers an alternative, creative and collective model of ecological, economic and social sustainability premised upon an affirmation and reconfiguration of existing abundance, an actualisation of latent potentials, and an orientation towards enabling the future flourishing of trees, neighbourhood connections, and access to fresh local fruit by those in need.

Not Far From the Tree's founder Laura Reinsborough describes how the shift in her perspective came while picking apples in a city orchard at a one-time event. This act of picking fruit in the city activated what she describes as her 'fruit goggles': all of a sudden, she became attuned to her milieu and began to see the city differently. Most notably, she began to see fruit trees – and their latent, unpicked potential – throughout the downtown core (an area often described by food activists as a 'food desert') (notfarfromthetree.org). This shift in perception – from seeing the given world in terms of scarcity (for example, downtown Toronto as a setting for wealth disparities, homelessness, poverty and hunger) to seeing it from the point of view of abundance – is the very kind of shift in perception and interpretation that Deleuze and Guattari advocated in their Spinozist focus on the capacities of things, their Nietzschean emphasis on joy, and their interest in affirming immanence (Thiele 2010). Although, for example, there can be little doubt that there are real shortcomings in the ways in which current food and social systems are organised, a Deleuzo-Guattarian response to such a situation would begin by advocating for an activation of desire in a productive mode, which begins with an ontological shift – an attempt to conceptualise the world differently in order to re-make it in a different way. Similarly, *Not Far From the Tree* engages with the world affirmatively – by creatively identifying what is possible in what is already immanently given, by experimenting with the virtual potential in every actual state of affairs, and by being oriented towards a future that does not merely attempt to 'solve problems' but, more importantly, enables environmentally and socially equitable flourishing.

Indeed, *Not Far From the Tree*, though it doesn't call itself a design or activist project, is nonetheless the type of project that designers interested in models of design for social innovation consider examples of the direction design can take in order to engage with emerging social, economic and environmental challenges. Ezio Manzini, leading theorist of design for social innovation, describes the challenging and yet promising transition that design as a discipline is currently undergoing:

> Design was born and has developed its conceptual and operational tools in a world that looked simple, solid, and limitless. This triad of concepts has been swept away by the force of new phenomena: by the discovery of system complexity, by the need to learn how to navigate in the fluidity of events, and, today, with reference to the transition towards sustainability, by the emergence of limits. It is in this new complex, fluid, limited world that design must operate today ... design for sustainability has to find its way and to define its concepts and tools. (Manzini 2008a: x)

Not Far From the Tree is one among many examples of design for sustainable social innovation. Some of the projects Manzini and Tassarini described in a working paper for a panel on 'Sustainable Social Innovation' at the Parsons New School for Design in 2012 included 'cohousing, collaborative housing, couch surfing, circles of care, elderly mutual help, social incubators, micronurseries, time banks, local currencies, carpooling, car-sharing, food coops, farmers' markets, zero miles food, CSA, street festivals, [and] community gardens' (Manzini and Tassarini 2012: 4). Though an in-depth critical engagement with each of these examples – though very important – is beyond the scope of this chapter, these kinds of projects exist in communities around the world, including in Toronto. Although each of these activities responds to a different set of 'wicked problems', and each arise from a specific context, many of them can be thought of as eclectic modes of design activism, though they may not identify in such a way. What is clear, however, is that they are of interest to designers interested in activist modes of re-making the world. According to Manzini, these kinds of initiatives demonstrate that 'already today, it is possible to do things differently' (Manzini 2008b: 18) from conventional mainstream economic, ecological and social paradigms and expectations (Deleuze and Guattari 1994: 85).

Of course, as one network in a much broader set of networks, *Not Far From the Tree* isn't single-handedly able to solve hunger, social cohesion, economic equity, or food waste issues in Toronto; however, it models at a local level a conceptual and a material mode of thinking and/as doing our environmental, social and economic system differently. As Reinsborough explains, 'it takes that first experience of getting over the social barrier', of entering a neighbour's yard, having a neighbour enter your yard as well as eating the fruit that grows in it (Interview 2013). *Not Far From the Tree* challenges the ways in which property lines and increasingly individualistic social systems have created divisions among people. It also challenges the notion that the 'urban' isn't also an 'environment' or a 'nature' capable of providing food for inhabitants, and it promotes not only individual food growing but also food sharing in a metropolis. *Not Far From the Tree* creates – even if just for a short time – a blurring of the boundary between private and common space, challenging the idea that we must live in an era of scarcity, and that economic austerity and increased competition among individuals are the ways to promote positive change (Gardiner 2000). Indeed, when someone regards cities as zones of austerity and scarcity – as concrete jungles of anonymous, uncaring and disconnected neighbourhoods – it takes a shift in perception and action to reveal the latent and actualisable abundance – an abundance of trees bearing fruit and an abundance of people willing to give their time to connect and transform their ecological, social and economic environments.[10] In other words, in the case of *Not Far From the Tree*, it's not about what's missing, but about creatively conceptualising, affirming and activating what's immanent in the environment – what's already here. In this way, *Not Far From the Tree* synthesises what Julier terms 'materialist and postmaterialist interests' by 'grappling with' both the 'everyday stuff of life' as well as 'ideas and understandings' (2013a: 146), and functions as what Svirsky calls an 'activist-machine' by creating 'alternative connections' through both the 'actualised world' and 'new imaginations' (2010b: 177).

The Problem Posed by 'Minor' Design: Affirmative Politics and Fruitful Futures

In this chapter I have invited us to read Deleuze and Guattari's domains of thought *intensively* and to consider the capacities of design activism as an 'intra-domain' discipline capable of effecting *intensive resistances* to the present – resistances that present ways to think and do otherwise. I contend that Deleuze and Guattari's return to 'categories' in their classification of the three domains of thought (not to mention their reduction of 'design' to its most narrow definition) is a critical response designed to defend the capacities of each domain and to target the way the creative force of the fields of art, science and, most importantly for them, philosophy (but also the 'disciplines of communication' such as design) have been captured by reductive thinking and practice. Although their critique remains pertinent to discussions about design today, especially as the ways in which we have been making and re-making the world are increasingly recognised for their problematic social, economic and ecological effects, contemporary expressions of activist design are also demonstrating potentialities that at once problematise the narrow way in which Deleuze and Guattari conceived of design, and, more importantly, respond critically and creatively to their prescient warnings.

Deleuze and Guattari's critical analysis of the way in which 'newness', 'creativity', 'concepts', and indeed 'design', often work as part of a difference-*diminishing* machine that leads to environmental degradation, economic monopolisation and social inequity, is instrumental in order to posit other modes of engaging the world, or worlding-otherwise. However, in their categorical dismissal of design, they failed to create a space for design as a potentially 'minor' mode. Given the understanding of activist design I've been describing in this chapter, I have sought to emphasise the ways that 'minor' or activist design poses a problem to Deleuze and Guattari's trifecta.

In this final section, I summarise some of the characteristics of design in a 'minor' mode. 'Minor' modes of design, like Deleuze and Guattari's modes of 'minor art' are 'collective enunciations' that challenge dominant paradigms and are thus always 'political' (Deleuze and Guattari 1986: 17). I emphasise the need to think the three domains of thought intensively – in terms of what they do, rather than what they are called – in order to do the kind of work Deleuze and Guattari advocate. Finally, I underscore the potential of design practices to effectuate difference in the way that Rosi Braidotti describes as 'putting the active back into activism' (Braidotti 2010: 45). That is, I highlight how design activism can enact an affirmative politics – a politics that engages the made world in order to re-make it in ways that promote the flourishing of future heterogeneous connections.

First, the primary 'problem' posed by design as practised today is that it is much more diverse, and also potentially much more like the kind of activity Deleuze and Guattari advocate than they recognised in *What is Philosophy?* Design in a 'minor' or activist mode enacts creative practices that are not simply part of a marketing machine churning out 'concepts', and instead challenge the underlying structures that territorialise creativity onto a plateau of profit at-all-costs. The design activist's role is to question whether the field of possibility that exists and has become taken for granted – the current way in which capitalism is operating – is the context within which one should continue to define sustainability, or whether sustainability as a paradigm must instead ask more difficult-to-answer questions such as: What is it we want to sustain? Does the economic, environmental, social and political framework within which we are operating allow for the conditions of possibility of a sustainable world (Hroch 2013b)? As Manzini points out, although we have been told that consumption 'turns the wheels of the economy and produces wealth . . . for everybody' (Manzini 2008b: 10), ecological and economic evidence suggests the contrary; as he explains, 'beyond a certain threshold, our conventional way of conceiving well-being, and the economy that supports it, produces disaster' (2008b: 11). Indeed, Manzini advocates for 'enabling solutions' that enhance the capacities of people and things and argues that sustainability, and the conservation and regeneration of environmental and social capital, means breaking with the currently dominant models of living, production and consumption and experimenting with new ones. If this experimentation does not take place, if we are unable to learn from the new experiences thus generated, then the historical pattern of disabling solutions will continue (Manzini 2008b: 16).

Second, the need to think Deleuze and Guattari's three domains of thought intensively extends to the way we think about design as an intra-domain modality of thought and/as action. Because of the border-crossing characteristic of most problems, design is, in its modes of analysis and engagement, a necessarily complex and interdisciplinary endeavour (Coyne 2005; Farrell and Hooker 2013). Design thus has the potential to offer us a set of complexity-embracing approaches and tools for dealing with the vagaries of 'sustainable' solutions or 'wicked problems'. Indeed, it is especially in the search for sustainable design solutions that, as Stuart Walker notes, 'the boundaries between the distinct disciplines can become barriers to change' (Walker 2008: 26–7). By following the flows of fruit through the circuitry of a city's citizenry, *Not Far From the Tree* is one example of an emerging form of design activism that expresses a response to a more broadly felt struggle about how to effectuate collective agency in the context of neoliberal structures of governance and their inherent processes of individualisation, fragmentation, competition and inequality. This kind of project not only challenges the status quo but also posits – at a local scale – alternative economic, ecological and social models that affirm what is immanent in the environment and activate more equitably fruitful futures.

In conclusion, designers reading Deleuze and Guattari's work need not despair at the harshness of their characterisation of design. Indeed, many modes of activist design have already incorporated Deleuze and Guattari's critical and creative modes of conceptualising and materialising – fabulating and fabricating – the world. At the same time, if we are to learn from Deleuze and Guattari's oeuvre, we should take seriously the political impetus of their work, attend to their expressed enthusiasms as well as to their warnings, and continue to reflect critically throughout the creative design process on the question: 'what does this do?' Indeed, Deleuze and Guattari are thinkers who have themselves designed formidable tools with which to fabricate concepts for thinking and doing differently. Thus, although they did not address design activism directly, design that aims to generate such a counter-narrative is very much the kind of problem-posing, counter-effectuating, convention-resisting mode that resonates with Deleuze and Guattari's description of art, science and philosophy in their most creative actualisations. Design activist responses to some of today's most pressing problems are already materialising intensive resistances to the present in their experimentation with different ways of thinking that draw on philosophical, scientific and artistic modes. We should not only include such design activist practices in our toolbox of 'concepts' but also put them to use.

Notes

1. Previous work on Deleuze and Guattari and design activism includes the special issue of *Design Culture* (2013) as well as the special issue of *Deleuze Studies* on Deleuze and Guattari and political activism (2010), based on the conference that took place at Cardiff University the previous year. More recently, more specific work has been done on Deleuze and the Occupy Movement by Thomas Nail (2013), and Brian Massumi (2013) has done work on activism and philosophy.
2. Deleuze and Guattari witnessed the beginning of the phenomenon we continue to see today – the predominance of 'design' as a synonym for innovative thinking. Their remark that the 'concept' is 'everywhere' (Dosse 2010: 457) or, even more boldly, that 'marketing appears as the concept itself' (Deleuze and Guattari 1994: 146) reveals their critical stance on the term 'concept' becoming a way of marketing a 'new' idea.
3. As François Dosse notes in his biography of Deleuze and Guattari, Deleuze attributed shared authorship of *What is Philosophy?* to Guattari despite their not penning the work together, out of a sense of gratitude and indebtedness to Guattari for friendship and previous collaborative work which made this text possible (Dosse 2010: 456). In this chapter, despite the book's noted 'ambiguous status', I follow this tribute by attributing the authorship of the text to both authors.
4. Stengers focuses in particular on the connections and disjunctions between philosophy and science. As she notes, she 'leave[s] art aside and concentrate[s] on

the differentiation between philosophy as a creation of concepts, and science as dealing with functions' (2005: 151).

5. Deleuze and Guattari describe all three domains of thought as creative in the following passage: 'If philosophy is this continuous creation of concepts, then obviously the question arises not only of what a concept is as philosophical Idea but also of the nature of other creative Ideas that are not concepts and that are due to the arts and sciences, which have their own history and becoming and which have their own variable relationships with one another and with philosophy. The exclusive right of concept creation secures a function for philosophy, but it does not give it any preeminence of privilege since there are other ways of thinking and creating, other modes of ideation that, like scientific thought, do not have to pass through concepts' (1994: 8).

6. This delineation presents a number of paradoxes. First, Deleuze and Guattari – thinkers of interdisciplinarity and the 'inter-breeding' of domains – in order to create a tripartite classification system, take a very reductive view of what 'science' is as well as what is considered 'art' (not to mention design) in their defence of a proper 'philosophy'. Commenting on what Deleuze and Guattari seem to have in mind when they refer to 'science', Stengers points out that these process philosophers paradoxically seem to privilege 'what is usually called "science made"' (2005: 153) – a definition of science focused on the 'achieve[ment of] result[s] as the direct consequence of a normal, rational method' (2005: 154) over 'the vivid, open, risky construction of "science in the making"' (2005: 153). Stengers remarks that this narrow characterisation of science as 'Royal science' is 'disappointing' at first, adding that 'this first disappointment . . . led [her] to a political reading of *What is Philosophy?*' (2005: 53). My argument that design is thought overly reductively in *What is Philosophy?* (design as 'discipline of communication' rather than a mode of conceptual-material fabulation and fabrication) resonates with Stengers's response of this text.

7. Although I include the work of ideology and conceptualisation in my understanding of design activism as also material, it is in material practice especially that in Julier's view the real work of design activism takes place (2013a, 2013b). Svirsky underscores the importance of both thinking and collective action for activism, stressing that the 'time activists spend on articulating ideologies will count for little if their practices are separated from a strategy that includes, at least partially, entering into joyous participation with others – meaning, pursuing compossible relations with them' (Svirsky 2010b: 176).

8. Examples of design activism that work within an economy of scarcity include projects such as Cynthia Hathaway's work in *Car Mekka* on the sustainability of skills and expertise as part of *Utrecht Biennale for Social Design No.4* and Darren O'Donnell's work in collaboration with the Catalyst Centre in *Beachballs41+All* in Toronto, Canada.

9. For example, the panel of 'Design Activism and the Production of Future Social Natures', organised by Damian White and Cameron Tonkinwise at the *Association of American Geographers Annual Meeting* in New York in 2012, as well as the *DESIS Philosophy Panel* on 'Emerging Aesthetics: Is Sustainable Social Innovation Generating a New Aesthetic Paradigm?' featuring panelists Clive Dilnot, Ezio Manzini, Victor Margolin, Cameron Tonkinwise, Virginia Tassinari, Tom Fisher and Marghertita Pillan at Parsons The New School for Design in New York in 2012.

10. Indeed, *Not Far From the Tree* has shown that what was once regarded as 'lack' (i.e. food deserts striated by private properties) can actually yield not only abundance but also over-abundance. There are more people interested in registering

trees than there is infrastructure to pick them, and there are more volunteers interested in picking fruit than are able to attend any single pick.

References

Braidotti, Rosi (2013), *The Posthuman*, London: Polity Press.

Braidotti, R. (2010), 'On Putting the "Active" Back into Activism', *New Formations*, 63:3, pp. 42–57.

Braidotti, Rosi (2006), *Transpositions: On Nomadic Ethics*, London: Polity Press.

Brown, Valerie A., J. Harris and J. Russell (2010), *Tackling Wicked Problems: Through the Transdisciplinary Imagination*, London: Earthscan.

Buchanan, R. (1992), 'Wicked Problems in Design Thinking', *Design Issues*, 8:2, pp. 5–21.

Coyne, R. (2005), 'Wicked Problems Revisited', *Design Studies*, 26:1, pp. 5–17.

Cross, N. (2001), 'Designerly Ways of Knowing: Design Discipline Versus Design Science', *Design Issues*, 17:3, pp. 49–55.

DeLanda, Manuel (2002), *Intensive Science and Virtual Philosophy*, London: Continuum.

Deleuze, Gilles (1992), 'Postscript on the Societies of Control', *October*, 59, pp. 3–7.

Deleuze, Gilles and F. Guattari (1994), *What is Philosophy?* trans. H. Tomlinson and G. Burchell, New York: Columbia University Press.

Deleuze, Gilles and F. Guattari (1987), *A Thousand Plateaus. Capitalism and Schizophrenia 2*, trans. B. Massumi, Minneapolis: University of Minnesota Press.

Deleuze, Gilles and F. Guattari (1986), *Kafka: Toward a Minor Literature*, trans. D. Polan, Minneapolis: University of Minnesota Press.

Deleuze, Gilles and F. Guattari (1983), *Anti-Oedipus. Capitalism and Schizophrenia 1*, trans. R. Hurley, M. Seem and H. R. Lane, Minneapolis: University of Minnesota Press.

Dilnot, C., E. Manzini, V. Margolin, C. Tonkinwise, V. Tassinari, T. Fisher and M. Pillan (2012), 'Emerging Aesthetics: Is Sustainable Social Innovation Generating a New Aesthetic Paradigm?', *Parsons Desis Lab.*, Desis Philosophy Talk no. 1, Parsons The New School for Design, New York.

Dosse, François (2010), *Gilles Deleuze and Félix Guattari: Intersecting Lives*, trans. D. Glassman, New York: Columbia University Press.

Farrell, R. and C. Hooker (2013), 'Design, Science and Wicked Problems', *Design Studies*, 34:6, pp. 681–705.

Fry, A. H. (2011), 'Getting over Architecture: Thinking, Surmounting and Redirecting', in I. Doucet and N. Janssens (eds), *Transdisciplinary Knowledge Production in Architecture and Urbanism*, Amsterdam: Springer, pp. 15–32.

Fry, A. H. (2009), *Design Futuring: Sustainability, Ethics and New Practice*, New York: Berg.

Fry, T. (1999), *A New Design Philosophy: An Introduction to Defuturing*, Sydney: University of New South Wales Press.

Fuad-Luke, Alastair (2009), *Design Activism: Beautiful Strangeness for a Sustainable World*, London: Earthscan.

Gardiner, Michael E. (2000), *Critiques of Everyday Life: An Introduction*, London and New York: Routledge.

Hardt, Michael and A. Negri (2009), *Commonwealth*, Cambridge, MA: Harvard University Press.

Harvey, David (2005), *A Brief History of Neoliberalism*, New York: Oxford University Press.

Hroch, P. (2014), 'Deleuze, Guattari, and Environmental Politics: *Ritournelles* for a Planet-yet-to-come', in M. Carlin and J. Wallin (eds), *Deleuze and Guattari, Politics, and Education: For a people-yet-to-come*, London: Bloomsbury, pp. 49–76.

Hroch, P. (2013a), 'Intensity', in R. Shields and M. Vallee (eds), *Demystifying Deleuze: An Introductory Assemblage of Crucial Concepts*, Ottawa: Red Quill Books, pp. 95–8.

Hroch, P. (2013b), 'Resilience versus Resistance: Affectively Modulating Contemporary Diagrams of Social Resilience, Social Sustainability, and Social Innovation', in G. Elmer and M. Tiessen (eds), *MediaTropes. Foucault/Deleuze: A Neo-liberal Diagram*, 4:1, pp. 17–46.

Julier, G. (2013a), 'Introduction: Material Preference and Design Activism', *Design and Culture*, 5:2, Special Issue on Design Activism, pp. 145–50

Julier, G. (2013b), 'From Design Culture to Design Activism', *Design and Culture*, 5:2, Special Issue on Design Activism, pp. 215–36.

Manzini, E. (2008a), 'Introduction: Designing for Sustainability and Strategic Design', in E. Manzini, S. Walker and B. Wylant, *Enabling Solutions for Sustainable Living: A Workshop*, Calgary: University of Calgary Press, pp. ix–xiv.

Manzini, E. (2008b), 'Design Context: Enabling Solutions for Sustainable Urban Everyday Life', in E. Manzini, S. Walker and B. Wylant, *Enabling Solutions for Sustainable Living: A Workshop*, Calgary: University of Calgary Press, pp. 1–24.

Manzini, E. and V. Tassinari (2012), 'Discussion Paper: Is Sustainable Social Innovation Generating a New Aesthetic Paradigm?' *Parsons Desis Lab.*, DESIS Philosophy Talk no. 1 (2 March), Parsons The New School for Design, New York.

Markussen, T. (2013), 'The Disruptive Aesthetics of Design Activism: Enacting Design Between Art and Politics', *Design Issues*, 29:1, pp. 38–50.

Massumi, B. (2013), *Semblance and Event: Activist Philosophy and the Occurrent Arts*, Cambridge, MA: The MIT Press.

Nail, T. (2013), 'Deleuze, Occupy, and the Actuality of Revolution', *Theory and Event*, 16:1.

Not Far From the Tree (no date), website; available at http://www.notfarfromthe-tree.org (accessed 1 October 2013).

Papanek, Victor (1995), *The Green Imperative: Natural Design for the Real World*, London and New York: Thames and Hudson.

Parr, A. (2013), 'Politics + Deleuze + Guattari + Architecture', in H. Frichot and S. Loo (eds), *Deleuze and Architecture*, Edinburgh: Edinburgh University Press, pp. 197–214.

Reinsborough, L. (2013), 'Interview', by P. Hroch (20 April).

Rittel, H. and M. Webber (1973), 'Dilemmas in a General Theory of Planning', *Policy Sciences*, 4:2, pp. 155–69.

Shedroff, Nathan (2009), *Design is the Problem: The Future of Design Must Be Sustainable*, New York: Rosenfeld Media.

Stengers, I. (2005), 'Deleuze and Guattari's Last Enigmatic Message', *Angelaki: Journal of the Theoretical Humanities*, 10:2, pp. 151–67.

Svirsky, M. (2010a), 'Introduction: Beyond the Royal Science of Politics', *Deleuze Studies*, 4, Deleuze and Political Activism (Supplement), pp. 1–6.

Svirsky, M. (2010b), 'Defining Activism', *Deleuze Studies*, 4, Deleuze and Political Activism (Supplement), pp. 163–82.

Teal, R. (2010), 'Developing a (Non-linear) Practice of Design Thinking', *International Journal of Art and Design Education*, 29:3, pp. 294–302.

Thiele, K. (2010), '"To Believe In This World, As It Is": Immanence and the Quest for Political Activism', *Deleuze Studies*, 4, Deleuze and Political Activism (Supplement), pp. 28–45.

Thorpe, A. (2012), *Architecture and Design versus Consumerism: How Design Activism Confronts Growth*, New York: Earthscan.

Trading the Future (2008) videotape, dir. b. h. Yael, Canada.

Walker, S. (2008), 'Sustainable Design', in E. Manzini, S. Walker and B. Wylant (eds), *Enabling Solutions for Sustainable Living: A Workshop*, Calgary: University of Calgary Press.

White, D. and C. Tonkinwise (2012), 'Design, Design Activism and the Democratic Production of Future Natures', *American Association of Geographers Annual Meeting*, 24–28 February, New York.

Notes on Contributors

Manola Antonioli
Manola Antonioli holds a PhD in philosophy and social sciences from EHESS (Paris) and previously held seminars at the Collège International de Philosophie. She currently teaches history and theory of design and architecture at ENSA Dijon and philosophy of architecture and urban studies at the Ecole Nationale Supérieure d'Architecture of Versailles. She recently directed a special report on Ecodesign, which appeared in the journal *Multitudes,* nos. 53–4 (January 2014). She has edited a book entitled *Théories et pratiques écologiques* (*Ecological Theories and Practices*, 2013), published by Presses Universitaires de Paris Ouest.

Vincent Beaubois
Vincent Beaubois is Lecturer in Philosophy at the Paris Ouest Nanterre University. He is currently doing a PhD in philosophy at Paris Ouest Nanterre University on the influences of industrial technology in the fields of art and culture in dialogue with contemporary philosophy, especially the philosophy of Gilbert Simondon. Vincent is also an engineer and a designer. He is member of the CIDES (International Centre for Simondonian Studies).

Jamie Brassett
Jamie Brassett has been working at Central Saint Martins, a college of the University of the Arts London, since 1995 across most of its subject provision – fashion design, graphics design, product design, textile design and fine art – and has been Subject Leader and MA Course Director of Innovation Management since 2008. Jamie has also consulted for a number of design and innovation agencies, and global commercial, public and voluntary sector organisations. He graduated with a PhD in Philosophy from the University of Warwick in 1993,

producing a thesis on Deleuze and Guattari, Kant and Bachelard called *Cartographies of Subjectification*, supervised by Nick Land. Jamie has published on a number of topics since 1991 and has spoken nationally and internationally at conferences since 1989, chairing 'Out of Control' the 8th International Conference on Design and Emotion in 2012. He is currently working on projects covering style and design, futures and trends, materialism and ontogenesis, sometimes all at the same time.

T. Hugh Crawford

T. Hugh Crawford is the author of *Modernism, Medicine, and William Carlos Williams* (1993) and former editor of the journal *Configurations*. He is an Associate Professor of Science and Technology studies at the Georgia Institute of Technology. He is also an amateur woodworker, a long-distance hiker, and is currently writing books on Melville and Deleuze, and walking and philosophy.

Derek Hales

Derek Hales is an architect and a principal lecturer in the School of Art, Design and Architecture at the University of Huddersfield, UK. He is engaged in researching the fictions of the technological object in electronic, aural and visual cultures. The fascination of his research is with the counterfactual, actual and fictional objects of unstable futures. Derek's current theory-fictions involve the designer as author of speculative culture. As guest editor of the journal *Digital Creativity*, he recently edited the special edition on Design Fictions (2013). He is currently editing a special issue on Speculative Hardware (forthcoming 2015).

Petra Hroch

Petra Hroch is a PhD Candidate, SSHRC Canada Graduate Scholar and Izaak Walton Killam Memorial Scholar in Theory and Culture (Dept. of Sociology) at the University of Alberta. Her interdisciplinary research on art and design, sustainability and materialist and posthumanist theory appears in *Walter Benjamin and the Aesthetics of Change* (2010), *Ecologies of Affect* (2011), *ETopia* (2011), *MediaTropes* (2013), *Demystifying Deleuze* (2013), *Journal of Curriculum and Pedagogy* (2013) and *Deleuze & Guattari, Politics, and Education* (2014).

Betti Marenko

Betti Marenko is Contextual Studies Leader for Product Design at Central St Martins, UAL London. Her work at the intersection of creative philosophy, materialities and design aims at developing lines of 'minor design', engaging issues of digital interaction, genealogies of technologies and animism. She is currently researching animism as the key post-human, post-user, post-cognitive mode of interaction with objects, digital and non-digital. She is on the editorial board of the journal *Design and Culture*.

John O'Reilly

John O'Reilly is an editor, consultant and educator. His clients include The British Council, Converse and Virgin Atlantic. He has contributed to *The Observer*, *The Guardian*, *Eye* and *Etapes* magazine. He is an Associate Lecturer in Innovation Management at Central Saint Martins, and lectures on illustration and philosophy at Camberwell College of the Arts and the Royal College of Arts. John is editor of *Varoom*, the journal of the Association of Illustrators (UK). He received his PhD in Philosophy from the University of Warwick.

Anne Sauvagnargues

Anne Sauvagnargues is Professor of Philosophy at the University of Paris, Nanterre, France, and specialises in the philosophy of Gilles Deleuze. She has published, among others, *Deleuze and Art* (Bloomsbury, 2013; first published in France in 2005) and *Deleuze and Transcendental Empiricism* (2010), and is preparing *Artmachines: Simondon, Deleuze, Guattari* (forthcoming with Edinburgh University Press).

Index

Main entries indicated in **bold**.